A GIFT IMPRISONED: THE POETIC LIFE OF
MATTHEW ARNOLD

A GIFT IMPRISONED: THE POETIC LIFE OF
MATTHEW ARNOLD

IAN HAMILTON

BLOOMSBURY

First published 1998
This paperback edition published 1999

Copyright © 1998 by Ian Hamilton

Bloomsbury Publishing Plc,
38 Soho Square,
London W1V 5DF

The moral right of the author has been asserted

A CIP catalogue record for this book is
available from the British Library

ISBN 0 7475 4287 2

10 9 8 7 6 5 4 3 2 1

Typeset by Hewer Text Limited, Edinburgh
Printed in Great Britain by Clays Limited, St Ives plc

It is a sad thing to see a man who has been frittered away piecemeal by petty distractions, and who has never done his best. But it is still sadder to see a man who has done his best, who has reached his utmost limits – and finds his work a failure, and himself far less than he had imagined himself.

Matthew Arnold,
Notes for his unwritten 'Lucretius'

CONTENTS

List of Illustrations   ix
Preface   xi
Acknowledgements   xiii

1 Dr Arnold of Rugby   1
2 'Crabby' in Childhood   13
3 Schooldays   26
4 Oxford   43
5 First Poems   55
6 'Days of *Lélia* and *Valentine*'   73
7 Lansdowne, Clough and Marguerite   92
8 *The Strayed Reveller*, *Obermann* and Marguerite,
  Once More   109
9 Marriage to Miss Wightman   128
10 *Empedocles* Renounced   148
11 'This for our wisest!'   164

Contents

12 A Professor of Poetry   179
13 Last Poems   197

Chronology   219
Notes   221
Index   237

LIST OF ILLUSTRATIONS

1. Dr Thomas Arnold

2. Mrs Mary Arnold

3. Rugby School from the Close

4. Fox How

5. A.H. Clough

6. Thomas Arnold

7. Jane Arnold

8. Matthew Arnold, 1856

PREFACE

Several years ago, I had the idea of trying to write a full-scale biography of Matthew Arnold. The ambition sprang chiefly from an interest in the poems, and in biographical questions relating to the poems. There were, it seemed to me, a number of intriguing puzzles. Chief among these, perhaps, was the much-pondered Marguerite. Who was she: a dream-girl, an invention born of too much exposure to the novels of George Sand, or a real person met in Switzerland in 1848, and fled from a year later? Then there was the question of Arnold's relations with his father, and his father's memory. Was Dr Arnold of Rugby a devitalising ogre or an inspiration: was it his fault that Matthew was so duty-bound? And, overarchingly, there was the matter of Arnold's attitude to his own gifts as a poet: why did he abandon the poetic life and settle for three decades of drudgery as an inspector of elementary schools? Was it a fierce love of obligation that took him down this path, or was it, rather, that all along he had insufficient faith in his own talent? Was the fear of being (by his own standards) second rate more powerful, in the end, than his commitment to the realm of duty?

There were other aspects of the Arnold life that seemed to be worth close-up study: his marriage, his relationship with his elder sister, his friendship with Arthur Hugh Clough, his youthful self-assertiveness and foppery, his fluctuating feelings about God, his Tennyson-phobia, the steady, slow-drip sadness that seemed to underlie even his most elegant and amiable sermons. In the very best of Arnold's poems – 'Dover Beach', 'The Buried Life', 'Empedocles', 'The Scholar-Gipsy', some of the lyrics addressed to Marguerite – the deepest impulse is towards repudiation: repudiation, often, of those very elements in his own nature which urged him towards poetry in the first place.

When Arnold got married and became an educationist, he also turned himself into a pedagogic neo-classicist; the age, he said, needed the kind of large-scale, objective, architectonic verse-constructions which he himself, he came to learn, had no real gift for. Or, to put it another way, what the age didn't need were more poems of the kind that Arnold did have a real gift for, and had indeed already written: lyric poems of the self, that Arnold self which, as he came to believe, had or should have had more important things to do than, well, write lyric poems.

Thus, most of my lines of biographical enquiry seemed to be focusing on Arnold's early years. I soon enough abandoned plans for a cradle-to-grave Life. The present book is an attempt to animate certain key moments, or turning points, in Arnold's passage from the poetic life to the prose life of his later years. Arnold, in those later years, spoke urgently of poetry's civilising capabilities, but he spoke thus at the expense of his own talent. 'He thrust his gift in prison till it died' was Auden's diagnosis. In the ensuing pages I attempt to tell, in detail, the story of that slow imprisonment. As Arnold came to see things, an all-out commitment to his art would have involved an 'actual tearing of oneself to pieces'. It might also have involved some other kinds of damage – to people, to principles, to his ingrained sense of social purpose. And would it have been worth it after all? We'll never know; as Arnold never knew.

Ian Hamilton
London 1997

ACKNOWLEDGEMENTS

I am grateful to the following for their advice and practical assistance during the preparation and writing of this book: Gillon Aitken, Liz Calder, Sarah-Jane Forder, Dan Jacobson, Karl Miller, Charis Ryder, Chris Sheppard (Brotherton Library, University of Leeds), Ahdaf Soueif, Ann Thwaite and Patricia Wheatley. I would also like to thank Balliol College Library, Oxford, and the Beinecke Library, Yale, for giving me access to manuscript material, and to acknowledge my indebtedness to biographies of Arnold by Park Honan and Nicholas Murray, to Kenneth Allott's edition of the *Poems*, and to Cecil Y. Lang's edition of the *Letters* (Volumes One and Two).

1

Dr Arnold of Rugby

Matthew Arnold was the eldest son of the most celebrated headmaster in England. As a boy, he was – uninterruptedly – a schoolboy. His Rugby classmates went home at the end of term and told their parents what it was like to be taught by the legendary Thomas Arnold. For them, schoolmasters were one thing; parents were another. Some might have spoken of Dr Arnold with resentment, having lately been on the wrong end of a flogging. Others might have sung his praises, having perhaps earned a word or two of commendation. One or two might have worn a strange glint in the eye, as if they had been through some glorious conversion. All of them were probably quite glad to take a break. For Matthew Arnold, there was no such respite. Just having the name 'Arnold' told the world where he belonged. For him, school holidays could never quite be holidays from school.

It was Thomas Arnold's mission to mark boys for life, and over the years he scored some notable successes. Rugby in the nineteenth century produced numerous judges and high-ranking clerics. The colonies were well stocked with Arnold-trained officials. The school's speciality, though, was the training of schoolmasters. By mid-century, Arnold's Old Boys were in charge of more than a dozen of England's leading public schools. And Arnold's own legend – the legend that Lytton Strachey would eventually labour to demolish – was largely constructed by worshipful ex-pupils: Arthur Stanley, who wrote Arnold's biography, a huge Victorian bestseller, and Thomas Hughes, who – in the even more successful *Tom Brown's Schooldays* – portrayed the Doctor, with a reverential shudder, as 'a man whom we felt to be with all his heart and soul and strength striving against whatever was mean and unmanly and unrighteous in our little world'.[1]

The tone here captures well the atmosphere at Rugby in the 1830s, the atmosphere from which Matthew Arnold, in his teens, so rarely managed to escape. The place crackled with moral fervour. Each day was alarmingly momentous; each day was a reckoning. Thomas Arnold, after all, was the civilised world's leading expert on boy-evil. 'I have known boys of eight or nine years old who did not so much as know what would happen to them after their deaths,' he used to say. He above all others understood the 'awful wickedness' of the half-men he ruled:

> When the spring and activity of youth is altogether unsanctioned by anything pure and elevated in its desires it becomes a spectacle that is as dismaying, and almost more morally distressing, than the shouts and gambols of a set of lunatics.[2]

Thomas Arnold's secret, perhaps, was that he never really liked small boys – or, rather, he never liked them when they were at their most instinctively small-boyish. He could too easily perceive 'the devil in most of them'. And he had the knack of persuading them, or some of them, not to like themselves. When they grew big enough to join his sixth form, his trick was to give them a taste of his own power, setting them up as praepostors with big sticks, 'fellow workers with him for the highest good of the school'. And he was intensely loyal to these juvenile lieutenants. They were encouraged to transmit to their juniors that 'abhorrence of evil' in which they themselves had been so painfully instructed. When anybody complained about his prefects' methods, Arnold would usually leap to their defence: 'There was no obloquy which he would not undergo in the protection of a boy who had, by due energy of this discipline, made himself obnoxious to the school, the parents, or the public.'[3]

Arnold's little Rugbeians had it drilled into them, day after day, that they were on the brink of an all-determining life-choice: they could seek promotion to the Arnold-controlled upper realm of 'moral thoughtfulness' or they could linger in the mire, as 'beasts or devils'. No boyish action was so insignificant that it could not be 'invested with a moral character'; no adolescent fancy so fanciful that it might not reveal the truth of a boy's personality. It was Arnold's habit, as a critic of his pointed out, to refer 'the most trifling matters to the most awful principles'.[4] It was 'his serious wish to bring boys to see a duty in every act of their lives'.

Dr Arnold expelled boys from Rugby not just for 'lying, or drinking, or habitual idleness', the three big sins to be watched for. Sometimes he kicked them out merely for exhibiting 'low wit' or 'carelessness of character'. He took pride in always being able to sniff out a bad egg. 'Evil being unavoidable, we are not a jail to keep it in but a place of education where we must cast it out.'[5]

Why then did so many boys worship this fanatic? Dr Arnold himself gives us a clue when he describes an incident from his first teaching post, before he took the headmastership of Rugby. In the schoolroom one day he lost his temper with a backward pupil. As he raged, the boy looked up at him and asked: 'Why do you speak angrily, sir? Indeed, I am doing the best that I can.' At this, Arnold was in disarray: 'I never felt so ashamed in my life: that look and that speech I have never forgotten.'[6] On another

3

occasion, at roll-call, an inattentive boy called out his 'Here' too loudly, making 'the windows rattle'. When reprimanded, he said that he was of 'a nervous disposition' and had been 'so frightened at hearing his name called, that his shout was involuntary'.[7] Instead of laughing off this explanation, Arnold consulted the school doctor. He wanted physiological corroboration.

Nobody seems to have thought of Arnold as unjust; how could he be since he so loved the truth? Indeed, some of his sharper students viewed him near-protectively as the arch-victim of his own judicial vehemence. All this really did hurt him more than it hurt them. And he was always ready to take the side of the slow learner. Mere 'intellectual acuteness, divested as it is, in too many cases, of all that is comprehensive and great and good' was to him 'more revolting than the most helpless imbecility'.[8] He was particularly contemptuous of rich boys who evinced 'insolence and want of sympathy . . . toward the lower orders'. When Arnold listed the three qualities he most prized in a boy, 'intellectual ability' came third. He placed 'gentlemanly conduct' second. 'Religious and moral principles' was first. In other words, he offered a curriculum that was in everybody's reach. He could also be surprisingly tolerant, at times, when boys fell into error. He could not bear the idea of a boy *choosing* to be evil, but if a boy was simply too young to understand what was required of him, Arnold was prepared to bide his time. Tom Brown thought of Rugby as 'the only spot in England well and truly ruled'.

Arnold was a ruler, but he was also an eminent scholar, editor of Thucydides, disciple of Niebuhr, and author of several works on Roman history. The example of Niebuhr, whose own history of Rome was appearing in English in the 1830s, led Arnold to construct a theory of history which was most useful to him in his dealings with small boys.[9] A nation, he would say, is 'like a person'. It has a moral consciousness that develops, stage by stage, from infancy, through adolescence, to full manhood. Nations grow up in different ways, as people do, and react differently to each stage of their development. Some have unhappy childhoods, others are moody and aggressive during adolescence. Few ever manage to achieve a balanced and virtuous maturity. Over the centuries, ancient Greece and Rome reached something like full adulthood. Now it was England's turn.

England in 1830 was, so to speak, still in the sixth form. There were signs, though, that the nation was getting ready to leave school. Looking around, Arnold thought he could perceive a new spirit in the land, a spirit suggestive of intellectual freedom, social justice, ecclesiastical reform. But he was troubled, too. He sensed a general 'superficiality of feeling', an absence of that moral self-awareness without which no reform could be meaningful, or made to stick. It was much the same with boys. When Arnold 'thought of the social evils of the country, it awakened a corresponding desire to check the thoughtless waste and self-ishness of schoolboys'.[10]

But schoolboys, like nations, could not learn to be grown up until they *were* grown up. This truism seems to have caused Arnold some perplexity, accounting perhaps for the 'puzzled expression' that Lytton Strachey detected in his portrait.[11] If small boys were indeed wicked by nature, by involuntary inclination, at what age should the devil in them be uprooted? A schoolmaster could hardly stand by and let the little horrors have their way. On the other hand, were there not dangers in catching them too young? 'My object,' Arnold said when he took on the Rugby job, 'will be, if possible, to form Christian men, for Christian boys I can scarcely hope to make; I mean that, from the natural imperfect state of boyhood, they are not susceptible of Christian principles in their full development upon their practice, and I suspect that a low standard of morals in many respects must be tolerated amongst them, as it was on a larger scale in what I consider the boyhood of the human race.'[12]

No boy, though, was so small that he did not know when Dr Arnold was displeased. In lessons, Arnold saw to it that his students learned to crave 'the pleased look and the cheerful

"Thank you" which followed upon a successful answer or translation', and to dread 'the fall of his countenance with its deepening severity, the stern elevation of his eyebrow, the sudden "Sit down" which followed upon the reverse'.

The Doctor's 'presence' has been variously described: magnetic, awesome, irresistible – these are the customary epithets. And yet there was more to it than mere intimidation. Somehow he made the boys not *want* to let him down. Arnold, says Arthur Stanley, never 'seemed to be on the watch for boys' and altogether he gave the impression of trusting their allegiance to his cause. For example, he despised liars. If a falsehood were discovered, he would punish it severely. But he could be oddly unsuspicious. ' "If you say so, that is quite enough – *of course*, I believe your word," ' he'd say, 'and there grew up in consequence a general feeling that it was a shame to tell Arnold a lie – he always believes one.'[13] (Not always, it so happened. On one notorious occasion, Arnold gave a boy eighteen strokes for lying and then discovered he was innocent. Abject public apologies ensued.[14])

Tom Brown was also flogged by Dr Arnold, but he of course was grateful. The Doctor had his reasons, as he always did.

The oak pulpit standing out by itself above the school seats. The tall gallant form, the kindling eye, the voice, now soft as the tones of a flute, now clear and stirring as the call of the light infantry bugle, of him who stood there Sunday after Sunday, witnessing and pleading for his Lord, the King of righteousness and love and glory, with whose spirit he was filled, and in whose power he spoke. The long lines of young faces rising tier above tier down the whole length of the chapel, from the little boy's who had just left his mother to the young man's who was going out next week into the great world rejoicing in his strength . . . But what was it after all which seized and held these 300 boys, dragging them out of themselves, willing or unwilling, for twenty minutes on Sunday afternoons . . . We couldn't enter into half of what we heard; we hadn't the knowledge of our own hearts or the knowledge of one another, and little enough of the faith, hope and love needed to that end. But we listened, as all boys in their better moods will listen . . . to a man whom we felt to be with all his heart and soul and strength striving against whatever was mean and unmanly and unrighteous in our little world. It was not the cold clear voice of one giving advice and warning from serene heights to those who were struggling and sinning below, but the warm living voice of one who was fighting for us and by our sides, and calling on us to help him and ourselves and one another. And so, wearily and little by little, but surely and steadily on the whole, was brought home to the young boy, for the first time, the meaning of his life: that it was no fool's or sluggard's paradise into which he had wandered by chance, but a battlefield ordained from on old, where there are no spectators, but the youngest must take his side, and the stakes are life and death. And he who roused this consciousness in them showed them at the same time, by every word he spoke in the pulpit, and by his whole daily life, how that battle was to be fought; and stood there before them their fellow-soldier and the captain of their band. The true sort of captain too for a boy's army, one who had no misgivings and gave no uncertain word of command, and, let who would yield or make truce, would fight the fight out (so every boy felt) to the last gasp and the last drop of blood. Other sides of his character might take hold and influence boys here and there, but it was this thoroughness and undaunted courage which more than anything else won his way to the hearts of the great mass of those on whom he left his mark . . .[15]

These sermons of Arnold's were dashed off in half an hour on Sunday mornings and perusers of his manuscripts have been surprised to find in them no crossings-out, no second thoughts. Some of his flintier harangues must indeed have been tough going for the younger boys. Were schools like theirs really 'the very seats and nurseries of vice'? Had they themselves already supped 'too largely of that poisoned bowl'? Would they in truth look back in years to come 'with inexpressible regret' on those 'hours which have been wasted in folly, or worse than folly'?

Arnold's voice, in spite of Tom Brown's testimony, was not in the least flute-like. Others have described his delivery as harsh and grating. But his sermons were always short and, although aimed for publication, they were not easy to sleep through. Even when Arnold was abstractly ranting about sin, punishment, eternal damnation and suchlike, he could give the impression that *this* sermon was meant especially for *you*:

> But how is it with you now? . . . Do you think of God *now*? . . . Do you say your prayers to Him? Do you still think that lying, and all those shuffling, dishonest excuses, which are as bad as lying, are base, and contemptible, and wicked? . . . Do you still love to be kind to your companions, never teasing or ill-treating them? – or have you already been accustomed to the devilish pleasure of giving pain to others; and whilst you are yourselves teased and ill-used by some who are stronger than you, do you repeat the very same conduct to those who are weaker than you? Are you still anxious to please your parents; and, in saying your lessons, do you still retain the natural thought of a well-bred and noble disposition, that you would like to say them as well as you can, and to please those who teach you?[16]

These interrogative lists were obviously calculated to keep each boy squirming in his seat. Now and again, though, Arnold answered his own questions, rather movingly. 'And where are our departed friends now?' he asked on All Souls' Day, 1834. This question, he said, could be answered with 'one word; but how much does that word contain!'. The boys must have expected the answer to be 'Heaven', but Arnold had a better word for what he had in mind:

> I cannot tell in what place they are, or with what degree of happiness or consciousness. I cannot tell if they regard us still, or if they can pray for us, or wish us any good. But they are in *safety* . . . and under Christ's care, and . . . we shall meet them when Christ comes again.

In 1834 Matthew Arnold was eleven, not yet enrolled at Rugby and not yet exposed to the full force of his father's public style. Nor, probably, did he know much of the Doctor's reputation in the world at large. By this date, Arnold was not only a well-known schoolteacher; he was also notorious as an intrepid controversialist. The grand gentlemen of Warwickshire who sat on the school's board of trustees could barely open a newspaper without coming across an attack on their danger-ously 'radical' headmaster. Arnold was what we would now speak of as 'good copy': on politics, on Church reform, on corporal punishment, on Catholics, Dissenters, Jews. It was not always easy to predict the line he would take. He was by no means straightforwardly liberal in his views. But, whatever his position, he was always ready to espouse it with energy and 'indiscretion'.

And this may have come as a surprise to his employers. When Thomas Arnold was offered the headmastership of Rugby in 1828, the trustees had no idea what they were getting. Arnold was well connected in Oxford, where he had been a Fellow of Oriel, then mightily prestigious, but for nine years he had been teaching obscurely at a private school at Laleham in Middlesex. Born in the Isle of Wight in 1795, the son of a customs inspector, he had reached Oriel by way of scholarships to Winchester, then Corpus Christi, Oxford. Great things had been predicted for him but even at Oriel he was found to be too scrupulously wayward, too rigorously zealous for the truth. He delayed his ordination because he had doubts concerning 'certain points' in the Thirty-Nine Articles. The doctrine of the blessed Trinity, for instance, gave him pause: he could not 'get rid of a certain feeling of objections'. His friends advised him to conquer these objec-tions by 'main force', but he preferred to bide his time. He married, moved to Laleham, had the first six of his nine children, and seemed to have opted for a life of studious, home-based seclusion:

> I have always thought that I should like to be *aut Caesar aut nullus*,
> and as it is pretty well settled that I shall not be *Caesar*, I am quite
> content to live in peace as *nullus*.[17]

So he said. But he also confessed to being 'one of the most
ambitious men alive'. He used these Laleham years to stock his
mind, to prepare for the great tasks that lay ahead. He worked on
his Thucydides, wrote articles on Roman history, published his
first *Sermons*, travelled a lot, learned German. In 1826 he wrote:
'I hope to be allowed, before I die, to accomplish something in
education, and also with regard to the Church.' His writings kept
him in the public eye, and his Laleham pupils – who tended to be
of sixth-form age – went on to university, where they spoke
glowingly of his teaching prowess. When he applied for the
Rugby headmastership, the Provost of Oriel wrote him a testimonial predicting that, if he got the job, he would 'change the
face of education all through the public schools of England'.[18]

It was this testimonial, some said, that gave Arnold the edge
over his fifty or so rival applicants. And the trustees had good
reason to be happy with their choice. The school's reputation was
transformed; under Arnold, enrolments shot up from 136 boys
when he arrived to 360 in his final year – a figure that might have
been higher if Arnold had not been so free with his expulsions.
Rugby's governors could not have predicted that their shy scholar
from the sticks – and Arnold *was* shy at first, by all accounts –
would turn into a firebrand pamphleteer.

In 1829 the new head raised eyebrows by publishing *The
Christian Duty of Conceding the Claims of the Roman Catholics*. He followed this a few years later with a plea for Church
reform which argued for an Established Church that would
assimilate all Christian sects, including the Dissenters, allow
the laity more power and cut back on the privileges and preten-
sions of the clergy. Arnold's Church of England would welcome
'great varieties of opinion and of ceremonies . . . while it
worshipped a common God'.

This was in 1834, the year after the emergence of the Oxford Movement, which of course wanted just the opposite. John Keble, the Movement's founder, was one of Arnold's closest friends – indeed, the Movement was largely Oriel-based and staffed by several significant 'friends of his youth' – but such loyalties, although still genuinely felt, did not stop him from penning a vitriolic magazine article, 'The Oxford Malignants', which lambasted Keble and his High Anglican associates. As Arnold saw it, the tracts put out by the Oxford Movement threatened to obstruct all his own designs for Church reform. If successful in their aims, these Tractarians would make the established Church even more inaccessible, more remote from social issues, than it already was. In his view, the whole enterprise was really a last-ditch attempt to protect the mystique of the priesthood, and to shore up the assumptions of authority and privilege that went along with that mystique. 'The fanaticism of mere tomfoolery,' he called it, and proceeded to denounce Newman, Pusey and the others as 'formalist, Judaising fanatics who have ever been the peculiar disgrace of the Church of England', causing Newman to enquire, with deadly *politesse*: 'But is Arnold a Christian?'

A good question, from the Oxford point of view. As the High Anglicans understood it, Arnold – once a good chap, one of them, though flawed – had turned into a rough-tongued liberal activist, ready to sweep away the 'one true Church', with its time-honoured rituals and doctrines, its apostolic birthright, its vestments and ceremonies (all of which they wished to see revitalised and re-enforced), for the sake of some vague, sleeves-up, utopia of Christian togetherness. The Oxford Movement, they would say, stood for the old poetry of belief. Reformers like Arnold represented the new prose.

As Arthur Stanley indicates in his biography, Arnold's stance earned him some influential enemies. The year of his 'Oxford Malignants' piece, 1836, was in many ways the low point of his career. His job at Rugby was under threat because of his pamphleteering, and he was viewed with suspicion, not to say with enmity, by several of his old admirers. Even former pupils, now at Oxford, and seduced – as most clever students were – by Newman's silver tongue, were made uneasy by Arnold's belligerent approach. In the coming years, this belligerence would soften. Arnold continued to stand firm against the Newmanites (as late as 1841 he was lamenting that 'I scarcely know one amongst my dearest friends . . . whom I do not believe to be in some point or other in grave error') but he came to regret the tone of some of his earlier pronouncements. 'The Oxford Malignants' marked the climax of his youthful vehemence. A year earlier, he had turned forty. A year later, his son Matthew enrolled at Rugby, aged fourteen.

2

'Crabby' in Childhood

Thomas Arnold married Mary Penrose in August 1820. She was four years older than he, the sister of a college friend and the daughter of a Nottinghamshire vicar, and he had known her for only a few months when he proposed. The Penroses were originally from Cornwall, and Mary is often credited with having introduced a 'poetic' or Celtic strain into the Arnold line of East Anglian fishermen and farmers. She was the dreamer, he the doer, it was said. The Penroses (and Trevenens, on her mother's side) were mostly clerics, one or two of whom wrote verse, as Mary herself did from time to time.

When the two married, Arnold was already running his private school at Laleham, which at first he co-owned with his sister's husband, the Reverend John Buckland, and it was here that they set up their first home. Money was short – Arnold had to borrow £1,000 in order to get married – but they rented a large red-brick mansion at the south end of the village: not far, it so happens, from the back lawns of Lord Lucan.

The Arnolds also had back lawns, on which the schoolmaster would sometimes romp with some of his more sporty pupils, 'for they are all alive in limbs and spirit, if not in mind'.[1] Writing to a teacher-friend years later, he advised: 'Have your pupils a good deal with you, and be as familiar with them as you possibly can. I did this continually more and more before I left Laleham, going to bathe with them, leaping, and all other gymnastic exercises within my capacity, and sometimes sailing or rowing with them . . . I enjoyed it myself like a boy, and found myself constantly the better for it.'[2]

The schoolroom was a two-house conversion big enough for about thirty pupils, some of whom turned out to be too sporty for the Doctor's liking. (On one occasion, he was obliged to quell a riot.) After a few years, it was agreed to dissolve the partnership with Buckland. Arnold elected to concentrate on older boys, preparing them for entrance to the universities. Buckland, a disciplinarian, took charge of the slackers and roughnecks.

Over his nine years there, Arnold became fond of Laleham: 'really a quiet village and not at all infested with Cockneys'. He was an enthusiastic walker and it was already his habit to holiday in the Lake District – where he had formed an acquaintance with Wordsworth – so Middlesex, in contrast, was always likely to seem tame. He took a Wordsworthian pleasure, though, in the 'entire loneliness' of his riverside expeditions to Staines or Chertsey Bridge, 'there not being a house anywhere near it [the river], and the river here has none of the stir of boats and barges upon it, which makes it in many ways as public as the high road'.[3]

To the Laleham natives it must sometimes have seemed that their village had been occupied by Arnolds. When Arnold first moved there, he had with him his widowed mother (her husband had died young, of a heart attack, when Arnold was just six), as well as an invalid sister and an aunt. Then there was Mrs Buckland and, in due course, small Arnold-Bucklands. Although Arnold had been the youngest of three sons, his two brothers had died by the time he, Thomas, had reached the age of twenty-five. Needless to say, Arnold took seriously his new role as male head of the clan.

In the first year of the Arnold marriage, a girl was born: Jane Martha, later nicknamed 'K', for reasons that seem to have gone unrecorded. Matthew came next, and a year later little Tom, his father's favourite; although he might not have been if Arnold had known that Tom would eventually convert – twice – to Rome: the first time with some assistance from Newman. Six more children followed, at intervals first yearly (a daughter was born in 1824, but died in a few days) then two-yearly through until 1835, by which date Mary was approaching her mid-forties. Matthew was born on Christmas Eve, 1822. One of his godfathers was John Keble, who gave the new baby a signed copy of the Bible.

Mary Penrose was reputed to be 'fragile' and sure enough the laudanum was kept to hand. She was also said to be 'anxious, even to nervousness, at the least indication of illness' in the family. But she was clearly a formidable organiser, both of the household and the school – and, seemingly, of Dr Arnold. He, in these first years of fatherhood, was given to upsurges of impatience with his young. Puzzled enough by growing boys, he was baffled by babies. At six months, infant Matthew was pronounced to be both 'backward' and 'badtempered'. The child was apparently incapable of lying still: 'He will not generally bear . . . to be laid on the floor on his back – although sometimes he is as good as possible.'[4] In this same 1823 letter, we are afforded an amusing glimpse of the Arnold discipline at work in a domestic setting. He is writing about K, now two years old:

> Poor little Jane is to Day in Disgrace for the first time in her life . . . she will not make a curtsey to her Mamma as she was told, and has persisted for two hours in her Disobedience, in spite of the Corner, and all sorts of tokens of our Displeasure. She understands quite well, but looks as dogged and obstinate when we mention it, as a little child can look:- her little Heart swelling with Pride. It has made

me think how truly Pride is our original and besetting Sin from the very first, – when it tempts such a little Creature to make herself and Friends so uncomfortable, rather than submit to lawful authority.

(*Two days later*) I find that I left off writing at an unhappy moment, just in the midst of Jane's Naughtiness:- I am happy to say however that she was at last overcome, and made her curtsey very obediently, and was a very good Child afterwards. She is usually very docile, and does every Thing that she is told, and is very fond of her little Brother, whom she kisses and fondles with the utmost Gentleness.[5]

When Matthew was two, it was noticed that one of his legs was 'greatly bent'. This disability, his father said, was the result of the boy's 'bad habit of crawling before he could walk'.[6] A London specialist was consulted and leg-irons were prescribed. These 'fetters' Matthew wore until the age of four, and when they were removed both legs were slightly out of shape. He had a 'clumsy manner of walking' and seemed in danger of developing 'inactive habits'.[7] Mary Arnold worried that the fetters might have been bad for him: 'I cannot help thinking that they would have been equally safe and efficacious if *much* lighter – and of course to a little child this would have been a great matter.'[8] At the same time, she consoled herself by reflecting on the 'great good' they had done: 'He should always be thankful when old enough to know the importance of what was done for him, that the prompt use of these incumbering irons probably saved him from permanent lameness or deformity.'[9] When he was six, though, she wrote in her journal: 'He does not get at all less clumsy, but rather his awkwardness strikes me more than ever as he gets older.' She thought of hiring 'a drill sergeant and a dancing master'.[10]

Dr Arnold, no humorist, had a facetious vein. He called his children 'fry' or 'dogs' and spoke of 'kennel rules'. He also gave each of them a nickname. Thus, son Tom was known as 'Prawn' and others were dubbed 'Bonze' or 'Quid' or 'Bacco'. Matthew he called 'Crab', because of the odd way he walked. The name stuck, so that in *Tom Brown's Schooldays* we catch a glimpse of one Crab Jones: 'The coolest fish in Rugby; if he were tumbled into the moon this minute, he would just pick himself up without taking his hands out of his pockets.'[11]

This pose of nonchalance was established early on. Crab was above the battle. None the less, he was a battler. He liked playing soldiers, building forts, organising skirmishes with mud-bombs, brandishing his wooden sword. Because of his awkwardness, he always had to hold back a bit, and keep to the margins of a scrimmage. Hence the pose. As brother Tom would say years later, Matthew entered into 'games and amusements . . . in a way peculiar to himself'.[12] Since he could not excel as a footsoldier, he instead took on the airs of high command. At Laleham, he was the oldest boy and his authority was never questioned. It was not long before Tom was calling him not 'Crab' but 'Emperor'.

In the meantime, though, Crab had his own emperor to contend with. From a very early age, Matthew seems to have been made aware that Father was difficult to please. In 1830, after the family had moved to Rugby, he presented Dr Arnold with his own in-pencil version of *The Pilgrim's Progress*. He had seen his father reading Bunyan's book and thought that he might enjoy a new edition:

Pimgrim's Progress in 4 Vols. 5th Edition. Vol Ist.
By Matthew Arnold, LATE Fellow of CHRIST CHURCH, OXFORD.[13]

On the flyleaf, the seven year old had written: 'from Matt to Papa, October 15 1830.' The book's dedication was 'to his Holiness Lord Man', which may not altogether have gratified Papa. The text itself strained somewhat for the bellicose but its heart was in the right place: 'Love manfully getting up again hit Cruel such a knock on his forehead that it quite killed him.'

If Dr Arnold was touched, he did not immediately show it. He had already decided that the languid Matt needed to be taught a lesson – several lessons. At Laleham and for two years after the

Rugby move, the three elder Arnold children were in the charge of governesses, none of whom lasted very long or made much headway – at any rate, not by Dr Arnold's standards. It was he who decided the children's day-to-day workload: lessons before and after breakfast, as well as in the afternoons. As soon as they could walk, Jane, Matt and little Tom were directed to the schoolroom.

By the age of five, all three were expected to be tackling a programme of studies covering Latin grammar, French verbs and exercises, arithmetical tables and sums, history, geography and scripture – this last requiring them to memorise a hymn and a short passage from the Bible every day. When the children were older – that is to say, when they were six – Greek, German and Italian were attached to the curriculum. On Sunday evenings they would be tested by their father. 'Those memorable examinations,' wrote Mrs Arnold, 'when your dearest father with eyes and words of love drew you around him and gently, yet accurately, examined you in the chapters he had given you to prepare for him. To me those evenings are delightful, loving as I do the *Teacher* and the *Taught*.'[14]

For a schoolmaster, Dr Arnold was oddly reluctant to send his children off to school. 'I am a coward about schools,' he told a friend, 'I am inclined to think that the trials of a school are useful to a boy's after character, and thus I dread not to expose my boys to it; but on the other hand the immediate effect of it is so ugly that, like washing one's hands with earth, one shrinks from dirtying them so grievously in the first stage of the process.'[15]

In 1830 Matthew was sent back to Laleham, to serve time in Buckland's school. The boy saw this as a banishment. He missed his mother and his sister, K, and would later speak of Buckland's academy as 'a really bad and injurious school'.[16] For two years, he said, 'We never left that detestable little gravel playground, except on Sundays.'

Buckland's reports on his progress at first seem to have been negative. 'My dear Crabby,' wrote Dr Arnold after a year, 'you have got a *Male* twice in one week . . . it makes me afraid that my boy Matt is an idle Boy, who thinks that God sent him into the world to play and eat and drink.'[17] And Mrs Arnold threatened to stop writing if his marks did not improve: 'You have only to write and tell me you have given proof of [?] necessary diligence, and our letter shall be written.'[18]

These snippets – often quoted – tend to make the Arnold parents sound more straightforwardly scolding than they really were. Their usual tone was affectionate-regretful. In September 1831, Dr Arnold wrote to his son as follows:

My dearest Matt,

I thank you very much for your long letter which we received this morning. To be sure there was a long Gap between the Beginning and the End of it, but still it was a very nice letter. I am sorry, my own Crabby, that you are in Trouble about your Greek Grammar – it puts me very much in mind of my own trouble when I was first put into Phaedrus. You cannot think how many Impositions I got, and how many hard knocks:- but still the end was that I learnt Phaedrus, and so will the end be, that you will learn your Greek Grammar. You know, Crabby, that nothing is to be done without Trouble – but I would have you cheer up your old Heart, and sit your Neck to the Collar, and pull very hard, and then the Coach will at last get up the Hill . . . work away, Crabby, and do your best, and be my own true Boy, and I shall love you always very dearly . . . My own Boy will think and remember that he must expect Trials in this Life – and whether the Trial be a hard bit of Greek Grammar to you at your present Age, still God loves us when we fight against our Temptations manfully and beg of Him to help us. And you who wrote so nicely about Pilgrim Love will understand that we are all Pilgrims, and must expect to meet with Enemies on our Way, and must fight with them as with great and bloody Giants. Your dearest Mamma will write to you soon, but we wished a Letter to go to you immediately, and to pat you on the Back, and say to you 'Never mind, Crabby', 'To it again, Crabby', and get through your work well. God bless you, my dearest Boy, we all join in kindest love to you, and believe me to be ever your most loving Father.[19]

After two years with Buckland, Matthew's marks did improve although – said Dr Arnold – grammar was 'still Pain and Grief to him, as I suppose it always must be to every boy'.[20] A breakthrough came by way of Virgil's *Eclogues*. It was Buckland's practice to make his boys learn these by heart. In his effort to oblige, Matthew found himself responding to the poetry and, by 1832, his father was calling him 'a grand Crab' who could 'construe Virgil and quote Ovid',[21] and writing to his sister – Crab's headmaster's wife: 'Crab certainly does construe Virgil very well . . . when made to think about it.'[22] It was decreed that the boy's exile should be ended. He would return to Rugby, 'to familiarise himself with home feelings' once again.

A tutor was engaged – for Matthew and for the much keener Tom. Herbert Hill, a cousin of the poet Southey, was – Tom later said – 'a good but rather a severe tutor: and we all made fair progress under him in Greek and Latin. Euclid he taught us also, but here the natural bent of my brother's mind showed itself. Ratiocination did not at that time charm him; and the demonstration of what he did not care to know found him languid.'[23] Even so, Hill remained as tutor for three years, from 1832 to 1835, after which it was decided to give the two boys a spell at Thomas Arnold's old school, Winchester, before enrolling them at Rugby. 'I think by and by that I shall put them in school here,' wrote Dr Arnold, 'but I shall do it with trembling. Experience seems to point out no one plan of action as decidedly the best; it only says, I think, that public education is the best when it succeeds. There is much chance about it.'[24]

In the meantime, Matthew was happy to be back on home ground – ground that was much extended and made perhaps more homely with the building of a Lakeland house, Fox How. Dr Arnold had always been an energetic traveller – to France, Italy, Germany, North Wales – and since moving to Rugby he had inclined more and more towards Scotland or the Lakes. He favoured mountainous terrain; he liked to climb. The Warwickshire countryside was boring, he would say: 'No hills – no plains – no heath – no down – no rock – no river – no clear stream – nothing but one endless monotony of inclosed fields and hedgerow trees.'[25] The Lake District, on the other hand, was endlessly various and thrilling. Of Rydal he exclaimed: 'The higher mountains that bound our view are all snow-capped, but it is all snug and warm and green in the valley – nowhere on earth have I ever seen a spot of more perfect and enjoyable beauty, with not a single object out of tune with it, look which way I will . . .'[26]

In 1833 the family rented a house in the Grasmere Valley and Arnold resumed his acquaintance with Wordsworth. He and the poet took long walks together and argued about politics, on which they found much scope for disagreement. But the Lakes became the focus of their friendship. Wordsworth was 'the perfect guide' and he warmed to Arnold's curiosity and vigour. And Dorothy, according to her journal, took pleasure in the Arnold children: 'good and wild and happy as it is possible for children to be'.[27] When Arnold expressed the wish for his own Lake District home, Wordsworth advised him on the location and helped to supervise the builders – the chosen site being a quarter of an hour's walk from the poet's home at Rydal Mount.

The grey stone house was to be on the bank of the River Rotha, at the foot of Loughrigg and not many yards from Fox Ghyll, home for some years of De Quincey. Wordsworth, says Mary Moorman, wanted the building 'to embody many of the principles which he had laid down for prospective house-builders in his *Description of the Lake Country*'.[28] The garden and grounds – some twenty acres – would be laid out and designed by the poet's sister-in-law, Sara Hutchinson.

Certainly Dr Arnold was delighted with Wordsworth's blueprints. He was soon writing excitedly to relatives and friends: 'It looks right into the bosom of Fairfield – a noble mountain, which sends down two long arms into the valley, and keeps the clouds reposing between them, while he looks down on them composedly with his quiet brow.'[29] A headmaster's landscape, to be sure. In another letter, he calls the view from Fox How 'a Picture that I can scarcely take my eyes from'.[30]

Fox How was also the perfect children's playground. The days there were always too short, Tom Arnold later wrote. The little Arnolds ran and climbed; they fished, rowed, skated, swam, played cricket; they built bonfires and took picnics by Lake Windermere. When it rained, they organised debates and charades. They published their own *Fox How Magazine*. Now and then they put on plays. On one occasion, the production was *Beauty and the Beast*, in which Matthew played the Beast. His mother remembered him 'with my cloak for his furry garment and a boa to complete his equipment as a tail'.[31] A visitor to the house recorded, with some ruefulness: 'I was often obliged to take refuge in my room, but that was simply because my quiet tête-à-tête life makes it difficult to attend to anything in a crowd of bee like or ant like activity such as goes on in the drawing room here.'[32]

In some of these activities, Dr Arnold was a jovial participant: jovial yet unfalteringly senior. 'My father,' Tom said, 'delighted in our games and sometimes joined in them. Stern though his look could be – and often he had to be – there was a vein of drollery in him, a spirit of pure fun.'[33] At the same time, it would have been a brave child who refused to join one of the Doctor's fatiguing two-hour hikes. 'In a sense,' Tom also said, 'we were afraid of him; that is we were very much afraid, if we did wrong, of being found out, punished and still worse of witnessing the frown gather on his brow, yet in all of us on the whole love cast out fear; for he never held us at a distance, was never impatient with us; always, we knew, was trying to make us good and happy.'[34]

Dr Arnold liked to lead his 'troop' on arduous cross-country rambles, and was adept at 'viewing the characteristic features of a country and its marked positions, or the most beautiful points of a prospect'.[35] These expeditions maybe served as correctives to the seductive overtures of nature. He sometimes feared that the Lake District should really be classed as a temptation: perhaps 'mere mountain and lake hunting' was actually 'time lost' in life's great struggle.[36] He would pray that 'the sense of Moral Evil be as strong in us as my delight in Natural Beauty'. Dr Arnold loved flowers – 'Flowers are my music,' he (who was deeply unmusical) once said – but at the same time he was impatient with Wordsworth's reverence for 'the meanest flower that blows'. Flowers were so *little*; was it not morbid to dwell on them so?

Dr Arnold would often argue that Fox How recharged his energies and allowed him time and space for contemplation. It also kept him fit. His father had died young, and – as he wrote in 1830 – 'The deaths of my two Brothers, who neither of them outlived my present age, ought to be sufficient to remind me that Health, even in a far more robust frame than mine, is no security.'[37] Even so, he was constantly suspicious of his own escapist pangs. A poem he wrote in 1839 is worth a second glance, not just because of what it reveals about its author's conscience but also because his son Matthew must have read it more than once:

How still this upland Vale!
How clear, how peaceful, is this infant Stream!
How blest in this untroubled Loveliness
Its sparkling Waters seem!

Yonder in Distance far
How gleams beneath the Light the mighty Sea!
Eternal Life is there, Eternal Power,
Eternal Purity.

Couldst thou at once be there,
O peaceful stream! thine were a Wondrous Story:
Here, to have Rest and Pleasure for thy Lot
There, Rest and Glory –

A GIFT IMPRISONED

Between this upland Vale
And yon far Ocean, canst thou nothing see?
  A wide Space parts the two – and there is set
    God's Task for thee –

A rich and busy Land!
Wide fruitful Fields, and many a Crowded Town –
  Thither, O stream, from this thy early Home
    God calls thee down –

Down with precipitous Fall
From this thy upland Vale thou must be hurled!
  Chafing and restless, tossed and broken, reach
    That busy World –

Soon from that wild Turmoil
Escaped, with fuller and with calmer Flow
  Lonely no more nor wandering, on thy Way
    I see thee go –

A straight embanked Line
Confines thee, wont to trace at will erewhile
  Thine own free Margin; and the Haunts of Men
    Thy spotless waves defile –

Calmly thou flowest now:
Singing no more, as erst, for mere Delight:
  But louder harsher sounds from Morn till Eve
    Thy banks affright –

So changed from what thou wast!
Curbed, soiled and troubled: yet thou must not grieve
  Knowing their better Wisdom, who their Good
    Give, not receive.

Better that sullied Stream
Than thy clear waters in thy upland Vale!
  Better that ceaseless Din, than thy blithe Song
    Answering the mountain Gale.

    Thy sullied Waters tell
Of others' stains which thou hast washed away:
  Thy straightened Course shows that where duty calls
    Thou wilt not play.

    Loud is that din of Sounds
Gloomy and close the Dwellings whence they rose –
  For Life and Freshness to the drearier Scenes
    Thy stream supplies.

    No more at Distance now,
The mighty Ocean calls thee to his Breast –
  Soiled in God's Task, there wash thy stains away –
    God grants thee rest.[38]

The upland vale, the far ocean, and – dividing them – the noisome realm of duty. This symbolic configuration we think of as Arnoldian, and so it is. Matthew Arnold may not have assented to his father's purposeful last stanzas, with their vision of a triumphant oceanic cleansing, but he did take heed of the poem's emotional topography. Here was a map of life that centred on the middle ground, the in-between.

3

Schooldays

The Arnolds could never quite pinpoint what it was that troubled them about their eldest son. He was loving and dutiful but never, they felt, wholly *serious* – not in the Arnold way. He 'flitters from flower to flower but is not apt to fix',[1] his father said. He liked fine clothes, jokes, smart company. In one letter, his mother lamented his 'vanity and love of ease – and admiration of rank and fashion'.[2] In another she wrote caustically about his adolescent passion for firearms:

Matt is not at home, having been invited to spend the day at Sir Grey Skipwiths – and the presence of a double barrelled gun for his entertainment so filled him with joy that I believe he has thought of little else since the invitation came – This shooting mania I cannot like but we have given him to understand that it must be indulged sparingly. His father does not think it right to debar him altogether from an amusement he so delights in. A gun is bought accordingly which is to go to Fox How, and live there – only with these

26

conditions that it shall be considered the gardener's gun and that there is to be no hedge-popping or slaughter of little birds.[3]

Matthew had poor eyesight and turned out to be a laughably inept marksman, but even so his mother fretted: 'I believe it is a vain hope that the want of success will sicken him of it.'[4] Dr Arnold was more sanguine. To the *Fox How Magazine* he contributed a poem, 'Crab', to be spoken in his indolent son's voice:

> Now welcome to the Rotha, where I stand and fish all day
> And where I shoot the birds, when they do not get away.[5]

This was in 1838. A year and a half earlier, Dr Arnold had sent his two eldest sons to Winchester. Before packing them off he wrote a prayer: 'Keep them, I beseech Thee, from evil ways – make them dare to do right.'[6] Matthew, though, got off to a bad start. In the spring term of 1837 he and Tom were invited to breakfast by the Winchester headmaster, George Moberly. When asked about the progress of their schoolwork, Matthew – who 'always talked freely' – declared it to be 'light and easy'. Tom later on described the outcome:

> A stupid boy from 'senior part' was present, and took the matter very seriously. Being older and stronger than my brother, he attacked him as soon as we had returned into Commoners, and practically impressed upon him the wickedness of making little to the headmaster of the difficulty of the form work. From this slight cause my brother became unpopular in the school; and when the time came on (in connection, I think, with the ceremony known as 'Cloister peelings') for the public exhibition of feelings of disapproval towards boys who were supposed to have deserved ill of the school-republic, my brother was brought out, placed at the end of the great school, and, amid howls and jeers, pelted with a rain of 'pontos' for some time.[7]

'Pontos', it should be said, were missiles 'made of the soft insides of a fresh roll'.

What Matthew thought of this ordeal is not recorded. Maybe it too was reckoned to be light and easy. We also know little of his response to another Winchester upset. In April 1837 he accidentally set fire to his right hand, perhaps when tinkering with one of his guns. His mother later wrote of her distress, 'All alone you had to bear the suffering of so severe a burn – actually seeing the light about your hand of the fire unextinguished by the lotion,'[8] but there is no description of the details. Matthew was sent for treatment and convalescence to his Aunt Buckland at Laleham, and seems to have recovered fairly swiftly. For a time, though, his mother feared 'a life long injury'. (Was she making too much of a small mishap? Park Honan believes that 'it was his mother who made Matthew a master of pathos' and amusingly recalls Mrs Arnold's reaction to an early portrait of herself, in which she appears to be 'on the point of starvation, with a thin bending torso and enormous eyes'.[9] Addressing her children, she commented: 'I rejoice to think that you my darlings might recognise something motherly in those eyes resting upon you, even if the eyes themselves . . . have closed for ever!')

By 1837 her droll fourteen year old had already started to write poems. Under the guidance of Herbert Hill, he had penned several verse exercises in English: 'Mary Queen of Scots on her Departure from France' and 'The First Sight of Italy' being perhaps the most polished and pretentious. When he wrote these two pieces, he had been neither to Italy nor France. There was also a birthday poem addressed to his cousin Martha Buckland, in which we get a glimpse of the precocious airiness that so disturbed his parents:

> A cough and a cold, and a weight at my chest
> (Mind not at my heart), not to speak of my breast,
> Have made me quite *low* for a season, and so
> You cannot expect any wit, you must know,

> *Your* facetiae and puns must atone for my folly,
> For I find that I cannot when unwell be jolly.[10]

Around this time (the summer of 1836), he also seems to have developed the interesting habit of disappearing for hours on end. More than once the alarm was raised because he had gone missing. When he reappeared he was of course coolly surprised by all the fuss. A calculated bid for centre-stage? Perhaps. Whatever the motives, the effect was to underscore his peculiar abstractedness. His mother indulgently records one of his disappearances. It happened just before his Winchester enrolment, when the family was holidaying on the Isle of Wight:

> Matt was missing (after breakfast). It was suggested that he might have gone down to the shore, and this was in fact the case, but I do not think it would be guessed what he was doing there. I did not know till as we were driving along he put in at the carriage window a pencilled paper which proved he had been poetising.[11]

The 'poetising' she speaks of here was 'Lines Written on the Seashore at Eaglehurst', the first of many Arnoldian essays in ambivalent sea-gazing, and perhaps the first poem of his that can be thought of *as* a poem, although it is clearly derivative from Thomas Gray:

> What though the murmur of the sea
> Beats gently on the sandy lea,
> And ever restless fills the ear
> With sounds which it is sweet to hear
>   On many a quiet shore.
> Yet here it seems as if the wave
> Were struggling with the sand to lave
> The foot of yonder wooded cliff,
> And then a barrier firm and stiff
>   Opposed the ocean's roar.[12]

Although Matthew enjoyed startling his mother, he approached his father with more caution. He knew that both parents believed him to lack 'sobriety of mind and manliness of character'[13] and from time to time he set himself to reassure them: the reassurance, though, was aimed at Father. A few days after his arrival at Winchester he wrote a poem, 'Lines written on first leaving home for a Public School',[14] that seems to have been meant for Dr Arnold's eyes:

> One step in life is taken,
> And we must hurry on
> And cheer our onward path as best we may . . .

The poem opens on a glum, forsaken note. The schoolboy feels 'deserted and alone'. And yet, 'e'en in this wilderness', there 'gleams one ray of light'. He calls to mind 'the sound of home', its 'fond, familiar' faces, and reflects that, however bad things get, we are always able to cheer ourselves with memories of those 'we know or love'.

Such is the drift of stanzas one and two. But then there is a change of tone, or tune, as if the poet has suddenly realised that homesickness is not the manliest of ailments. 'The sound of home will cheer the mind when naught beside it can.' *Naught* beside it? In stanza three, he remembers, just in time, that there are other, more exalted consolations:

> Yet a still firmer pillar let us rear
> On which our sinking hopes to prop:
> Though all human aid forsake us
> And naught appears our way to cheer,
> Though conflicting passions shake us,
> Do thou, O Lord, be present still
> And aye direct us with Thy guiding hand,
> That, as we labour up life's toilsome hill,
> Or with a slower step descend, we may be found,
> Mid all the storms that shake the world around,
> Not to have built our temple on the sand.

All the same, it took Dr Arnold less than a year to decide that the Winchester experiment had failed. Moberly was a sound enough man who would later praise Arnold for bringing about 'a general improvement of our generation in respect of piety and reverence' but he had evidently not yet made his mark at Winchester. 'To speak confidentially,' said Dr Arnold to a friend, 'I do not think that the state of Winchester is as satisfactory as that of Rugby with all our faults. I think evil among the boys is more powerful than it is with us.'[15]

In the summer of 1837 Matthew was removed from Winchester and enrolled in the fifth form at Rugby (Tom would follow three months later). During the summer holidays, the family took a ten-day trip to France, as if in preparation for this new turn of events, a turn which – as Mrs Arnold saw it – would complete the family circle.[16] Dr Arnold's French schedule was crowded but well planned. He would take his troop to Paris via Abbeville, Beauvais, Chartres, Evreux, Montreuil and Rouen and show them 'six of the best churches of France'.[17] When he was about Matthew's age, it had been his hobby to tour the English cathedral cities ('at the end of each visit he carefully noted down the architectural merits and demerits of the buildings in a special notebook')[18] and as a young man he had visited France with similarly purposeful intent.

The travel journal Matthew kept of his 1837 trip was meant for his left-behind younger brother Edward and has little in it about architecture: 'nothing remarkable' and 'nothing particular' are two of his judgements.[19] He now and then notices the 'gewgaw ornaments and worthless pictures' of these Roman citadels, but is usually more inclined to comment on the human aspect. In one churchyard, he 'was struck . . . at the inscriptions on the wooden crucifixes which are the monuments here. The form is thus: "Ici repose" – then follows the name and age etc., and it thus concludes: "Priez Dieu pour le repose de son âme" or "Requiescat in Pace. Amen." The simplicity of this is very beautiful.' At Abbeville, he and his family visit the cathedral at dusk and he finds 'many people kneeling at their devotions in the aisle . . . the solemn stillness of everything around, together with the indistinctly seen altar at the upper end, had a very imposing effect'. Even at Chartres, it was the worshippers who caught his eye rather than the architecture or the statuary – although these, he had to say, were 'most beautiful'.

Versailles failed to excite him – 'absolutely enormous' but 'of modern appearance'; nor, in Paris, did the Louvre: an 'immense picture gallery'. He lists the famous paintings but comments only on 'the Egyptian porphyry vases'. His most thrilling moment in the French capital came when he accompanied his mother to a draper's shop 'and assisted her with my exquisite taste in forming a selection of Pelerines, Lace, Cambric, Silks, etc., a tasteful assortment of which it would have been impossible to have procured without my assistance'. In London, before setting out, Matthew had bought himself a monocle.

All in all, it is French 'taste' that most beguiles him – the simple wooden crosses as well as the fine shops (in Paris, the 'jewellers in particular were beautiful') – so that when, along the road, he notices a hidden aqueduct, 'It seems to me to show the taste of the French, that . . . the banks, which were steep and high, seemed more like a low well wooded Range of even hills than a bricked aqueduct for a canal, of all unromantic things . . .' And in his final verdict on Paris, he calls it 'a capital in size only inferior to London, and that but slightly – in fashion, elegance, public buildings the inferior to none – superior almost to any in Europe'.

Matthew's first-hand knowledge of other European capitals was, at this stage, zero. In 1837, though, his journal was intended for the eyes of an admiring younger brother. It grandly concludes:

No 10-days tour ever gave more gratification. To you my dear Didu I take the liberty of inscribing it, trusting that if ever you make the same tour, you will find it useful to your travelling propensities in mentioning towns, routes, etc., and to your no less Natural Piggish

Propensities in its being in no small measure a 'journale Gastro-nomique'.

When Matthew, in September 1837, became his father's full-time pupil, he knew all too well what was required of him. In the abstract, he would be expected to work hard, behave himself, and seek always to bring honour to the school. Specifically, he would be expected to take notice of Arthur Hugh Clough. Clough was Dr Arnold's pride and joy. He had come to the school, aged ten, a year after Arnold's appointment as headmaster, and had fair claim to be thought of as the first Arnoldian, the first exemplar of Rugby's new solemnity of purpose. A prize-winning scholar, a capable athlete, a vehement Christian wholly committed to the school's ideals, he was expected to go forth and show the world what Arnold's Rugby men were made of. In 1837 he had just won a Balliol scholarship and had carried off almost every honour Rugby had to offer. His triumphant exit coincided with Matthew's enrolment in the school's fifth form. During the younger boy's first term at Rugby all the school-talk was to do with Clough's achievements and prospects. In October 1837, Dr Arnold wrote to Clough's uncle:

> I cannot resist my Desire of congratulating you most heartily on the delightful close of your Nephew's long career at Rugby: – where he has passed eight years without a Fault, so far as the school is concerned, where he has gone on ripening gradually in all excellence intellectual and spiritual – and from whence he has now gone to Oxford, not only full of Honours – but carrying with him the Respect and Love of all whom he has left behind – and regarded by myself, I may truly say, with an Affection and Interest hardly less than I should feel for my own son.[20]

Clough's parents lived in America, where he himself had spent his infant years. When, in 1829, he was sent to England for an education, he felt bewildered and bereft. During school holidays he was farmed out to uncles and aunts, none of whom he particularly warmed to. Now and again, though, he would be asked to stay with the Arnolds at Fox How. This, he found, was more like home. Over the years, the headmaster and his wife took on the role of his 'real' English parents. Later on, Clough would remember his childhood as divided between 'the blessing of being under Arnold' and 'the curse of being without a home'.[21] In England, though, Rugby *was* his home; he made it so. During term he was allowed to spend much of his free time in the Arnolds' private quarters in School House. For Dr Arnold, he was the dream-pupil; for Mrs Arnold, he was the pitiable orphan. She 'marked his somewhat delicate health' and 'conceived a great liking for him'.[22] By 1837, he was viewed almost as an honorary tenth Arnold child.

Matthew was four years younger than his parents' admired adoptee: too large a gap for envy, it might seem. At the same time, he could hardly have failed to take an interest in the Clough phenomenon. After all, he – Matthew – was supposed to be the eldest son. As Clough had flourished in the Arnolds' favour, Matthew's star had continued to decline: he had found himself banished to Winchester, an object of puzzlement and glum prognostication. Where he was languid and prankish, Clough was tense and gloweringly troubled; where he was idle, inconsistent, vain, Clough was tirelessly high-purposed. Later on Matthew would write in praise of Clough's 'genuineness and faith' and contrast them with his own 'not want of faith exactly – but invincible languor of spirit, and fickleness and insincerity even in the gravest matters'.[23] This harsh comparison was probably established early on, at Rugby. Looking at Clough, the fifteen-year-old Matthew might easily have thought: so *that* is what my father wants from me.

And he might also have asked himself: do I really want to model myself on this strange, brilliant youth whose 'clear black eyes, under a broad, full and lofty forehead, were often partly closed – as if through the pressure of thought; but when the problem occupying him was solved, a glorious flash would break from his eyes, expressive of an inner joy and sudden illumination, which fascinated any who were present'?[24] The problems Clough grappled with were as Dr Arnold would have wished: problems of conscience, problems of evil, the kind of problems Dr Arnold had forced to the centre of school life. 'There is a great deal of evil springing up in the school,' the boy Clough wrote in 1835, 'and it is to be feared that the tares will choke much of the wheat.'[25] And a year later: 'I verily believe that my whole being is soaked through with the wishing and hoping and striving to do the school good.'[26]

During his last year at Rugby, Clough kept a journal in which he recorded his own sins and those of his schoolfellows, some of whom went in for 'drunkenness and brawling'. To combat these evils, he founded *The Rugby Magazine* and wrote in his first editorial:

> O all-wise God . . . let thy purifying influence so continually dwell in me, that this work may be indeed done unto the Lord, that I may seek in it not the selfish gratification of my own desires, but the increase of reputation to this *my* school.[27]

'I have been in one continued state of excitement for at least the last three years,'[28] he told his mother in 1838, and there are those who have blamed Dr Arnold for 'over-stimulating, prematurely developing' Clough's adolescent conscience. The young man was sent off to Oxford, an impassioned champion of virtue, with every school prize in his grasp. He was manifestly destined for great things. Nobody at the time seems to have worried that he was perhaps already at the limit, and that Oxford in the 1830s was the last place in England to help cool him down.

Matthew the schoolboy could not compete with Clough, and hoped he would not have to. Even so, he badly wanted his father's good opinion. Virtue, on the vehement Clough model, was clearly out of reach. So too, it seemed, was scholarship. Poetry perhaps offered an alternative way forward. He was reading Byron in his school spare time. His one Winchester triumph had been winning the verse-speaking prize, with a speech from *Marino Faliero*. And at Fox How there was the eminence of Wordsworth to be savoured. 'Clough's head ... was beautiful,' Tom Arnold wrote, 'but Clough's head was not equal to Wordsworth's.'[29] Clough's 'seemed hardly equal to the burden and stress of thought which it sometimes had to bear'; Wordsworth's 'was equal to *all* thoughts, and incapable of being disturbed from the just balance in which its Creator had poised it'.

Wordsworth was held in high esteem by both the Arnold parents. Sister K had early on formed a friendship with the ailing Dorothy, and Matthew sometimes went with her when she paid her calls. At Rydal Mount the atmosphere was heavily literary, with talk not of evil but of Keats, Shelley, Coleridge and the like. And when poetry was not under discussion, there would be Lakeland practicalities – arguments about the coming railroads, or suggestions for new hiking routes that might be tried.

At Winchester, during breaks from school work, the most exciting thing the Arnold boys had to look forward to was paying visits to John Keble's nearby residence at Hursley. Keble, author of *The Christian Year*, was a poet of sorts. Mrs Arnold used to copy out his verses, in spite of her husband's private objections to their 'feebleness and want of power'.[30] 'Think not of rest, though dreams be sweet/Start up and ply your heavenward feet' was a couplet she liked to urge upon her children whenever they felt inclined to slacken into states of 'careless peace'. Matthew, not surprisingly, was unimpressed by his celebrated Tractarian godparent, with his 'flibbertigibbet, fanatical, twinkling expression'.[31] Certainly he had no time for Keble's 'poems': were they not *hymns*, really? And in any case, 1836 – the year of the boys' Keble visits – was also the year in which Keble would break off relations with the Arnolds, in the aftermath of Dr Arnold's 'Oxford Malignants' essay.

Literary sightings in the Lake District were of a different order, more authentic, and nothing to do with hymns or clerical disputes. There were encounters with Southey, who once told the unamazed young Arnolds, 'So, now you've seen a live poet!' Less exaltedly, there were glimpses of Coleridge's son Hartley, lately expelled from Oriel for drunkenness and well along the road to his eventual 'melancholy ruin'. Hartley might not have lasted long at Rugby (he had recently been dismissed from a schoolmastership) but at Fox How, whenever he begged Dr Arnold for a drink, he was likely to be given one. And there was Henry Crabb Robinson, who remembered the young Matthew Arnold as 'a very gentlemanly young man with a light tinge of the fop that does no harm when blended with talents, good nature and high spirits'.[32]

Crabb Robinson's judgement would come later, but it seems that even in 1837 the foppery was well established. In the fifth form, Matthew was admired for the elegance of his detachment. As Dr Arnold's son, he was of course observed closely by the other boys, and was usually described by them as 'cool' or 'jocund'. He was often late for class and in general evinced 'a singular constraint towards his father'. During Dr Arnold's history lessons, Matthew seems to have been careful not to shine. There is even a story of him pulling faces behind the headmaster's back. With other masters, though, he was less fidgety. He performed well in English composition and at the end of his fifth-form year he won a prize for Latin verse. He failed to excel, though, in Greek or mathematics ('the mathematics were ever foolishness to me')[33] and the parental verdict, after his first Rugby year, was that his 'attitude' was still not satisfactory. His mother continued to lament his lack of a 'decided sense of duty'.

Perhaps Byron was somewhat to blame. Matthew was deep in *Childe Harold*, and his own verses at this time were inclining to the oriental-elegiac. In 1838 he read Julia Pardoe's *The City of the Sultan*, and worked on a poem based on one of that book's chapters. Set in Constantinople, the poem tells of a young Greek girl whose lover is 'smitten with the plague'. In spite of the danger, and in spite of all senior advice, she insists on nursing him in his last hours. When he dies, she flees to the mountains, where 'her body was found a few days afterwards . . . in a doubled-up position, as though the last spasm had been a bitter one'. Matthew's response, published in the *Fox How Magazine*, extols her magnificent self-sacrifice and promises recompense in heaven, but for him the real power of the story is its pathos: 'She died – unwept, perchance unknown,/She laid her calmly down to die./By mountain cliff she stood alone/As Death came gradually nigh.'

Dying lovers, fallen empires: these are the seductive themes. There is a dallying with notions of surrendered happiness, lost power, and a pervasive atmosphere of doom. The poem 'Constantinople'[34] bemoans the city's invasion by the Turks (or infidels) and insists on a proper reverence for its vanished 'days of old':

> Oh smile not on, thou glittering sun, for ever
>> So beautifully bright;
> Oh, flow not on, thou sparkling ocean river
>> Serenely calm in darkness as in light.
>>> Poetic fancy paints thy form
>>> In clouds and dreariness and storm . . .

The determinedly elegiac tone of 'Constantinople' may have come as a surprise to the readership of the *Fox How Magazine*; to its younger elements, especially. There were now nine Arnold children. Besides Jane, Matthew, Tom and Edward, there was Mary (b. 1825), William Delafield (b. 1828), Susannah (b. 1830), Frances (b. 1833) and Walter (b. 1835). Matthew's gloomy 'Constantinople' was probably written in 1839, when he was sixteen. A year later, with his eighteenth birthday coming up, he gave the family magazine a poem which his brothers and sisters (and his parents) would have reckoned to be more 'in character'. Called 'The Birthday, or Eighteen Years Ago',[35] it is in his jocund, Crabby mode. The poem is signed C.F.L.R.F.H., which

Schooldays

Kenneth Allott suggests means 'Crab, floruit Laleham, Rugby, Fox How', and is accompanied in the magazine by some verses, probably by Tom, in which Matt's still-inept marksmanship is mocked: 'He takes the gun/To have some fun/He shoots a Duck/But O, bad luck.' Matthew's poem is an affectionate rejoinder:

> Just eighteen years ago, a happy child
> Blind to my future woes, I lay and smiled;
> Now sadly I commit to faithful lays
> Dear reminiscences of early days.
>
> One only rival did my friends possess
> To share their table and their tenderness.
> No crowding then, no turns were in my way
> Large was my room by night and large by day.
>
> 'Tis true that many a whipping was my lot;
> Yet – seeing what I am – I murmur not,
> But mourn the weakness of the modern school
> Which governs boys and girls by milder rule.
>
> And see the consequence – one, two, three, four,
> Five, six and seven increase our household store.
> Pity their father! Pity their poor mother!
> But, above all, pity their eldest brother!
>
> For when my gun some hard earned triumph gains,
> Then do they flout and gibe me for my pains
> And say that all the creatures which I slay
> Will live to fly and fall another day.
>
> Yet were I happy if with this they'd cease,
> If I might breakfast, dine and sup in peace.
> But little tables are my father's passion
> And having all the nine my mother's fashion.

O! that these ribs had language! that these arms –
Jostled so oft by Edward's rude alarms –
Could paint their sorrows! That these elbows too
Could shew their various bruises, black and blue!

But no, it must not be! Only if e'er
My little Arnolds dare to come so near,
Then shall their Father's woes be brought to light
And all the tribe shall vanish from my sight.

Matthew Arnold's first published poem – or, rather, his first printed poem – was composed in this same year. In June his 'Alaric at Rome'[36] won the Rugby Sixth Form Poetry Prize, and the reward was to have his poem printed in 'a pamphlet of eleven pages, with preface, bound in a rose-coloured paper' (a rare item of Victoriana which in later years would be the target of one of T.J. Wise's notorious forgeries). If, as some have claimed, Arnold was hoping with this triumph for 'his mother's astonishment and Wordsworth's approval', he was disappointed. Wordsworth made no comment, so far as we know, and Mrs Arnold was perfunctory in her acknowledgement of the success. More important, in her view, was Matthew's immediate academic future. In November he would be trying for an open scholarship to Balliol College, Oxford. Nobody gave him much of a chance, but who could tell?

'Alaric at Rome' was probably written in May 1840, and it reflects Matthew's reading at that time: Byron, Gibbon's *Decline and Fall*, and – presumably – his father's own *History of Rome*. The first volume of Dr Arnold's monumental work had appeared in 1838. Also, under the headmaster's guidance, he had been pondering Niebuhr and Vico – his father's pet 'cyclical' historians – and reading up on the French Revolution, hoping to fathom it from the French point of view.

'Alaric' is a poem about worldly triumph – its substance and its hollowness. Stiff and trite most of the time, the work is usually dismissed as a Byronic exercise, but there is little in it of Byron's appetite for bustling heroic action. When the poem opens, the action is already done. Alaric was the Visigoth leader who conquered Rome in AD 410, a Rome fatigued by its own glories and excesses. Instead of portraying Alaric as an energetic warrior-figure, Matthew sees him as a solitary, uncertain introvert. What did this lone barbarian *feel* as he surveyed his prize, won at the third attempt?

> Perhaps his wandering heart was far away,
> Lost in dim memories of his early home.

The poet is helped in this portrayal by his knowledge that Alaric's Roman victory would not last long. In the very year of his conquest, the Goth died young, 'of a sudden illness'. Rome's glory is the stuff of history and legend: it will last. Alaric's vanishes, almost as soon as it is won.

The poem is thus a double-elegy: an elegy for Rome and an elegy for Rome's conqueror. The real conqueror is Time:

> Oh! it is bitter, that each fairest dream
> Should fleet before us but to melt away!

And yet 'glory', if it is glorious enough, can resist Time. There are figures in history whose stories are 'registered on high'. There are 'deeds that shall live when they who did them, die'. At the same time, though – and here we can half-hear a cadence that is sharply personal – there are those who do nothing much, who leave nothing much behind:

> Yet some there are, their very lives would give
> To be remembered thus, and yet they cannot live.

During the summer before Matthew's Balliol exam, a tutor was engaged. The appointee was William Lake, a 23-year-old Rug-beian – a friend of Clough's and favourite of Dr Arnold – who had in 1838 been appointed to a Classics fellowship at Balliol. Lake was a distinguished scholar but was thought of as old for his years, inclining to pomposity and cunning. In years to come, he would be Dean of Durham.

Matthew, accompanied by the ever-willing Tom, joined Lake for a 'reading party' in Wales during the first week of August 1840, but seems to have gained little from it. He could not warm to Lake – 'a perfect child – if all does not go as he wishes, he can neither keep his temper, nor conceal that he has lost it'[37] – and soon grew 'heartily tired' of the Welsh rain. At the end of the summer, Lake submitted a negative report to Dr Arnold, who replied:

> Matt does not know what it is to work because he so little knows what it is to think. But I am hopeful about him more than I was: his amiableness of temper seems very great, and some of his faults appear to me less; and he is so loving to me that it ought to make me not only very hopeful, but very patient and long-suffering towards him. Besides, I think that he is not so idle as he was, and that there is a better prospect of his beginning to read in earnest. Alas! that we should have to talk of prospect only, and of no performance as yet which deserves the name of 'earnest reading'.[38]

In November Matthew sat his Balliol exam – four days' written work followed by a lengthy *viva voce*. There were over thirty candidates for two £30-per-year awards. When it was learned at Rugby that Matthew was one of the two winners, Dr Arnold wrote: 'I had not the least expectation of his being successful . . . The news actually filled me with astonishment.'[39] For the headmaster, a Balliol scholarship meant Clough or – before him – Lake, or A.P. Stanley, his own biographer-to-be. It meant, surely, a more strenuous Christian commitment than was evident so far in the always amiable Matthew. What did this triumph signify? A lowering of standards at Balliol? An error of judgement at Rugby? How was it that Matthew had managed to pretend to be his father's son? Had he been practising, in secret?

4

Oxford

The Matthew Arnold who arrived at Balliol in October 1841 was certainly welcomed – and inspected – as his father's son. Oxford was well stocked with Arnoldians but in any case everyone knew Dr Arnold's name. And in 1841, the year of Newman's notorious *Tract 90*, that name stood for more than mere headmastership. Oxford was riven by theological controversy, and the university's established churchmen badly needed a champion to counter Newman's rise. Thomas Arnold's 'Oxford Malignants' essay was remembered fondly by those who viewed the Tractarian movement as a threat to the university's power structure.

Oxford, after all, was a religious institution. As things stood, no undergraduate could matriculate without subscribing to the Thirty-Nine Articles of the Church of England: atheists, Dissenters, Roman Catholics and the rest were strictly not allowed. Newman's *Tract 90* caused a great scandal because it argued that the Articles were 'patient of a Catholic interpretation'. In other words, Roman Catholics could join the university without surrendering their faith. Or, even more alarmingly, Newmanites could join the Roman Church without surrendering their jobs.

Newman, of course, was not yet a Roman Catholic but his drift towards Rome seemed irresistible. So too did the appeal he held for undergraduates and for certain of Oxford's younger clerics. His services at St Mary's were always packed and his sermons were listened to with awe. In 1841 the streets of Oxford thronged with his disciples – who, it was said, could be spotted at a glance: 'All hold their heads slightly to one side, speak in very soft voices, all . . . make long pauses between their sentences, and fall on their knees exactly as if their legs were knocked out from under them.'[1]

Fully fledged converts of this sort would not have relished having Newman's sermons compared to those of Dr Arnold, his arch-foe. For Rugby men, though, the similarities were unmistakable – unmistakable, and troubling. In St Mary's Dr Arnold's acolytes could re-experience the thrill of Rugby Chapel. And this surely was not right. Arthur Stanley – Rugby's first-ever Balliol scholar and Clough-like in his attachment to the Arnold ethos – more than once found himself shaken by the inspired pulpitry of Newman. With Newman, as with Arnold, he received 'the same overpowering conviction that he was a thorough Christian'.[2]

Stanley 'dreaded a collision' between his Rugby mentor and the university's High Anglicans, and eventually drew back from the brink of a Tractarian conversion. Clough also feared a clash. At the same time, he too was touched by Newman's spell. In one of the first letters he wrote from Oxford, he asked a friend: 'Have you ever read Newman's sermons? I hope you will soon if you have not, for they are very good.'[3] This slight wavering from the Arnold line was for Clough like the first tremor of a spiritual earthquake. He could not afford to be drawn to Newman; he could not afford to call Arnold into question.

At Balliol Clough fell under the influence of his mathematics tutor, W.G. Ward, a one-time Arnoldian who – en route to full-scale Newmanism – lingered for a season in the realm of doubt. During this period, he took pleasure in getting his most susceptible students to re-examine their beliefs from 'logical' perspectives. His 'supreme delight was to make proselytes by starting a destructive line of thought, to be replaced, if the experiment turned out happily, by constructive notions'.[4] As it transpired, no one was more susceptible than Clough. Ward fastened on to him with an intensity and possessiveness that went far beyond the merely pedagogic: 'Many hours of almost every day he would keep Clough in his room, arguing theology and craving for comfort and affection.'[5] The immediate effect was to plunge Clough into a fever of despairing self-analysis. His journals no longer itemised the sins of others; they now turned the full weight of his reproachfulness on to his own 'misdeeds and mixed motives'.[6] Ward's method left him stranded at Stage One.

Arthur Stanley once wrote: 'I know of no system to which I can hold except Arnold's; and if that breaks down under me, I know not where I can look.'[7] Clough might well have said the same during his high-pressure tutorials with Ward. Ward overcame his own doubts and became a Roman Catholic but he left poor Clough in a state of emotional and spiritual bewilderment. The brilliant scholar's academic career collapsed, along with his religious certainties. Rugby's most celebrated pupil ended up with a second-class degree. 'I have failed,' Clough said to Dr Arnold.[8] As a result, he did not secure the Balliol fellowship that had no doubt been reserved for him. He did gain refuge for a time at Oriel, but he would never again be anyone's star pupil.

When Matthew Arnold took up rooms at Balliol, he would have been vividly aware of Clough's predicament, even though he and Clough were not yet the close friends they would soon become. He would have known too of Stanley's waverings, of Ward's conversion. (Ward, after all, was stripped of his tutorship after writing in support of *Tract 90*.) Matthew had no taste for theological dispute: it was all so solemn and extreme. He resolved, it seems, to keep his distance. From the outset, it would have been clear to Balliol's Arnoldians that the head-master's amusing son was unlikely to be numbered in their ranks.

As if to underscore the point, Matthew visited St Mary's and allowed himself to be impressed by Newman's style:

> Who could resist the charm of that spiritual apparition, gliding in the dim afternoon light through the aisles of St Mary's, rising into the pulpit, and then, in the most entrancing of voices, breaking the silence with words and thoughts which were a religious music – subtle, sweet, mournful?[9]

This was his recollection, forty years after the event. At the time, he said not very much, but he did make further visits to St Mary's. Did he too find something of his father there? It seems unlikely. Indeed, he may well have found the opposite. For him, Newman's potency was not to do with *what* he said; the impact was aesthetic. As Tom put it: 'The perfect handling of words, joined to the delicate presentation of ideas, attracted him powerfully . . . but, so far as I know, Newman's *teaching* never made an impression upon him.'[10] Of Dr Arnold's sermons, Matthew always spoke respectfully but he was inclined to stress their moral content, their magnetic power for good. Dr Arnold was an inspiring leader in the all-important field of 'conduct'. Newman seemed to be touched by a spark of the divine:

> In vain, all, all in vain,
> They beat upon my ear again,
> Those melancholy tones so sweet and still.
> Those lute-like tones which in the bygone year
>   Did steal into mine ear –
> Blew such a thrilling summons to my will,
>   Yet could not shake it;
> Made my tossed heart its very life-blood spill,
>   Yet could not break it.[11]

Matthew's method of keeping aloof from local passions was much as it had been at Rugby. At Oxford, though, he no longer had to face his father's frown. Or so he thought. November brought news that Dr Arnold had been named as Oxford's new Regius Professor of Modern History. He would remain at Rugby for the time being, perhaps renting a house in Oxford during the weeks when he was giving lectures. For him, the appointment was a triumph. He had long coveted an Oxford niche but had supposed that his enemies would keep him out. 'It vexes me,' he once said, 'to be shut out from the very place where I fancy that I could do most good.'[12] When his appointment was secured he vowed to 'lecture . . . neither hostilely nor cautiously, not seeking occasions of shocking men's favourite opinions, yet neither in any way humouring them, or declining to speak the truth, however opposed it may be to them'.[13] His Inaugural lecture was scheduled for early December.

If his son was at all disconcerted by this news, he did not show it, except whimsically. Nor did he modify his stance. Already, 'Matt Arnold' stories had begun to do the Oxford rounds, most of them pointing up the extraordinary contrast between stern father and facetious son. There was a legend that had the once-crippled Matthew leaping over Wadham's high spiked railings for a five-pound bet, and another in which, rebuked by a clergyman for bathing in the nude, he asked: 'Is it possible that you see anything indelicate in the human form divine?' There was talk too of his hunting exploits, his wine-bibbing, his card-playing, his exotic taste in clothes.

By Christmas, his sister Jane was writing in the *Fox How Magazine* of 'a 'fine young Oxford gentleman' with 'an eye-glass round his neck hung by a silken string':

Eau de Mille Fleurs, Eau de Cologne and twenty eaux beside
Rowland's Odonto, scented soaps, jostle his books aside.[14]

This was the image, and at Balliol's Scholars' Table, where the talk was of Ward, of *Tract 90*, of Dr Arnold's professorship and so on, he must now and then have been in danger of striking a wrong note. Was this scented wit really the eldest son of the most earnest man in England?

Sometimes it was as if this was the very question that he *wanted* them to ask. On the other hand, he seems to have been popular, even with the most solemn of his fellow-students. On occasions, he would admit, 'I laugh too much and they make one's laughter mean so much.' Mostly, though, according to his brother Tom (who joined him at Oxford in 1842): 'Things which said by anyone else would have produced a deadly quarrel were said by him with such a bright playfulness, such a humorous masterfulness, that the victim laughed before he had time to feel hurt.' Matthew, said Tom, 'could have become a formidable satirist if he had chosen' but he was essentially 'too good-natured'. When it came to 'banter', though, 'no one surpassed him'.

In a poem about Balliol in the 1840s, Campbell Shairp later portrayed Matthew Arnold as 'one wide-welcomed for his father's fame' who none the less 'entered with free bold step that seemed to claim/Fame for himself, not on another lean':

> So full of power, yet blithe and debonair,
> Rallying his friends with pleasant banter gay,
>   Or half-adream chanting with jaunty air,
> Great words of Goethe, catch of Béranger,
> We see the banter sparkle in his prose,
> But knew not then the undertone that flows
>   So calmly sad, through all his stately lay.

His fellow-students may not have known about the 'calmly sad' Matt Arnold who would write the poems but they evidently suspected that in some way he was living in disguise.

Goethe and Béranger were not, of course, on the syllabus at Oxford. To Rugby men, the curriculum at Balliol in parts seemed all too 'light and easy'. Most of the Greek and Latin texts, for instance, they had already learned at school. Although Matthew attended lectures conscientiously, he approached his routine college-work in 'desultory' fashion. Richard Jenkyns, the Master of Balliol, used to keep a term-by-term report book on his students, in which he assessed each of them under the headings: Divinity, Greek, Latin, Maths, Exercises and Morals. Under 'Morals' he would record his overall view of a student's attitude and performance. Matthew Arnold is described as 'indolent', 'not uniformly regular' and 'not sufficiently attentive to the rules of the college'.[15] His best results are for the 'English essay': his writing is here praised for its 'considerable power and skill'. But this is a rare commendation. Compared to the best students, who are routinely called 'regular and exemplary' or 'uniformly excellent', he made an average showing. At the bottom end of the scale, a student called Hibbert is described as 'very irregular and unsatisfactory in every respect'.

So, 'could do worse' was Jenkyns's verdict; although it should be said that the Master's judgements do seem rather off-the-cuff. When stumped, he invariably falls back on a 'respectable'. It is unlikely, though, that Matthew and his associates were too troubled by such ratings. If we can believe John Duke Coleridge, an Etonian whom Matthew had first met at Buckland's school and who was now one of his closest Balliol friends, the important intellectual action was always likely to be extramural. At Balliol there was a debating society called The Decade, which Matthew attended fairly often – as did Stanley, Clough and Shairp, together with some of the younger college Fellows: Benjamin Jowett, William Lake, Frederick Temple, Archibald Tait. (The roll-call includes two future Archbishops of Canterbury – Tait and Temple, a Master of Balliol – Jowett – as well as Coleridge himself, who would eventually be Lord Chief Justice.) 'There was a society called The Decade,' wrote Coleridge,

which I think did a good deal for the mental education of those who belonged to it, of those of us, at least, who came from public schools, where we were taught to construe, to say by heart, to write verses, and Greek and Latin prose, but where our minds were allowed to lie fallow and to grow on, unclouded by thought, in an atmosphere of severe and healthy unintelligence ... We met in one another's rooms. We discussed all things, human and divine. We thought we stripped things to the very bone, we believed we dragged recondite truths into the light of common day and subjected them to the scrutiny of what we were pleased to call our minds. We fought to the very stumps of our intellects, and I believe that many of us, I can speak for one, would gladly admit that many a fruitful seed of knowledge, of taste, of cultivation, was sown on those pleasant, if somewhat pugnacious evenings.[16]

No records of The Decade's proceedings have survived, although we know from Tom Arnold, and from other sources, that Clough was one of the society's most forceful speakers: not on theology, however, but on social and political affairs – 'the future politics of the world, the connexion of the world and of the Church' was one of his most memorable topics.

It was probably through Tom and The Decade that Clough and Matthew Arnold became friends. Tom wrote:

After I came up to University in October [1842], Clough, Theodore Walrond, my brother and I formed a little interior company, and saw a great deal of one another. We used often to go skiffing up the Cherwell, or else in the network of river channels that meander through the broad meadows facing Iffley and Sandford. After a time it was arranged that we four should always breakfast at Clough's rooms [at Oriel] on Sunday morning.[17]

It may be thought that Clough's tortured earnestness would have repelled Matthew at this bantering stage of the younger man's career. Not so: Clough, it seems, was never boringly down-in-the-mouth. Indeed, Tom thought of him as 'jolly'. He was also a 'tremendous' talker and, as his faith cracked, he became more and more preoccupied with current politics. Early on, Matthew was drawn to this side of him, if somewhat sheepishly: he would not have wished to acknowledge that the real bond between the two of them was Dr Arnold.

Dr Arnold's Inaugural was a stunning success. Stanley describes it well; for him, it was as if Oxford was welcoming its true redeemer. In an Oxford torn by doubts and factions, Rugby had arrived to save the day:

> Even to an indifferent spectator, it must have been striking, amidst the general decay of the professorial system in Oxford, and at a time when the number of hearers rarely exceeded thirty or forty students, to see a Chair, in itself one of the most important in the place . . . filled at last by a man whose very look and manner bespoke a genius and energy capable of discharging its duties as they had never been discharged before; and at that moment commanding an audience unprecedented in the range of Academical memory . . . The oppressive atmosphere of controversy, hanging at that particular period so heavily on the University, was felt to be broken, at least for the time, by an element of freshness and vigour . . . But to many of his audience there was the yet deeper interest of again listening to that well-known voice, and gazing on that well-known face, in the relation of pupils to their teacher, – of seeing him at last, after years of misapprehension and obloquy, stand in his proper place, in his professorial robes, and receive a tribute of respect, so marked and so general, in his own beloved Oxford . . . [18]

In January 1842 Dr Arnold had agreed to give a course of eight lectures over a two-week period. This duty involved moving his family to Oxford, where he had rented a house in Beaumont Street. At Christmas, in the family magazine, Matthew had anticipated the arrival in 'a dramatic fragment' called 'The Incursion', in which Oxford is portrayed not as redeemed but as invaded by 'barbarian hordes' – that is the Arnold kids, seen here as rowdy urchins:

What sights of horror hast thou late beheld!
From Beaumont Street the frighted citizens
Rush in disordered crowds, and the pale Proctor
Arrays his Bulldogs at the accursed house door
That holds this strange, unmannered family.[19]

And Tom, not yet an undergraduate, remembered the family descending on Matthew in his Balliol rooms: 'My brother, in all the glory of a scholar's gown and three months experience as a "University man", welcomed his rustic *geschwister* with an amused and superior graciousness.'[20] It was not easy, packing his parents and eight siblings into his not spacious college quarters. 'When he had got us all safely in, he is said to have exclaimed, "Thank God, you are in!" and when the visit was over, and he had seen the last of us out on the staircase, "Thank God, you are out!" But this tradition is doubtful.'

Arnold's 1842 lectures were as well attended and admired as his Inaugural had been. By the end of the spring term he could reflect that all was indeed well with him these days. He was forty-six; Rugby was now thought of as one of the nation's two or three best schools and Oxford had given him the prize he had yearned for. Even better, those Oxford figures whom he feared would be implacably against him had turned out to be – if not forgiving, at any rate respectful. 'Every Body was very kind,' he wrote not long after his arrival, 'and certainly it satisfied me that in returning to Oxford I was going to no place full of enemies.'[21]

Also, his family was in settled order. Matthew, for all his foibles, was showing signs of an emerging earnestness: in one of his characteristically surprising bursts of academic brilliance he had almost carried off the Hertford Latin Scholarship. Tom was about to enter University College, where he would be under Arthur Stanley's wing, and Jane had become engaged to be married. Her fiancé was a Rugby teacher called George Cotton (the 'Young Master' in *Tom Brown's Schooldays*), a favourite of Dr Arnold's. Cotton was, by some accounts, an awkward, unengaging figure – noted, we note, for his monocle, with which he was 'forever fidgeting'. 'A more unattractive youth I never saw' was Wordsworth's comment.[22] Still, he was as 'morally thoughtful' as could be, and Jane evidently loved him. During the months of their engagement she was 'as happy and carefree as a kitten'. The wedding would take place in June, in the headmaster's Rugby garden.

In May, though, everything went wrong. Cotton suddenly cancelled the engagement, telling Dr Arnold that he 'was not in love with Jane'. Jane plunged into a severe depression: she could neither eat nor sleep and, when comforted, could barely bring herself to speak. Dr Arnold was appalled by her unhappiness – and was also perhaps enraged by Cotton's conduct, though he showed the young man only 'extreme tenderness and kindness'. On 17 May, out walking with his wife, he suddenly collapsed: 'A light, feverish attack,' he called it, 'brought on by my distress and anxiety about dearest Jane.'[23] After a few days' rest, he was thought to have recovered, but his journal during this time is the work of a man who knows he is about to die:

Another day and another month succeed . . . I would wish to keep a watch over my tongue, as to vehement speaking and censuring of others. I would desire to be more thoughtful of others, more thoughtful of my own head . . . I would desire to remember my latter end to which I am approaching, going down the hill of life, and having done far more than half my work. May God keep me in the hour of death . . .

Ten days later there was a second seizure, then a third. Arnold died on 12 June, twenty-four hours before his forty-seventh birthday. The diagnosis was angina pectoris, the illness that had killed his father at roughly the same age.

Tom was at Dr Arnold's bedside when he died and heard his father thank God for sending him such terrible chest pains. 'I have suffered so little pain in my life, that I feel it is very good for me: now God has given it to me, and I do so thank him for it.'[24]

Matthew was at Fox How when he heard of his father's death. He had gone there directly from Oxford, in preparation for the summer holidays. The news was brought to him by William Lake, who then travelled back to Rugby with Matthew and the four youngest Arnold children. By the time they arrived, the mourners were already assembling. Stanley was there, and it was he who read the funeral service; Dr Arnold was buried in the chapel vault that he himself had built. Afterwards, said Stanley, 'Matthew spoke of one thing which seemed to me very natural and affecting: that the first thing which struck him when he saw the body was the thought that their sole source of *information* was gone, that all that they had ever known was contained in that lifeless head. They had consulted him so entirely on everything, and the strange feeling of their being cut off for ever one can well imagine.'[25]

5

First Poems

Six weeks before he died, Dr Arnold was visited at Rugby by Thomas Carlyle. For Carlyle, the trip to Warwickshire was an irksome duty or, as he put it, 'a desperate effort of conscientious martyrdom'.[1] Arnold, on the other hand, felt honoured. For him, as for so many others, Carlyle had the status of a contemporary prophet. Indeed, it had been in terms of almost grovelling adulation that Arnold had written to Carlyle two years before, in the hope of gaining the great man's support for a new Arnold brainchild: the formation of a society 'the object of which would be to collect information as to . . . the condition of the poor throughout the kingdom'.[2] Carlyle had refused, even though he was about to begin work on his 'Chartism', an essay in which he would complain bitterly about the middle class's general ignorance of working conditions in the industrial north: 'Why are the Working Classes discontented: what is their condition, economical, moral, in their houses and their hearts?' He replied to Arnold that he sympathised with his aims but was on principle against joining societies: did not most of them 'turn out very soon to be rather empty things, swollen mostly with cant, vanity and wind – the main reality in them the *dinners* they eat!'?[3]

In 1842, though, it was Carlyle who needed Arnold's help. By this date, he was researching his *Cromwell* and wanted to take a look at Naseby battlefield, near Rugby. It was arranged that he would dine at Rugby, stay overnight, and go to Naseby in the morning, with Arnold and two of his senior schoolboys. Although it is said that Carlyle was led to the wrong field, there was no mistaking his response. He was mightily inspired: 'I pray daily for a new Oliver,' he said.[4] As to Arnold's Rugby, it was 'a triumph of industrious peace'. Against the odds, the visit was counted a success.

Matthew was not at home when Carlyle came to call, and would have been sorry to have missed him. Like most Oxford undergraduates of the day, he was a passionate admirer. Just as many Rugbeians were drawn to Newman, so they saw something of Dr Arnold in Carlyle. Even Tom Brown had 'scarcely ever in his life been so moved by a book' as he had been by Carlyle's *Past and Present*.[5] 'In and from 1840 Carlyle's name was running like wildfire through the British Islands and through English-speaking America; there was the utmost avidity for his books wherever they were accessible; phrases from them were in all men's mouths.'[6] And it was precisely Carlyle's quality of wildfire that so excited these young readers. 'He carries one off one's legs like a hurricane,' said one.[7] 'His daring theories moved me like electric shocks,' testified another.[8] There was talk of his language having 'the electric effect of a moral discharge', his voice resembling 'ten thousand trumpets'. When Matthew Arnold, in the 1880s, looked back on his undergraduate career, he spoke of 'voices . . . in the air which haunt my memory still'. One of these voices was Carlyle's.

Carlyle's *Heroes and Hero-Worship* appeared in 1841, 'a history of what man has accomplished in this world'. It offered a seductive counterbalance both to Dr Arnold's theory of historic cycles and to the clerical preoccupations of the Newmanites, and yet at the same time it did not insist on repudiating either. Carlyle's hero-worshipping could easily be reconciled with Arnold's cycles. As to the Tractarians, Carlyle and Newman were surely agreed that the Church of England needed a spiritual recharge, and Newman may even have perceived something of himself in Carlyle's portrayal of the Priest as Hero.

Carlyle's power, his vividness, was in his subjectivity. He was not speaking on behalf of God but for himself: these insights have been suffered for, he seemed to say. And, with *Heroes and Hero-Worship*, he seemed also to be saying: you too can suffer as I have, as these great figures of the past have – you too can be a leader. And this, of course, was stirring stuff for earnest young undergraduates whose own leaders had led them into a wilderness of introspection and hair-splitting theological debate. Carlyle had no time for the inert or the compliant, the languid or the pusillanimous. He had no time for squabbling clerics. In his universe, human beings are possessed of godlike energies and strengths. Well, one or two are: 'The Hero is he who lives in the inward sphere of things, in the True, Divine and Eternal, which exists always, unseen to most, under the Temporary, Trivial.'[9]

Chief among Carlyle's list of hero-types was, of course, the Poet. Poetry, he said, was 'the highest form of the Godlike in Man's Being'. To the ears of such as Clough and Matthew Arnold, the rhetoric could not have been more timely. Each of them, after Dr Arnold's death, felt suddenly adrift, cut loose – not just from a habitual source of 'information' but from the innocence and stability of the headmaster's Christian faith; perhaps even from the refuge it afforded. So long as Dr Arnold lived, his disciples could be both errant and 'in safety'. Matthew's affectations served as a means of keeping Dr Arnold's extreme earnestness at bay, but they also protected him from his *own* earnestness. What now, if anything, did that earnestness amount to? What could, or should, be done with it?

Clough was asking the same questions. The two friends, though, the two beginning poets, were not yet comparing notes. Their shared response to Carlyle's vehemence, his magnificent big-talk, was an important bond for them to build on. It was similar to their response to Newman's vocal music. In each case, the seduction was aesthetic but with Carlyle 'aesthetic' was not second best. He did not expect poets to sign up to any creed. 'The Great Man,' he said, 'was always as lightning out of Heaven':

> But I liken common languid Times, with their unbelief, distress, perplexity, with their languid doubting characters and embarrassed circumstances, impotently crumbling down into ever worse distress towards final ruin; – all this I liken to dry dead fuel, waiting for the lightning out of Heaven that shall kindle it. The great man, with his free force direct out of God's own hand, is the lightning. His word is the wise healing word that all can believe in.[10]

To those who feared that they had lost, or were losing, their belief in God, Carlyle would say: be Godlike and you *do* believe in God. Even Newman had to admit that Carlyle was 'quite fascinating as a writer'.[11]

In 1843 a curious set of circumstances brought Matthew Arnold even closer to the spirit of Carlyle. The subject for Oxford's Newdigate Prize poem was announced to be 'Cromwell' – Cromwell, the reason for Carlyle's visit to Rugby, a hero of Carlyle's *Hero as King*, and now the subject of Carlyle's next eagerly awaited work. To many, the choice of subject was provocative, aimed so as to irritate those Newmanites who made a cult of Charles I. Matthew Arnold would have been aware of this political backcloth but made little of it in his rather laborious entry. Arnold's 'Cromwell' is part-borrowed from Carlyle but is more reflective and resigned. He might almost be described as Tennysonian. Tennyson's *Poems* came out in 1842, and there are echoes of 'Ulysses' in Arnold's 'Cromwell'.[12]

Arnold's verdict on the Protector's place in history, however, is not unlike Carlyle's: 'Peace to him. Did he not, in spite of all, accomplish much for us?' Arnold, mourning his dead father, underscores Carlyle's memorial with his own private grief:

> A daring hand, that shrunk not to fulfil
> The thought that spurred it; and a dauntless will,
> Bold action's parent; and a piercing ken
> Through the dark chambers of the hearts of men,
> To read each thought and teach that master mind
> The fears and hopes and passions of mankind;
> All these were thine – Oh thought of fear! – and thou,
> Stretched on the bed of death, art nothing now.

In another poem, 'Mycerinus' [13] – probably begun in this same year – the presence of Dr Arnold is even more touchingly explicit. It is a poem about early death. The Egyptian ruler Mycerinus has six years to live: an oracle has told him so. But why is he thus condemned? After all, he has been a pious ruler – unlike his forebears, who were allowed to live much longer. Where's the justice? 'The Gods declare my recompense today./I looked for life more lasting, rule more high;/And when six years are measured, lo, I die!'

Mycerinus devises an ingenious stratagem for extending his lifespan: he will devote his remaining years to non-stop revelry, so that 'by turning night into day he might make his six years into twelve'. Arnold does his best to make the ensuing merriment seem fun – 'flushed guests, and golden goblets foamed with wine' – but his heart is not in it. Nor is the heart of Mycerinus. Every so often, the king's drinking arm is stilled by the reflection that, at any moment, 'some pale shape/Gliding half hidden through the dusky stems/Would thrust a hand before the lifted bowl,/Whispering: *A little space, and thou art mine!*' At such moments:

> It may be on that joyless feast his eye
> Dwelt with mere outward seeming; he, within

> Took measure of his soul, and knew its strength,
> And by that silent knowledge, day by day,
> Was calmed, ennobled, comforted, sustained.
> It may be.

Matthew's father had died young, in his forties. So too had his father's father. The fear that he himself, known for his mirth, might have inherited a deadly family trait seems to have been present from an early age. But how early? His brother Tom later on refers to Matthew's lack of prowess at school sports: 'Probably his heart gave him trouble even then.'[14] He also says that, at the age of twenty-four (that is to say, in 1846), Matthew 'knew that he was in a certain sense doomed – an eminent physician having told him that the action of his heart was not regular, and that he must take great care of himself'.[15] And Max Müller, who knew the Arnolds well, has said that Matthew 'knew for years that though he was strong and looked very young for his age, the thread of his life might snap at any moment'.[16]

In leg-irons as a baby, Matthew had had a lot to do with doctors. It seems likely that some notion of his own fragility would have got through to him in childhood. 'Mycerinus' is a poem of mourning: the king is in mourning for his own doomed self. But it is also a poem about Dr Arnold's death. Was it wasted, all that virtue, all that faith? If not, then where was the reward? Matthew Arnold liked to revel – so he thought – but, as with Mycerinus, he was not built for it, full time. And his father, of course, had not been built for it at all.

Arnold's 'Cromwell' poem won the 1843 Newdigate Prize and was printed in an edition of 750 copies. The title-page claims that the poem was recited by its author in the Sheldonian Theatre on Commemoration Day, but this scheduled event was in fact disrupted by a student riot. The reasons for the riot are obscure – something to do with an unpopular Proctor and the awarding of an honorary degree to a visiting Low Church American. The scene, according to The Times, was 'impossible adequately to describe. What business took place was transacted in dumb show.'[17] There is no evidence that Arnold's prize-winning poem was transacted in this way.

Apart from 'Mycerinus' – if that poem was indeed begun in 1843 – Arnold's two most ambitious works so far had been set-pieces. He had written both 'Alaric' and 'Cromwell' more or less to order – or rather as ways of showing his seniors that he was more substantial than he seemed. They were strictly academic pieces: more to do with scholarly self-advancement than with any really concentrated testing-out of his resources as a poet. But then: *was* he a poet? He felt as though he should be one: he seemed to have the temper, the sensibility, the cast of mind. But was he, so to speak, a natural? Writing in 1843 about his 'Cromwell' piece, he feared that some key element of spontaneity was missing:

> As a boy, I used to write very quickly and I declare that at first it was with an effort that I compelled myself to write more slowly and carefully, though I am ready to confess that now I could not write quicker if I would . . . But if people are to be allowed to write very slow, they ought, I confess, to write very constantly, or there is a great stiffness about their productions when they are complete. This is a great fault in my Poem, and is, ludicrously enough, united with the fault of over-rapidity in the last part, which I had to finish in two or three days. However, some of it, I think, is fairly good . . .[18]

The poems Arnold wrote, or drafted, in 1844 combine 'great stiffness' with signs of 'over-rapidity' of composition. He seems to be labouring for spontaneity – and for subject matter, too. There are argumentative pieces that might go down well at The Decade, and there are verses in annotation of the books he happens to be reading: 'Written in Emerson's Essays', 'Written in Butler's Sermons'. Of these, the Emerson sonnet is by far the liveliest. It adds the American's 'voice oracular' to those other Oxford 'voices in the air . . . as new and moving and unforgettable as the strain of Newman, or Carlyle or Goethe'. Like Carlyle, Emerson is 'scornful and strange, and full of bitter knowledge' yet inspiringly insists on mankind's boundless capability: 'The seeds of godlike power are in us still/Gods are we, bards, saints, heroes, if we will.' And the sonnet 'To Shakespeare' also has Carlyle and Emerson in view. The greatest of poets is presented as wondrously *self*-made: 'And thou, who didst the stars and sunbeams know,/Self-schooled, self-scanned, self-honoured, self-secure.'

'To Shakespeare', though, is also a poem about biography, a topic which in 1844 was much on Arnold's mind. Stanley's *Life of Thomas Arnold* appeared in the early summer of that year and attracted widespread notice, most of it approving. What Matthew Arnold thought of the book is not entirely clear. He seems to have been both glad of it and privately resentful: once again he was sharing his father with a doting pupil. Stanley had done a decently reverential job, but his Dr Arnold was very much the public hero, the hero of good works. Matthew could see that his dead father *had* been heroic in this way: self-made and selfless, a schoolmaster, social reformer and good Christian. But these styles of heroism were not the styles that Matthew found himself aspiring to these days. Perhaps they should have been. On the other hand, he – the loving son – was still in mourning. Stanley's *Life* was a good thing, to be sure, but not much help. It was not, finally, *poetic*.

The letter Matthew wrote to his mother about Stanley's book was a letter he was not sure how to write. It begins with an apology for not writing sooner and ends with a grumble about money: 'I am in an awful state of want, with absolutely only one shilling and sixpence in the world.' In between, his words on Stanley are distinctly measured:

> There is not much for me to say – except as to the body of letters which I had not seen and which delight me: I did not know, even if I may have thought, that he had felt or entered upon many of the

difficulties there discussed: and on whatever subjects he touches he seems in these letters, above all other Places, to have got a free full expression of himself: the compass of a letter constrains him to be pithy, and the writing to one man instead of to the world lets him open his heart as wide as he likes. It often does happen that the rough sketch a man throws off says more about him than the same sketch filled up and transferred in all its fulness into a book: but with him it is not only more characteristic, but infinitely more pregnant with meaning: to us particularly who can supply what is absolutely necessary, from having known him, and no more than we want, on questions of Church, and of religious belief . . . I could not have believed I should find anything to enjoy so fully and so fully to go along with. What I have always thought clean conclusive, as he would have said, against the completeness of Newman's system, making it impossible that it should ever satisfy the whole of any man's nature . . . is most characteristically put out in the CXXXth Letter . . . I think myself there is a little Repetition in the Letters: so many on the same subject, for which things said and done by him might well be substituted. The sale in Oxford seems to have been very good . . . Men whose names you do not know, and who knew his works but little, or gathered little of his Greatness from them, speak, I believe, most warmly: I of course, hear less than others. Temple, a fellow and Tutor here, says he discovers in this Book the substance of all he has ever heard any Rugby man ever say.[19]

Stanley's *Life* was in some ways Mrs Arnold's book about her husband. She had assisted with the project and Stanley was anxious to provide a memorial that met with her approval. Hence Matthew's caution. And yet the letter is revealing, with its suggestion that the public Dr Arnold was not always as pithily self-expressive as he might have been, and with its overall assumption that self-expression *matters*: the opening of the heart, the responsiveness of an individual's 'whole nature', 'the writing to one man instead of to the world'.

This letter to Mrs Arnold was unusually straight-faced and to the point. Arnold's correspondence at this time tends to be full of flighty apologies for not being a good correspondent. He was accustomed to his friends' grumbles on this score, to their 'miserable insinuations about laziness, carelessness, and so on' and every so often he tried to 'astonish' them with 'swift and immediate' replies to their communications.[20] To be really swift, though, he usually needed the stimulus of a reproach, or some intimation of 'doubt and distrust' from those he wrote to. In more than one area of life, Arnold enjoyed this kind of teasing. He liked to lull people into exasperation, then confound them with a burst of sober purpose.

The technique did not always work. The tetchy Coleridge, for instance, was once not amused by some Arnold jokes about the Devon countryside – Arnold had called it 'lumpy' but no doubt 'nice when it had the sun upon it'. Hearing of Coleridge's annoyance, Arnold moved to make amends: his *mea culpa*, though, had an easy offhandedness which might well have further grated on the Coleridge nerves:

> See what it is to say rash things: . . . I must be altogether wrong about Devonshire: for dining the other Evening with the Reverend Hamilton Southcombe, our Curate, he and a man of the name of Grainger (so I took it) decided positively and authoritatively that Devonshire was pre-eminent in beauty among the English Counties, and teemed with great Men: and remarkt, at the same time with great force and shrewdness on the singular Insensibility of Devonshire Men to their own merits and their County's, and the very reprehensible silence they maintained on the subject. Undoubtedly they must know that being Devonshire men: and so of course I must have been quite wrong.[21]

There is a similar jauntiness when he tries to congratulate Coleridge on his impending marriage, although Arnold is here *trying* not to smile:

It is difficult for me to know in what terms to express myself after your last letter: so completely is it penetrated with that unfortunate error as to my want of Interest in my Friends which you say they have begun to attribute to me. It is an old subject which I need not discuss over again with you: the accusation, as you say, is not true: I laugh too much, and they make one's laughter mean too much. However, the Result is that when one wishes to be serious one cannot but fear a half suspicion on one's Friend's Parts that one is laughing: and so the difficulty gets worse and worse: so much so that it is impossible for me to say more about your marriage than that I congratulate you, which I do very sincerely. I know you are shaking your head. You told it me, you know, as briefly as you could, and as late as you could, and it is a delicate subject at best. If it had been left, though, for some of your Friends to tell me, the Congratulation would have been left for a personal Interview: for I was not likely to hear of it in this deep seclusion [he is writing from the Lake District], and should have gone back to Oxford in Ignorance. It was a great surprise: I had heard you speculate too in so disengaged a way, but a few months before, on the Desirableness of Marriage. Mais nous avons changé tout cela. I see I shall be incurring fresh Suspicions, so I shall quit the subject: I could speak on it more freely than I can write.[22]

'Matt utters as many absurdities as ever, with as grave a face, and I am afraid wastes his time considerably, which I deeply regret – But advice does not go much with him, and perhaps I am not qualified to give it.'[23] The mildly avuncular voice here belongs to Manley Hawker, a Winchester friend now also at Balliol. It was on a visit to the West Country with Hawker that Arnold had issued his quip about the Devonshire terrain. The trip, it seems, was laughter all the way: 'We arrived,' said Hawker, 'on Friday evening after sundry displays of the most consummate coolness on the part of our friend Matt, who pleasantly induced a belief into the passengers of the coach that I was a poor mad gentleman, and that he was my keeper.'[24]

The note of concern in Hawker's letter was echoed by other

Arnold friends. Clough, in particular, was troubled: it seemed to him that Arnold was heading for an academic failure even more striking than his own. If only for the sake of Dr Arnold's memory, something should be done. In July 1844 Clough took Arnold to the north of England for a 'reading period' – in other words, a cramming-session in preparation for his Finals in November. After a few days, Clough's progress reports were comically disconsolate:

> For this evening, Matt is away; a party of Oxford visitants from Ambleside and Grasmere came over last night to spend the weekly holiday; hospitalities were required ... so Matt improvised a necessity to visit his Penates, and left the *onus entertainendi* upon me ...

> Matt has gone out fishing, when he ought properly to be working ... I rejoice to think that he will get a good wetting.[25]

By November Clough was more or less resigned to Arnold's failure: 'I think he is destined for second; this is above his deserts certainly, but I do not think he can drop below it, and one would not be surprised if he rose above it in spite of all his ignorance.'[26]

This time, however, there would be no last-minute saving-of-the-day. A second-class degree it was, and for Arnold – as for Clough before him – this spelled trouble. Arnold had no money and, with this result, no solid prospects. A university teaching post, which he had vaguely expected for himself, would now be almost impossible to get. The only alternative would be to set up as a freelance tutor, but pupils would be hard to come by. They 'avoided me as a suspected Person,' he later recalled, 'I was by no means safe of a livelihood.'[27]

Again, though, Clough's example could be kept in mind. On becoming certain that his friend would fail to get a First, Clough wrote: 'May he also tread in my steps next Easter.'[28] By this he meant that Arnold could put in for a fellowship at Oriel, as he had done. The Oriel exam was stiff, but Arnold had a few months to prepare for it. Also, a lot would depend on the attitude of the incumbent Fellows. In the end, fellowships were awarded by election, and Arnold could at least count on one enthusiastic vote. The reckoning was that the setback of Arnold's second-class degree would jolt him into a last, clinching spurt of diligence.

And so it proved. Clough was delighted when the news of Arnold's fellowship came through – delighted as much for an anxious Mrs Arnold as for her still seemingly unruffled son. Arnold himself, announcing the success, supposed that it would 'in some measure atone for the discredit of a second class in the eyes of those who felt most discredit for it'.[29] In other words, *he* was not bothered about academic grades. After all, Wordsworth had got a Second and Newman – so he understood – had got a Third.

Even so, the Oriel appointment bought him time and, in spite of his disdain, it maintained his reputation as an effortless achiever – as someone who could do it if he tried. And Oriel had a special significance. So too did the date of his success, 28 March:

> . . . the time was the 30th anniversary exactly from the day Papa was elected at Oriel. We had nothing but modern prayerbooks at hand in my rooms, which did not give dates of Easter so far back as 1815: so Tom went through an elaborate computation, and discovered that Easter in that year fell within a day or two of Easter 1845: and the time of Election is always the same.[30]

Much of Arnold's preparation for the Oriel exam was done at Rugby, where – after his Balliol disappointment – he had taken work as a 'temporary assistant master'. The new headmaster there was Archibald Tait, one of his Balliol tutors, a staunch anti-Tractarian who at Oxford had kept a special eye on Dr Arnold's son. Tait put Matthew in charge of the fifth form, where – according to at least one account – his approach to the shaping of young minds was not at all Arnoldian: 'The little creatures,' he is reputed to have said, 'whom I have the honour of teaching, by a whim of our good Tait, must be treated like young pigs, poked at and prodded everlastingly, until they are taught to squeak intelligibly.'[31] At the same time he did not expect that prodding would achieve much. Children were either clever or they were not clever: that was that.

The following exchange is supposedly based on a real-life conversation between Arnold and one of his more earnest colleagues. The pair of them are discovered on a Rugby lawn, eating strawberries. Arnold is lolling in an easy chair, stroking the head of a great staghound, and can barely rouse himself to meet the challenge of young Fulton, 'erect and keen as ever' and intent upon rebutting Arnold's snooty views. Surely, says Fulton, the giving of marks was one way to 'stimulate and encourage' the less-able student. Arnold lazily demurs. In his system:

> . . . you would put the clever boys comfortably at the top of the form, and feed them with nectar and ambrosia, while stupidity sat staring at the bottom. That . . . would be my way. Indeed, it is the only way to teach the world. Give wings to the few: the many will pick up a gay feather or two, which the few have moulted.[32]

Fulton is appropriately nettled and protests that 'it is just the many we have to do most for. Nectar and ambrosia for the Fifth and Sixth! Something, anything, to awaken appetite for knowledge in the Lower School.' To this, Arnold replies:

> Appetite, my dear Fulton! I assure you their appetite is enormous. They gather round me after lesson to know what marks I give them – it's the only thing they are for – with an eagerness, a ferocity, which is quite appalling. If ever I don't return to breakfast, you'll know what has become of me: but, enough! These strawberries are delicious. I observe, by-the-by, you take the smallest ones. I understand . . . Are they the sweetest?[33]

Fulton points out that he has taken the small strawberries only because Arnold has already seized the big ones. Arnold lifts a strawberry from his plate and stares at it admiringly: 'I do like big things, certainly, and this strawberry . . . is an imperial one, quite the grand style. Ripe too all over! I wonder how much of me would ever come to ripeness if I was a Schoolmaster!'[34]

This episode is recorded in a novel, *The Three Friends: A Story of Rugby in the Forties*, by A.G. Butler, a former housemaster at the school. In the same book, two fifth-formers are heard discussing Arnold's performance as a teacher: 'He's not the stuff to make a Master of . . . There's not a bit of the Dominie about him. He's much too great a swell.' Once, when a half-holiday was announced in class, Arnold said aloud 'Thank Heaven' and was cheered by the whole form. 'He'd never be a Fulton,' one of the boys says, 'you always feel as if Fulton would do for you just all that he could.' And yet, the other boy replies, 'Arnold, if he got something he liked, might make you feel . . . well, something that Fulton couldn't.'

This Matthew Arnold of 1845 is a perplexing figure, poised between dandyism and melancholia, between a burgeoning aestheticism and a declining faith in God: a son in mourning who made everybody laugh; a youth marked for early death who appeared to have all the time in the world. People liked him well enough but few could make him out. The general feeling seems to have been that he was still living in disguise. But what was he disguising? When his father was alive, he needed to hold himself at a remove from virtuous instruction; he could adopt styles that were provisional, play-acting. These styles seemed now to have become habitual and in an adult – Arnold was now twenty-one – sometimes took on the appearance of superiority and arrogance. The aimed-for demeanour was one of amiable condescension.

For friends like Clough, though, who were able to study him close up and in detail, and who read the poems he was writing, there was a real danger that Arnold might turn into the fop he seemed to be. Without Dr Arnold to lean on and lovingly rebel against, Matthew's schoolboy pose of languor and detachment might all too easily settle into a mere frippery: a disguise that had nothing to disguise. Being undutiful is not the same as being duty-less. As for Matthew himself, he felt that there were 'other ways to go', ways that led not to Balliol, nor Oriel, nor Rugby. On the one hand, there were Carlyle and Emerson insisting on the high-souled, the impassioned path of creative self-fulfilment. On the other, there was the immediate real world of family, Fox How, society at large. There was also the matter of his father's legacy: the question of 'what would Papa have done, had he been spared?' Matthew knew himself to be in many ways the creature of his background. He had an inborn disposition to good conduct – or, at any rate, an inborn need to give a good account of himself *to* himself. How powerful was this need? Which way to go? And to what end?

Something of Arnold's inner disarray breaks through in a letter he wrote to Clough shortly before the all-important Oriel exam – an exam for which Arnold claims he is unfitted: 'for wisdom I have not, nor skilfulness . . . no, nor yet Learning'. After some amusing persiflage about the drudgery of his Rugby teaching job – 'True, I give satisfaction – but to whom?' – he launches into a lively, and Carlylean, account of his own character deficiencies:

> But, my dear Clough, have you a great Force of Character? That is the true Question. For me, I am a reed, a very whoreson Bullrush; yet such as I am, I give satisfaction. Which you will find to be nothing – nor yet is a patent Simulation open to all men, nor to all satisfactory. But to be listless when you should be on Fire; to be full of headaches when you should slap your Thigh; to be rolling Paper Balls when you should be weaving fifty Spirits into one: to be raining when you had been better thundering: to be damped with a dull ditchwater . . . to be all this, and to know it – O my Clough . . .[35]

His Oriel fellowship secured, Arnold was once again leaving Rugby for Oxford, but this time would be different. His new tutors were Carlyle, Emerson and Goethe, whom he had lately been reading in Carlyle's translation. These men spoke not of serving God but of becoming godlike. The dandy-scholar perhaps had a vocation after all. It was in 1844 that Arnold began seriously to think that he might be a poet. Being Arnold, though, he would hardly be content simply to write poems. He needed to have *faith* in poetry, he needed to believe that, as a vocation, it might have value in the 'general life' – as teaching, for example, surely did.

The 'general life' of England was of course going through a period of cataclysmic change. The Industrial Revolution had begun three decades earlier but it was not until the 1840s that politicians and intellectuals in the south began to fasten on to its life-altering significance. Thomas Arnold had been among the first to draw attention to the miserable plight of the new industrial working class, and Carlyle in the 1830s had railed against the soul-destroying monsters of the new materialism. But it was only in the 1840s that real anxiety began to bite among the ruling class. A new England seemed to be in the making, but what would it be like, and who would run it? The Chartist riots of 1839 provoked fears that unless the old aristocratic-ecclesiastical establishment came up with some answers – both material and spiritual – England might turn out to be sitting on a revolutionary 'volcano'. Carlyle's *French Revolution* had portrayed France's upheaval as predestined. Was England, inevitably, next in line?

A young poet at this hour would have to ask himself: what use does poetry have? To which Carlyle, at any rate, would answer:

The uses of this Dante? We will not say much about his 'uses'. A human soul who has once got into that primal element of *Song*, and sung-forth fitly somewhat therefrom, has worked on the *depths* of our existence; feeding through long times the life-*roots* of all excellent human things whatsoever – in a way that 'utilities' will not succeed in calculating.

And in Goethe's *Wilhelm Meister*,[36] the poet is presented as serenely wise, above the human struggle and yet intimately *of* it: 'as if he were a god'.

> He has a fellow feeling of the mournful and the joyful in the fate of all human beings . . . from his heart, its native soil, springs up the lovely flower of wisdom; and if others while waking dream, and are pained with fantastic delusions from their every sense, he passes the dream of life like one awake, and the strangest of incidents is to him a part of both the past and of the future. And thus the poet is at once a teacher, a prophet, a friend of gods and men.

These were the texts that Arnold was reading, and taking heart from, we assume. If he already had an ideal of the poetic calling, it would have been on these exalted, and yet mysteriously *useful*, lines. But there would have been misgivings. The kind of poet Goethe described was a rare flower indeed. Of the living poets Arnold knew about, only Wordsworth could plausibly be thought of in such terms.

Still, setting off for Oriel in October 1845, Arnold was perhaps happy enough to reflect that, for a time at least, he had escaped the tedium of regular employment. On this topic, Goethe also had some words of wisdom:

> And thus the poet is at once a teacher, a prophet, a friend of gods and men. How! thou wouldst have him to descend from his height to some paltry occupation? He who is fashioned like the bird to hover round the world, to nestle on the lofty summits, to feed on buds and fruits, exchanging gaily one bough for another, *he* ought also to work at the plough like an ox; like a dog to train himself to the harness and draught; or perhaps, tied up in a chain, to guard a farm-yard by his barking?

6

'Days of *Lélia* and *Valentine*'

At Oriel College 'men were elected to Fellowships rather upon their abilities than upon their scholarship'. According to one of the college's former Provosts, writing in 1843:

> Every election to a fellowship which tends to discourage the narrow and almost technical routine of public examinations, I consider as an important triumph. You remember Newman himself was an example. He was not even a good classical scholar. Yet in mind and power of composition, and in taste and knowledge, he was decidedly superior to some competitors who were a class above him in the Schools.[1]

It had been by these criteria that Thomas Arnold had won his fellowship in 1815; indeed it was Dr Arnold's vacated berth that Newman was up for in 1821. Arnold quit Oriel because of his scruples about signing the Thirty-Nine Articles. For him this had been a painful and determining moment in his early life, and Matthew would lately have read of it – perhaps for the first time – in Stanley's biography. And it might have been strange for him to find his father described there as a man of doubt: 'It is a defect of his,' a contemporary said, 'that he cannot get rid of a certain feeling of objections.'[2] At the same time, said another, 'One had better have Arnold's doubts than most men's certainties.'[3]

In 1846 people were saying much the same thing about Clough. He too was in trouble with the dreaded Articles and by the time Matthew Arnold arrived at the college, his friend was already heading for an honourable, if tortured, exit. Matthew would not have to sign the Articles just yet. His first year at Oriel was 'probationary' – a title that would have appealed to him, since so many things in his life seemed to be on trial. As a probationary fellow, he lived in college but was not required to teach.

In Oxford 1846 was a dramatic year. The Tractarian turmoil was moving to its climax, with Newman and Ward converting finally to Rome. And in Arnold's own circle, there was a deep restlessness. Clough was in the last stages of a total break with Christianity and even Tom Arnold was undergoing a crisis of belief. He would shortly be renouncing Oxford – and England – altogether. There was plenty to talk about, but how much of it impinged on Arnold's daily life we cannot know. Whereas Clough and brother Tom have left fairly detailed accounts of their spiritual travails, of Arnold we have only a few reading lists, some obscure aphoristic jottings and summaries of his gambling losses. He was still the enigmatic Matt. Now and again in his journal there is a gloomily sentimental moment: 'After all why am I restless because I have no one to say with tearful eyes to – I am wretched – and to be answered by mon pauvre enfant?'[4] As usual, though, he gives little of himself away – even, it seems, to himself.

Oriel's social life had nothing much to offer an elegant young aesthete beyond the 'grimaces' and 'affectations' of the 'born-to-be-tight-laced', and Arnold's closest companions seem to have been the philosophers he pored over in his study: Kant, Herder on Kant, Descartes and Bishop Berkeley. 'The true world for my love to live in,' he told Clough, 'is a general Torpor, with here and there a laughing or crying Philosopher. And while my misguided Relation [brother Tom] exchanges the decency God dressed him in for the déshabillé of an Emotee, we, my love, lovers of one another and fellow worshippers of Isis, while we believe in the universality of Passion as Passion, will keep pure our Aesthetics by remembering its one-sidedness as doctrine.'[5]

This letter to Clough ends: 'Oh my love suffer me to stop a little . . . Oh my love goodnight', a sign-off which has given pause to Arnold scholars over the years, and which they have now and then silently excised. It was Arnold's habit in his youth to throw out endearments like 'darling' and 'my love' to his male friends. Although these now seem over-fulsome, they were at the time taken to be symptoms of dandiacal grandeur. There is no evidence of any homosexual leanings. At Rugby, it should perhaps be said, homosexual scandals were almost unheard of. Boys slept two in a bed (single beds cost extra) and would openly declare their 'love' for one another but physical lusts seem to have been well sublimated by means of the school's 'manliness' doctrines. It was not until the second half of the century that public schools came to be spoken of as dens of vice. According to Stanley, whose own nickname was Nancy, Dr Arnold did have to deal with one or two cases of sexual indiscipline, and was sympathetic: 'At times on discovering cases of vice, he would, instead of treating them with contempt or extreme severity, allow the force of the temptation, and urge it upon them as a proof brought home to their own minds, how surely they must look for help out of themselves.'[6]

'Help out of themselves' was no doubt the solution. Clough's Oxford journals dolefully asterisk the days on which he falls victim to the 'wretched habit' of masturbation, 'the worst sin'. (In C.Y. Lang's edition of Arnold's *Letters*, Volume One, there is an appendix listing the occasions on which Arnold marked his pocket diary with a cross. Lang believes that Arnold's crosses have the same significance as Clough's asterisks: they denote his surrenders to 'the coercions of the post-pubertal, pre-marital libido'.) The early Victorians were huggers and kissers. They did not shrink from social ardour. Same-sex intensities and jealousies could flourish publicly without observers assuming that the two friends had gone to bed.

Even so, Oxford in those days was a kind of priesthood – Fellows were not permitted to be married – and quite often a crisis of belief was in reality a crisis of frustration. Most colleges were, we presume, seething with several varieties of sexual indecision. How else, we might wonder, could the novels of George Sand have captivated so many of the earnest young? For a dozen or so years, 'tight-laced' critics had been fulminating against Sand's 'immoral tendency and licentious descriptions'.[7] The heroine of her novel *Lélia* had been condemned as 'a monster – a Byronic woman . . . a bold, brazen paradox born, fostered and nourished . . . in a whirl and turbulence of Parisian politics, manners and questionable morality'. John Wilson Croker wanted her books labelled 'Poison' if they could not, as he wished, be banned. *Lélia* he called 'a work altogether such as in any country in the world but France would be burned by the hangman'.

Lélia was Arnold's favourite among Sand's books – but then he liked them all. By the 1840s, though, highbrow reviewers were rallying to Sand's defence. G.H. Lewes was her most influential champion, calling her in 1842 'the most remarkable writer of the present century'. Her style, he said, was 'the most beautiful ever written by a French author . . . Poetry flows from her pen as water from the rock.' Her steamy reputation he dismissed as 'giving a dog a bad name and hanging him':

Madame Sand has been known to travel in androgynous costume; smokes cigars; is separated from her husband, and has been the theme of prolific scandal. The conclusion drawn was, that from such a person nothing but anti-social works could possibly be expected.[8]

The discriminating reader, though, would see that Sand was a deeply moral writer. Her heroines, unlike Balzac's, were chaste, and usually pro-marriage. What they rebelled against was the 'abuse' of marriage: 'She puts forth *convictions* . . . It is incumbent on an author, not that he speak the truth, but what he holds to be the truth.'

Lewes's efforts established Sand in England as a writer to be taken seriously and by the mid-1840s she was almost respectable. Certainly she was hugely popular: 'the most widely read of all foreign authors except Goethe' according to one analyst.[9] In Matthew Arnold's Oxford set she was from the beginning an established favourite and a regular topic of discussion at Clough's Sunday breakfasts. Arnold himself knew parts of her work by heart and later on he would wistfully recall the impact of her books on 'those who, amid the agitations, more or less stormy, of their youth' had found inspiration in Sand's 'cry of agony and revolt, the trust in nature and beauty, the aspiration towards a purged and renewed human society'.[10] These, he said, were the 'days of *Lélia* and *Valentine*, days never to return!'.

Sand's appeal to Arnold was on several levels. When he first came across her, she was almost a forbidden writer: it was smart to be found with a copy of *Consuelo*. But there was more to his admiration than mere chic. For all their heavy breathing, Sand's books often turned on conflicts between passion and duty, with duty of one sort or another usually carrying the day. In *Lélia*, the poet Stenio is the voice of pure feeling – 'only what we feel we know' – and Lélia herself speaks for dutiful renunciation. And in *Indiana*, it was the heroine's exaltedly stoical letter to Raymond, her lost lover, that Arnold learned by heart. In this letter, the pursuit of high romantic passion is seen as deluding and destructive. Eventually, personal feeling must be surrendered to the general good, the higher good, whatever these might be. Sand's fiery heroines rebel against their stupid husbands and mendacious lovers but they have no Church they can turn to, nor any clearly defined system of belief. Even so, their noble agitation gives them

access to a serenity and wisdom that would have been unreach-
able by any other route. Writing to Clough, Arnold quotes a
fragment of Indiana's testament – 'from memory', and in his own
translation:

> Believe me, if a Being so vast deigned to take any Part in our
> miserable Interests, it would be to raise up the weak, and to beat
> down the strong: – it would be to pass his heavy hand over our heads,
> and to level them like the waters of the Sea: – to say to the Slave,
> 'Throw away thy chain,' – and to the Strong, 'Bear thy Brother's
> burden: for I have given him strength and wisdom, and thou shalt
> oppress him no longer.'[11]

Nothing could sound worthier, more socially purposeful. In
certain moods, Dr Arnold might have read this with approval.
In Sand's book, though, the letter goes on to speak not of slaves
and tyrants but of high-souled individuals who dream of finding
for themselves 'another life, another world', a world 'where
resistance and flight will not be crimes . . . where man can
escape man as the gazelle escapes the panther'. Not long after
penning her letter of renunciation, Indiana undertakes a ludi-
crously hazardous sea-voyage in pursuit of her lover, whom we
know to be unworthy.

In the summer of 1846, Arnold himself set sail for France,
bound for a holiday in Switzerland. On the way, he decided to
pay his respects to Madame Sand:

> From Boussac I addressed to Madame Sand the sort of letter of which
> she must in her lifetime have had scores, a letter conveying to her, in
> bad French, the homage of a youthful and enthusiastic foreigner who
> had read her works with delight. She received the infliction good-
> naturedly, for on my return to La Châtre I found a message left at the
> inn by a servant from Nohant that Madame Sand would be glad to
> see me if I called. The midday breakfast was not yet over when I
> reached the house, and I found a large party assembled. I entered

with some trepidation, as well I might, considering how I had got there; but the simplicity of Madame Sand's manner put me at ease in a moment. She named some of those present; amongst them were her son and daughter, the Maurice and Solange so familiar to us from her books, and Chopin with his wonderful eyes. There was at that time nothing astonishing in Madame Sand's appearance. She was not in man's clothes, she wore a sort of costume not impossible, I should think (although on these matters I speak with hesitation), to members of the fair sex at this hour amongst ourselves, as an out-door dress for the country or for Scotland. She made me sit by her and poured out for me the insipid and depressing beverage, *boisson fade et melancolique*, as Balzac called it, for which English people are thought abroad always to be thirsting – tea. She conversed of the country through which I had been wandering, of the Berry peasants and their mode of life, of Switzerland whither I was going; she touched politely, by a few questions and remarks, upon England and things and persons English – upon Oxford and Cambridge, Byron, Bulwer. As she spoke, her eyes, head, bearing, were all of them striking; but the main impression she made was an impression of what I have already mentioned – of *simplicity*, frank, cordial simplicity. After breakfast she led the way into the garden, asked me a few kind questions about myself and my plans, gathered a flower or two and gave them to me, shook hands heartily at the gate, and I saw her no more.[12]

George Sand would later remember Arnold's visit and call him 'un Milton jeune et voyageant'[13] – by which she may have meant that he was a young poet of somewhat Puritan aspect. As for Arnold, his admiration for Sand would cool over the years but he followed her writing career through to the end and would always remain grateful to her – not just for her own books but for the French authors she directed him towards: the poet Maurice de Guérin, the critic Charles-Augustin Sainte-Beuve and, most of all, the novelist Etienne de Senancour, whose *Obermann* would be as important to Arnold in his mid-twenties as *Lélia* had been in his late teens. Arnold's first encounter with *Obermann* would be in an edition containing a preface by George Sand.

The Sand visit took place in July 1846 and was the high-spot of a largely rural holiday. Arnold spent most of his month's stay touring 'Sand country', identifying places he had read of in her novels: 'Those old provinces of the centre of France, primitive and slumbering, – Berry, La Marche, Bourbonnais; those sites and streams in them, of name once so indifferent to us, but to which George Sand gave such a music for our ear – La Châtre, Ste Sévère, the *Vallée Noire*, the Indre, the Creuse . . .'[14] A key element of Sand's appeal was in the intensity and detail of her natural descriptions: 'She gives us the wild-flowers by their actual names.' More important than the detail, though: 'She regarded nature and beauty, not with the selfish and solitary joy of the artist who but seeks to appropriate them for his own purposes, she regarded them as a treasure of immense and hitherto unknown application, as a vast power of healing and delight for us all . . .' Arnold wrote this in middle age. In 1846 he may have been more indulgent of the artist's 'selfish and solitary joy'. Maybe not, though. From the beginning, he responded to Sand because, for all her daringness, she never went too far: she always made ecstasy seem to have a *function*.

In December, Arnold was back in France again, having perhaps raised funds with a brief teaching stint at Rugby during the autumn term. For six weeks he was based in Paris, where – once again – his mission was that of ardent young disciple. This time he had come to pay homage to Rachel, the celebrated Comédie Française tragedienne. Arnold had watched Rachel perform in London during the summer and had instantly become a devotee. In later years, he would say that it was Rachel's 'intellectual power' that most excited him. In the 1840s, writing to Clough, he took a humbler line: 'What do you think of Rachel – greater in what she is than in her creativity, eh? Exactly the converse of Jenny Lind. By the way, what an enormous obverse that young woman and excellent singer has.'[15]

When he was in Paris Arnold 'never missed one of [Rachel's] performances' in plays by Racine and Corneille, and wished only that her material had been equal to her gifts. Rachel's genius, he reckoned, was far greater than those of the French classical dramatists whose work she was obliged to serve. Not everyone would have agreed with him; few, certainly, would have described the tempestuous actress as a 'high and severe' intellectual presence. To Charlotte Brontë, she was a wild, demonic figure: 'She made me shudder to the marrow of my bones; in her some fiend has certainly taken up an incarnate home. She is not a woman, – she is a snake . . .'[16] And other witnesses tended to quail before her 'sublimely Jewish' talent. 'Her vocation,' said one, 'is for malediction, imprecation, bitter and hate-bearing irony.'[17]

All in all, it is easy enough to see why a young Englishman from Oriel might have been held spellbound by her antics:

Wicked, perhaps, she is, but also she is strong: and her strength has conquered Beauty, has overcome Grace, and bound both at her side, captives peerlessly fair, and docile as fair. Even in the uttermost frenzy of energy is each maenad movement royally, imperially, incedingly upborne. Her hair, flying loose in revel or war, is still an angel's hair, and glorious under a halo. Fallen, insurgent, banished, she remembers the heaven where she rebelled. Heaven's light, following her exile, pierces its confines, and discloses their forlorn remoteness.[18]

In *Villette* the 'cool young Briton', Dr Bretton, is asked what he thinks of the above. He answers merely 'Hmm-m-m', and then 'such a strange smile went wandering round his lips, a smile so critical, so almost callous'. (Matthew Arnold, when he read *Villette* in 1853, also pulled a face, calling it 'one of the most utterly disagreeable books I have ever read', and its author 'a fire without aliment . . . one of the most distressing barren sights'. But then Brontë, when she met *him*, was none too thrilled. In 1850 she found him foppish and insincere, full of 'assumed conceit' and 'superficial affectations'.)[19]

There is no evidence that Arnold sent a stage-door note to Rachel or had any social contact with her. As with George Sand, though, he would always remember her respectfully. After Rachel's death – in 1858, aged thirty-six – he wrote three awkwardly reverential sonnets in her memory.[20] By that time, he could barely recall why he had liked her. 'Sprung from the blood of Israel's scattered race', but born in Germany, she had given life to the dramatic works of France, Rome, Ancient Greece:

> Ah, not the radiant spirit of Greece alone
> She had – one power, which made her breast its home!
> In her, like us, there clashed, contending powers.
>
> Germany, France, Christ, Moses, Athens, Rome.
> The strife, the mixture in her soul, are ours;
> Her genius and her glory are her own.

In addition to his theatre-haunting, Arnold found time in Paris for one or two high-society distractions. He 'paid his respects to Lady Elgin and went to the Embassy Ball and the Opera Ball'.[21] He also took a course of French lessons; his pronunciation, he had learned, was faulty. By some accounts it remained so all his life, although his written French was said to be word-perfect. On his return to Oriel in February 1847, he was thought to have become almost comically Frenchified. Clough was pleased to see him but he had to smile:

Matt is full of Parisianism: theatres in general, and Rachel in special: he enters a room with a chanson of Béranger's on his lips – for the sake of the French words almost conscious of tune. His carriage shows him in fancy parading the Rue de Rivoli – and his hair is guiltless of English scissors. He breakfasts at twelve, and never dines in Hall, and in the week or eight days rather (for a Sunday must be included) he has been to Chapel *once* . . .

Arnold was not alone in seeming out of place. As it turned out, 1847 marked the break-up of that 'small interior company' that had sustained him since his Balliol days. Both Clough and Tom were straining to break free, and Matthew was aware that he too must shortly decide on a career. Certainly his mother took this view. A newly installed Whig government had opened up several avenues of influence. Both Lord John Russell, the new Prime Minister, and Lord Lansdowne, President of the Council, had been admirers of Dr Arnold. When approached by his widow, they were pleased to do something for his eldest sons. Tom was fixed up with a clerical job at the Colonial Office and, in April 1847, Matthew found himself installed in Berkeley Square as Lord Lansdowne's Private Secretary: a sinecure, he was assured, and one that offered scope for his social ambitions. Lansdowne House, where Arnold had his office, was a meeting place for bright young politicians and at Bowood House, Lord Lansdowne's Wiltshire seat, there would be smart gatherings of intellectuals and artists: the President of the Council was also a patron of the arts. Clough, on hearing of Arnold's glittering new job, was not impressed. 'Quite a mistake, I think' was his verdict.[22] On the other hand, he did not expect his friend to stick it out for very long: 'He has no intention of making this his permanent line.'

The same could have been said of Tom, for rather different reasons. At this point in his life, Tom hardly cared what he did, or what happened to him. In a burst of Sandian enthusiasm – for he too was a disciple – he had proposed marriage to Henrietta Whately, daughter of one of his father's closest friends. Spurned – perhaps on account of his 'radical' opinions: that is to say, his admiration for George Sand – the young lover saw himself as cast into a 'premature old age', a victim of 'the sad fate of a love which had inwoven itself into every fibre of my existence'.[23] At twenty-four, he was 'deadened to both pain and pleasure'.

Tom's intense earnestness had all along been something of a foil to Matthew's affectations of detachment. To know Tom was to know something of what went on behind his brother's mask.

The two were much closer than they seemed. But Matthew did use Tom. When the Arnold parents fretted about their eldest son's idleness and superficiality, they were always able to console themselves that their second boy was a true Arnold. And Tom, in his turn, was never inclined to skirt or suppress the Arnoldian inheritance. On the contrary, he embraced it with an endearing and at times bewildered fervour.

In 1847, though, Tom was unsure where his duty lay. During the few weeks he spent at the Colonial Office, he found himself for the first time living in a modern English city. He was appalled by what he saw there. Visiting London's poor, he encountered 'the extremity of human suffering and degradation'. Suddenly 'all other subjects seemed to fade into insignificance beside this one, all other evils to be as nothing compared with this monstrous and unutterable woe'. At the same time, he felt overwhelmed by a sense of 'utter powerlessness, and the futility of all individual efforts to stem the stream'.[24]

What could an Arnold *do*? For a young man of Tom's class and education there were of course a number of realistic possibilities. He could, for example, look the other way, as so many of his Oxford friends did, sign the Articles, take orders, marry the daughter of a bishop. He could become a Christian Socialist, like Charles Kingsley and F.D. Maurice. His sister Mary would eventually take this route. Or he could choose the law, or politics, and look to change things 'by the agency of actual governments, and by the help of a public opinion increasingly powerful and enlightened'.

None of these appealed either to his conscience or to his sense of the dramatic:

. . . satisfy yourself that you may honestly defend an unrighteous cause, and then you may go to the Bar, and become distinguished, and perhaps in the end sway the counsels of the State; prove to yourself, by the soundest arguments which political economy can furnish, that you may lawfully keep several hundred men, women, and children at work for twelve hours a day in your unwholesome factory, and then you may become wealthy and influential, and erect public baths and patronise artists. All this is open to you; while if you refuse to tamper in a single point with the integrity of your conscience, isolation awaits you, and unhappy love, and the contempt of men; and amidst the general bustle and movement of the world you will be stricken with a kind of impotence, and your arm will seem to be paralysed, and there will be moments when you will almost doubt whether truth indeed exists, or, at least, whether it is fitted for man. Yet in your loneliness you will be visited by consolations which the world knows not of; and you will feel that, if renunciation has separated you from the men of your own generation, it has united you to the great company of just men throughout all past time; nay, that even now there is a little band of Renunciants scattered over the world, of whom you are one, whose you are, and who are yours for ever.[25]

Thus Tom became a radical-renunciant. But it was England that had to be renounced, England where on every side he witnessed 'selfishness increasing', the pursuit of wealth hardening into brutal tyranny, industrialism – 'as the French call it' – causing 'our common human nature' to become 'prostrate and debased'. Nothing could be done in England; it had become 'a land for the rich' and Tom was, whether he liked it or not, one of the rich: 'I have *servants* to wait upon me; I am fed and clothed by the labour of the poor, and do nothing for them in return. The life I lead is an outrage and a wrong to humanity.'[26]

In the summer of 1847, Tom astonished friends and family by announcing that he planned to emigrate. In an unspoiled New World, he would pursue his dream of 'Freedom, Equality, Brotherhood'. It so happened that in the 1830s Dr Arnold had bought 200 acres in New Zealand. He had toyed with the idea of settling there himself. Tom's emigration could therefore be presented as a fulfilment of his father's vision. The unclaimed Arnold acres in 'Van Diemen's Land' might perhaps mend his fractured sense of purpose. Before he left, Tom asked himself, as he so often did, what Dr Arnold would have said. He knew that there were those who took the line that Dr Arnold's first concern would be with his son's loss of faith: 'How strange and sad that the son should depart thus widely from the father's faith, and seek to undo the father's work.' To voices such as these Tom would reply:

> Oh, if it were so indeed, it would be truly sad; a sadder and more unnatural sight could not be witnessed upon earth. But it is my comfort to believe that at the bottom it is not so, but the very contrary. If thou, my father, from thy place of rest, couldst still behold the scenes of thy pilgrimage and look into thy son's inmost heart, do I not believe that thou wouldst bless me, and bless also the work which I have chosen? Is not thy spirit with me? Do I not, like thee, hate injustice and falsehood with a perfect hatred? like thee, await and hope for the establishment of that 'glorious Church', that divine Society, which shall unite men together in a common faith and in mutual love? . . . The form, the outward vesture of thy faith – it is only this which I cannot accept.[27]

Tom embarked for New Zealand in November 1847, and was seen off at London Docks by Matthew, Clough and brother Edward, who was now an undergraduate at Balliol. The voyage would take five months. At the last moment, Edward asked Tom 'if he felt in the least inclined to change his mind':

> He said not the least, that when he had made his mind up fully, he looked upon the thing as inevitable; besides that, his wish to go was as strong as ever. What he felt most, I think, was the parting with Matt. I saw the tears in his eyes when it came to that.[28]

At Fox How there was of course a sense of loss. Tom was much loved in the family. There was also a fair amount of anxiety on his behalf. He had set off with hardly any money and no job. His only asset was his father's land. And there were other Arnold worries too in this strange year. Mary, the second girl (b. 1825 and known as 'Bacco'), had in April got married to a young physician who almost immediately fell victim to a fatal illness; William Twining would die within a year. Edward's career at Balliol was not going well: his health was poor and during the 1847 summer term he was mainly at home. William, the fourth son, was also having trouble at Oxford. He had rather reluctantly accepted a place at Christ Church – his ambition was to join the East India Company – and had got into some kind of scrape: all we know of it is from a letter in which his mother assures him that 'this is one of those lessons of life from which we may date much good'.[29] And even little Walter, the youngest child, was causing some concern. At thirteen, he had joined the Navy as a boy-sailor and by the end of the year was thought to be in Lisbon, on his maiden voyage. Of the nine children, then, only the girls were still at home: Jane (now twenty-six), Susannah (seventeen) and Fran (fourteen). Two of the five boys had gone abroad, and one more seemed about to follow. William would leave for India in 1848.

In these family anxieties, Mrs Arnold had a redoubtable lieutenant. For both Matthew and Tom, their sister Jane – or K – was an important confidante. Intuitive and sweet-tempered, and no stranger to suffering herself, Jane was the family's fount of sympathy and understanding. However, she was no sentimentalist. She invariably spoke her mind. When Tom's love affair with Henrietta Whately failed, K assured him that the marriage he yearned for would surely have failed too: 'She ought not to have been the wife of a man of very original or independent character.'[30] If Matthew showed her poems that she did not like, she told him so. And he, who believed her to be his best critic, would always be in a hurry to forgive her.

One of Arnold's most important early poems was addressed to K – or Fausta, as the poem calls her. 'Resignation'[31] is Arnold's first significant first-person work, and it was probably written over a period of years. Internal evidence suggests that he began writing it in 1843, the year after Dr Arnold's death and the breaking of Jane's engagement to George Cotton. He may well have revised and finished it in 1847. Its preoccupations are post-Sand, post-Goethe, and – very possibly – post Tom's decision to leave England. Set in the Lake District, the poem lovingly recalls the Arnolds' childhood walks, and in particular a long hike the family took in 1833, to Keswick from Wythburn. Ten years on, Matthew and Jane once more 'tread this self-same road', ghosts of their former selves:

> The self-same shadows now, as then,
> Play through this grassy upland glen;
> The loose dark stones on the green way
> Lie strewn, it seems, where then they lay;
> On this mild bank above the stream,
> (You crush them!) the blue gentians gleam.
> Still this wild brook, the rushes cool,
> The sailing foam, the shining pool!
> These are not changed; and we, you say,
> Are scarce more changed, in truth, than they.

And yet, of course, both of them had changed a lot. And Dr Arnold was no longer there to head the troop.

The poem urges on Jane a wise, stoical acceptance of her fate. Like the poets, she should seek to rise above 'the conflicting tumult of the passions'. Look around you, the poem seems to say, look at the 'solemn hills', the incessant stream, the 'lonely sky'. All of these 'seem to bear rather than rejoice'. It is possible, though, to bear *and* to rejoice. The poet, for example, stands to one side of life's bustle, but he 'does not say: *I am alone*':

> He sees the gentle stir of birth
> When morning purifies the earth;
> He leans upon a gate and sees
> The pastures, and the quiet trees . . .

He contemplates nature's round, the detail of her awakenings and closures, and although 'tears/Are in his eyes' he none the less rejoices in the world's unfathomable continuity:

> Before him he sees life unroll,
> A placid and continuous whole –
> That general life, which does not cease,
> Whose secret is not joy, but peace;
> That life, whose dumb wish is not missed
> If birth proceeds, if things subsist;
> The life of plants, and stones, and rain,
> The life he craves – if not in vain
> Fate gave, what chance shall not control,
> His sad lucidity of soul.

On the face of it, Arnold's plea in 'Resignation' is anti-romantic, calling for a transcendence of the self, for detachment and impersonality. The poet, though, does not just stand to one side of the turbulence and mediocrity of ordinary life: he stands above it, he beholds it from on high, 'as if he were a god'.

What Jane made of the poem, as consolation, no one knows. It is unlikely that she saw it, or any part of it, in 1843. And in any case she would have seen that Arnold, in 'Resignation', is not actually addressing *her*. Yet again, though here most nakedly, he is straining to construct for himself a poetic that will resist accusations of escapist self-absorption. 'Not deep the poet sees but wide', and to this end he needs to sit on high. Just as Tom had to present his flight to New Zealand as a search for social purity, so Matthew had to make out a case for his sad-souled aestheticism, his sense of estrangement from 'men's business'. If this poet withdraws to a mountain-top, he does so with a purpose.

In 'Resignation', the poet sees from his hillside vantage point a band of gipsies wandering below. Outcasts from the general life, they seem to have no purpose, no destination, no complaints. Are they to be envied as 'natural' or are they to be pitied? In an earlier poem, 'To a Gipsy Child by the Seashore', Arnold impulsively responded to the 'pitiful wan face and dark eyes' of a baby girl he caught sight of in a pier-side throng. What, he asked then, could be signified by such depths of misery in one so young? 'No exile's dream was ever half so sad/Nor any angel's sorrow so forlorn':

> Is the calm thine of stoic souls, who weigh
> Life well, and find it wanting, nor deplore;
> But in disdainful silence turn away,
> Stand mute, self-centred, stern, and dream no more?

He sees in the gipsies not the nobility of stoicism but the pathos of dumb acquiescence. This is not what he recommends for Jane, or for himself. He cannot live as gipsies live, who 'rubbed through yesterday in their hereditary way' and will 'rub through . . . tomorrow on the self-same plan'. At the same time, he knows all too well the enticements of disdain.

Arnold's chief reading passion in 1847 was *Obermann*, the epistolary novel/journal/treatise/or prose-poem by Etienne de Senancour to which George Sand had alerted him. *Obermann* first appeared in France in 1804 and by the 1830s had come to be viewed by connoisseurs as a minor classic of the post-Revolution sentimental-melancholic genre: the book had reputedly served as a model for Chateaubriand's *René* and for Sand's own *Lélia*. Aside from the Sand connection, it is not difficult to see why Arnold responded so ardently to Senancour's epic of depressed self-scrutiny. *Obermann*'s eponymous hero is a high-souled escapee. Raised strictly as a Christian, and intended for the priesthood, he breaks free from the seminary and flees – penniless and prospectless – to the Swiss Alps, where he wanders, hermit-like, and broods on the various conflicts and confusions in his nature: reason versus feeling, materialism versus idealism, duty versus art, belief versus . . . well, what? His agonising tos and fros are experienced against a lovingly described background of stern, spacious mountain landscapes.

In *Obermann*, the turbulent self is contrasted with the serene continuities of nature. Obermann's awed reveries are constantly brought 'down to earth' by enervation and ennui – reminders of his worldly uselessness, his broken will. 'What can be the advantage of existing rather than existing not?' he asks; and gets no answer.[32]

7

Lansdowne, Clough and Marguerite

It is not easy to imagine Obermann taking a job in the big city. Happily, though, Arnold's duties with Lord Lansdowne allowed plenty of scope for solitary contemplation: more, surely, than would have been permitted had he stayed in teaching.

Indeed, the very grandeur of his new workplace, together with the elevated contacts it afforded, probably intensified young Arnold's sense of separateness from the main, dreary drift of 'general life'. It may also have inflamed his underlying restlessness, his fear of not knowing how this sense of being separate might or should be used. A different job at this stage of his life – a humbler, more demanding one – might well have shelved such fears or rudely squashed them. We might have lost Arnold altogether as a poet. Whatever else he did or didn't do at Lansdowne House, these were prolific years for Arnold's verse, yielding a large proportion of the poems that went into his first book. They gave him too the anxieties that predominate in that first book: am I really a poet? If I am, what kind of poet should I be? Do *real* poets ask themselves such questions?

Lord Lansdowne had more than one factotum and Arnold's job, it seems, involved little more than translating the odd letter or from time to time supplying scraps of 'literary information': to what purpose, we cannot be sure, since Lansdowne was, for a politician, quite well read. Several of Matthew's working hours at Lansdowne House, as he described them to his brother Tom, were spent admiring the surroundings:

> Here I sit, opposite a marble group of Romulus and Remus and the wolf, the two children fighting like mad, and the limp-uddered she-wolf affectionately snarling at the little demons struggling on her back. Above it a great picture, [Rembrandt's] the Jewish Exiles . . . On my left two great windows looking out on the court in front of the house . . . The green lawn which occupies nearly half the court is studded over with crocuses of all colours – . . . delightful for the large still-faced white-robed babies whom their nurses carry up and down on the gravel court where it skirts the green. And from the square and the neighbouring streets, through the open door whereat the civil porter moves to and fro, come sounds of vehicles and men, in all graduations, some from near and some from far but mellowed by the time they reach this backstanding lordly mansion.[1]

There was leisure time also in which Arnold could scrutinise his patron: Henry Petty-Fitzmaurice, the 3rd Marquis of Lansdowne. For Arnold, Lansdowne over the years came to embody an ideal of the *de haut en bas*. Cultivated, kindly, worldly-wise – and very, very rich – the Marquis oozed 'distinction' of the sort to which Matthew, at this time, was thoroughly susceptible. Now and then Arnold railed in his letters against the typical capitalist who 'understands by *fair profits* such as will enable him to live like a colossal Nob'. Just as often, though, during this period with Lansdowne, he savoured the privileges of his position. He liked to refer casually to 'my man's' (Lansdowne's) private views on headline issues of the day. He enjoyed letting his friends know that he, Crabby, was now in the know: 'I wish you could have heard me and my man sneering at the vulgar officiousness of that vulgar fussy Yankee minister at Paris';[2] 'Later news than any of the papers have, is, that the National Guard have declared against a Republic.'[3]

At not much more than Arnold's age – Arnold was now twenty-five – Lansdowne was Chancellor of the Exchequer (under Grenville) and since then, for forty years, he had been in or near the topmost seats of government. Aged sixty-seven when Arnold went to work for him, he was by this time very much the *grand seigneur*: esteemed as a stylish weekend host, a patron of the arts, and – in political circles – a capable backstairs 'enabler'. According to Harriet Martineau, the Lansdowne Arnold knew was 'busy doing what he delighted in doing through life, helping people to a position, or fitting people and places to each other'.[4] Another contemporary called him 'the last of a remarkable generation of statesmen, combining political wisdom with literary accomplishments and high position, and wealth with taste'.[5]

Dubbed 'Nestor of the Whigs', presumably on account of his seen-it-all sagacity, the Marquis was admired even by his Tory foes. But then, for all his moderate-Whig standpoint on, say, slavery or education or electoral reform, Lansdowne was still one of England's wealthiest landowners. In a crisis he could be relied on to think first of his acres. Thus, on the matter of Ireland, where his acreage was vast (some 120,000), he took a firm line, during the Great 1846–7 Hunger, against government intervention. Too much state aid, he thought, would discourage the charitable agencies. In the worst years of the Irish Famine (years in which he himself was predicting an eventual death-toll of some '1,000,000 of persons'), Lansdowne provided funds to help scores of ruined tenants to emigrate to the United States: this, he believed, was charity in action, helping Irishmen to help themselves – helping them, in short, to disappear.

There is evidence that Arnold was troubled by what he knew of Lansdowne's line on Ireland, but none that he protested. Nor do we really know what view he took of his employer's languidly amused response to the revolutionary turmoil that was erupting across Europe at this time. On France, Lansdowne is said to have remarked (and this has been quoted as an instance of his 'wit'): 'I wish the French could produce something more useful to themselves though less amusing to others than the "mobs" with which they contrive to season all their calamities.'[6] Like others of his age and rank, Lansdowne had lived in fear of French-style mobs for nearly half a century, but by 1848 he seems to have decided that England was immune to full-scale revolutionary upheaval.

And Arnold, from his somewhat different situation, did not disagree. He witnessed the Chartist riots in Trafalgar Square in March 1848 and came away convinced that 'it will be rioting here, only'. Although 'the hour of the hereditary peerage and eldest sonship and immense properties' had, he believed, 'struck',[7] his hunch was that the English masses were too stupid to organise their version of events in France. Unlike the French, the English lower orders cared nothing for ideas. Also, they lacked visionary leaders. (Not that Arnold would have admired such leaders if they had appeared: always ready to praise France at the expense of England, he could – when not comparing – be fairly scornful of Parisian barricades-*pensants*.) A few days after the Chartist riots, he wrote to K:

What agitates me is this: if the new state of things succeeds in France, social changes are *inevitable* here and elsewhere – for no one looks on seeing his neighbour mending without asking himself if he cannot mend in the same way: but without waiting for the result, the spectacle of France is likely to breed great agitation here: and such is the state of our masses that their movements now *can* only be brutal plundering and destroying. And if they wait, there is no one, as far as one sees, to train them to conquer by their attitude and superior conviction: the deep ignorance of the middle and upper classes, and their feebleness of vision becoming if possible daily more apparent. – You must by this time begin to see what people mean by placing France *politically* in the van of Europe: it is the *intelligence* of their *idea-moved* masses which makes them politically as far superior to the *insensible masses* of England as to the Russian Serfs . . .[8]

This, for the youthful Arnold, was an unusually direct appraisal. But then he was here writing to his elder sister, who – he knew – had little taste for persiflage. When discussing politics with Clough, Matt sang a different tune. His manner tended usually to the affectedly oblique and/or the brusquely condescending. In 1848 Clough was in a condition of high radical excitement, and hoped that Arnold would be similarly thrilled by what was going on in Europe. He even travelled to France to witness the February upheavals at first hand. This sort of madcap spontaneity made Arnold wince. Clough, he kept saying, needed to *calm down*.

Arnold's letters to Clough at this time alternated between mild mockery (addressing him as 'Citizen Clough') and heavy wisdom, with Arnold liking to present himself as the deep-thinking quietist, as one who stood back and analysed the enduring 'tendencies' of nations, and would not be 'sucked even for an hour into the Time Stream': in other words, the shallow here and now. Not surprisingly, this 'detachment' of Arnold's was sometimes taken for complacency, or cynicism. A letter to Clough from J.A. Froude (who in this same year saw his book, *The Nemesis of Faith*, publicly burned in Oxford) suggests that Matt's dandy-charm was beginning to wear thin:

> I admire Matt – to a very great extent. Only I don't see what business he has to parade his calmness and lecture us on resignation when he has never known what a storm is, and doesn't know what he has to resign himself to – I think he only knows the shady side of nature out of books.[9]

Froude's irritation would not, we suspect, have been assuaged if he had known (perhaps he did) which books Arnold was currently absorbed in. In 1848, at the height of the European dramas, Matthew had sent Clough a copy of the *Bhagavadgita*, recommending that holy book's preoccupation with the virtues of 'reflectiveness and caution'. Clough was not so easily becalmed and later on would chide his friend, in a review, for holding too comfortably to what he called a 'dismal cycle of . . . rehabilitated Hindoo-Greek philosophy'. Arnold's orientalism (he was also reading exotic Eastern travel books around this time) struck Clough as just another aspect of his Oxford foppery.

While Arnold was perusing the *Bhagavadgita*, Clough was in a state, he said, of 'suppressed volcanic action'. Before heading off to France, he resigned his Oriel tutorship (and shortly afterwards his fellowship; and thus his only income) on the grounds that he could no longer honestly subscribe to the Thirty-Nine Articles. Indeed, he could no longer wholeheartedly assert that he believed in God:

> We are most hopeless, who had once most hope,
> And most beliefless, that had most believed.

In 1848, beliefless, he was 'loose on the world'. After Paris, he went on to Italy, to defend Mazzini's Rome against the French. Returning to England, he secured – though not for long – an appointment as Principal of University Hall London, a non-sectarian foundation and a useful refuge for young scholars who could not in conscience toe the Oxbridge line. 'Doubting Castle', Arnold called it.

Clough was also planning his first book of poems, *Ambervalia*, a joint volume with a friend of his called Thomas Burbridge. Both the politics and the poetry were viewed by Arnold with impatience. The politics, as seen from Lansdowne House, were reckoned to be puerile. The poems were mere fragments. They revealed, said Arnold, 'a deficiency of the beautiful'. 'I doubt you being an artist,' he went on.[10] And as for Burbridge: 'He lives quite beside the true poetical life, under a little gourd. So much for him.'[11]

Arnold understood Clough's restlessness, and shared it, but it frightened him: 'With you,' he wrote, 'I feel it necessary to stiffen myself – and hold fast my rudder.' And there was, to be sure, a stiffness in the mini-lectures he repeatedly dished out to Clough during these Lansdowne years, and for a spell thereafter. Stiffly, or offhandedly, Arnold never preserved Clough's answers to his letters, and this one-sidedness makes the younger man sound more grandly pedagogic than perhaps he would have wished. Even so, it is for Clough that we are often made to feel protective as we read the two friends' 'correspondence'. Every so often, Arnold apologises for his sharpness, and now and then there are expressions of affection, and even small bouts of personal confession. On the whole, though, the Arnold manner is distinctly 'senior'. Clough, he would pronounce, was too hectic, too impulsive. He had no deep personal direction, either as a radical or as a writer. He merely reacted to events as they occurred.

Some of these criticisms were made teasingly. Arnold could lightly patronise Clough the political hothead. He could indulge Clough's too-conscientious anxieties about the Articles. It was when the discussion turned to poetry that a certain edginess began to show itself. With poetry, Arnold seemed almost to resent Clough as a trespasser. Maybe this was to do with literary politics. Arnold was perhaps piqued by the suspicion that his friend's inclination towards some kind of wordy up-to-dateness was influenced by the example of the then-glamorous 'Spasmodic' school of poets. Arnold's own need to define an attitude to notions of modernity was in part a resistance to the easy topicality of rising poetic stars like Alexander Smith and Philip James Bailey – forgotten now but big names of the day. Such figures were being touted at the time as the true heirs of Keats and Shelley, and Arnold was determined not to be grouped with them. Hence his excessive suspicion of excess. The Spasmodics, as their name suggests, were all excess. Their mission, according to the satirist William Aytoun, was 'to exhibit the passions in that state of excitement which distinguishes one from the other'.

In the 1840s, a young poet looked either to the Spasmodics or to Tennyson, then in his thirties. Arnold had no fears that Clough would become Tennysonian but was perhaps not quite so sanguine on his own behalf. For Arnold, Tennyson was already a seductive presence, a presence to be kept strictly at arm's length. Poetry, he told Clough, was not an instrument for registering transient bewilderments. Nor was it a proper vehicle for philosophical discourse. 'To solve the universe as you try to do,' he complained, 'is as irritating as Tennyson's dawdling with its painted shell is fatiguing to me to witness.'[12] At other, slightly later, times he would go even further, accusing Clough of always 'poking and patching and cobbling', always 'looking for this and that mode of being':

> You have I am convinced lost infinite time in this way: it is what I call your morbid conscientiousness – you are the most conscientious man I ever knew: but on some lines morbidly so, and it spoils your action.[13]

When Clough's first solo book, *The Bothie of Toper-na-fuosich*, appeared and was applauded, Arnold was openly annoyed:

> I have been at Oxford the last two days and hearing Sellar and the rest of that clique who know neither life nor themselves rave about your poem ['The Bothie'] gave me a strong almost bitter feeling with respect to them, the age, the poem, even you.[14]

Clough's slack, amusing, bustlingly sociable mock-epic was, like his political excitements, too 'flippant':

> If I were to say the real truth as to your poems in general, as they impress me – it would be this – that they are not *natural*.
> . . . You succeed best, you see, in fact, in the hymn, where man, his deepest personal feelings being in play, finds personal expression

as *man* only, not as artist: – but consider whether you attain the beautiful, and whether your product gives PLEASURE, not excites curiosity and reflexion . . . Reflect too, as I cannot but do here more and more, in spite of all the nonsense some people talk, how deeply *unpoetical* the age and all one's surroundings are. Not unprofound, not ungrand, not unmoving: – but unpoetical.[15]

Once Clough had mastered his annoyance – and we can deduce from Arnold's letters that Clough did from time to time strike back – he might well have found it difficult to fathom his censorious young friend's position here. On the one hand, Arnold was ever-ready to glamorise his Lansdowne House worldliness; on the other he seemed to believe that he outranked Clough as an otherworldly thinker. In this letter – as Clough may well have pointed out – Arnold could easily have been writing to himself. After all, his own verse at this time could hardly be described as 'natural'. Stiff neo-classical constructions like 'The Strayed Reveller' and 'The New Sirens', each of them to do with keeping experience at bay, were more likely to generate 'curiosity and reflexion' than the 'pleasure' he scolds Clough for not providing. These verse-debates, in which Arnold somewhat incoherently labours to define his ideal of the poetic life, were, Clough might have noted, deeply preliminary to the actual writing of good poems; they were poems about how to be a poet. And as to the pleasure-giving motive: Arnold did not, could not pretend that his own works were easy to enjoy. Soon enough he would be telling sister Jane that 'you – Froude – Shairp, I believe the list of those reading me with any pleasure stops there or thereabouts'.[16]

Arnold's verse, pre-1848, for all its earnestness, has in it traces of the undergraduate poseur. Too often we get the feeling that he is first of all concerned with sorting out his poetic *demeanour*, with determining which bardic robes he should be putting on today. Am I to be a gourmet of the senses or am I to be wise, spacious and instructive? Should I be like de Guérin, one who 'hovers over the tumult of life but does not really put his hand to

100

it',[17] or should I – like the warrior-sage Ulysses – engage directly with real-life experience? The gods, says the Strayed Reveller, 'see below them/The earth and men'; they know it all, but from a distance. Poets are all-seeing, too, but – unlike the gods – they have to suffer for their wisdom:

> These things, Ulysses,
> The wise bards also
> Behold and sing.
> But oh, what labour!
> O prince, what pain!
> They too can see
> Tiresias; but the Gods,
> Who give them vision,
> Added this law:
> That they should bear too
> His groping blindness,
> His dark foreboding,
> His scorned white hairs;
> Bear Hera's anger
> Through a life lengthened
> To seven ages.
>
> They see the Centaurs
> On Pelion; then they feel,
> They too, the maddening wine
> Swell their large veins to bursting; in wild pain
> They feel the biting spears
> Of the grim Lapithae, and Theseus, drive,
> Drive crashing through their bones; they feel
> High on a jutting rock in the red stream
> Alcmena's dreadful son
> Ply his bow; such a price
> The Gods exact for song:
> To become what we sing.[18]

The alternatives Arnold set up in poems like 'The Strayed Reveller' were, unavoidably, post-Romantic, a designation which he would doubtless have refused. He did not want to be post-anything, in his poetic life. His was an age in flux, he would have said: an old world breaking up into a new, a forward-looking age whose finest souls preferred the backward view. Wordsworth, Keats and Byron had been able to speak out with conviction on behalf of the *lived* life, the instinctual life: each in his different way had been a 'natural'. The beliefless young mid-century Victorian was obliged to fabricate a personal identity, a style-of-being to get by with as he waited to discover what 'beliefless' really meant. And in the meantime, he was doomed to fret: the passive victim of a range of in-between, provisional emotions – vague discontents, vague prohibitions, vague recollections of bygone ideals, lost certainties, old hopes: 'wandering between two worlds, one dead/The other powerless to be born':

> Ah, if it *be* passed, take away,
> At least the restlessness, the pain;
> Be man henceforth no more a prey
> To these outdated stings again! –
> Ah, leave us not to fret alone!
>
> But – if you cannot give us ease –
> Last of the race of them who grieve,
> Here leave us to die out with these
> Last of the people who believe!
> Silent, while years engrave the brow;
> Silent – the best are silent now.

'The best are silent now.' Arnold wrote this slightly later on but in 1847 the urge in him to silence was probably as powerful as the urge to eloquence. It all depended on his mood, and in this prolific year his mood was rarely stable. Behind the posturing, the sermons and the jokes, the only constant was dissatisfaction. But how much of 'the restlessness, the pain' was personal and how much of it was 'in the air', he had no way of knowing. His youthful inclination was to blame 'the age'. But what if there was something wrong with *him*?

According to Arnold's medical doctors, there was something wrong with him. We know very little about the health warning Arnold is said to have received in 1846, a year before he took employment with Lord Lansdowne. He says nothing of it in his letters and as a result biographers have tended to make light of the whole question. It gets mentioned, and then left. But what if Arnold really did believe that time, his time, was short, that he was marked for early death, just like his father? If the doctors' diagnosis was correct, his life – at twenty-five – was more than halfway through. There was a lot he did not know, and had not done.

So far he had had no close relationships with women, or none that have been divulged to posterity. There are hints aplenty, though, in his letters to Clough that sex was on his mind (or was it simply that he knew it was on Clough's mind – some of the jests about posteriors or 'superbes filles' seem rather forced?). On the whole, Arnold's current style was either to be chucklingly vulgar about sex or to represent it as a threat, an undermining of the high-toned intellectual life. The women he had met had not impressed him: too often the 'pretty faces' he was drawn to had turned out to wear a 'half-alive look', suggesting 'something very like stupidity'. 'A proud-looking Englishwoman,' he said, 'is the hardest looking thing I know in the world.'[19] Of women in general, he opined: 'We know beforehand all they can teach us: yet we are obliged to learn it directly from them.'[20] As so often, Arnold's instinct was to talk in teacher–pupil terms.

To date, we can be pretty certain, this pupil had been under-taught. Arnold's fellowship at Oriel depended on his remaining unmarried, and at the moment he could not think of abandoning this, his one secure financial base. Unlike Clough, he was prepared to pay lip-homage to the rule-book until he could be sure of some alternative prospects. Even so there was a question to be settled 'with regard to (I hate the word) women'. In September 1848, holidaying in Switzerland, Arnold sent to Clough a fragment of Shakespearean pastiche:

'Say this of her:
The day was, thou wert not; the day will be,
Thou wilt be most unlovely; shall I choose
Thy little moment life of loveliness
Betwixt blank nothing and abhorred decay
To glue my fruitless gaze on, and to pine,
Sooner than those twin reaches of great time
When thou art either nought, and so not loved,
Or somewhat, but that most unlovable,
That preface and post-scribe thee?' –[21]

Arnold places these bleak lines between quotation marks, and calls them 'curious', as if they were perhaps by someone else. However, the sentiments are typically his: sexual love seen as a distraction, and a fruitless one at that, since beauty, the deceiver, does not last. Love is a poor investment: why do we permit it such subversive power? In an earlier poem called 'A Horatian Echo', Arnold had been similarly caustic:

The day approaches, when we must
Be crumbling bones and windy dust;
And scorn us as our mistress may,
Her beauty will no better be
Than the poor face she slights in thee,
    When dawns that day, that day.[22]

'That day, that day', we note, is anticipated with some equanimity, perhaps even with a certain relish: a woman's vaunted and intimidating beauty will in time 'no better be/Than the poor face she slights in thee'. Had Arnold already experienced such slights?

Had there been a particular 'proud-looking Englishwoman . . . the hardest looking thing I know in the world'? Or was he speaking here as a discriminating aesthete? Art's beauty is both durable and improving. Woman's beauty does not last and makes its worshippers *less* serious.

The pastiche Arnold sent to Clough was in a letter dated 29 September 1848. He was writing from the Baths of Leuk in Switzerland and had, he said, just completed a few days of Alpine hiking. His summer holiday was almost done: he was about to journey back to London, and Lord Lansdowne. Before leaving, though, he planned to stop off at the hotel in nearby Thun from which he had begun his expedition. 'Tomorrow,' he said, 'I repass the Gemini and set to Thun.' There he would 'linger one day at the Hotel Bellevue for the sake of the blue eyes of one of the inmates'.[23]

For more than sixty years, ever since this Baths of Leuk letter was first published, Arnold scholars have been trying to identify the owner of these eyes. It is generally accepted that they must have belonged to the 'Marguerite' who, shortly after the Swiss holiday, became the addressee of some of Arnold's most direct and heartfelt lyrics. But who *was* Marguerite? Theories have abounded; none, though, has been thoroughly convincing. Sleuth-academics have travelled to Thun only to find that the hotel register for 1848 has mysteriously gone missing. Arnold's pocket diary for this year is also lost. In the end, apart from the 'blue eyes' letter, we have nothing biographical to go on; nothing, that is, except what we can dig out from the poems. These, it must be said, do bristle with particulars: we know that Marguerite was pale-faced, wore a kerchief and was French; we know that she loaned her poet-lover a copy of Ugo Foscolo's *Letters of Ortis* (Ortis was 'an unhappy lover and a Wertherian misfit who finds the universe incomprehensible and eventually commits suicide in despair'); we know that, a year after the two lovers met, they went their separate ways. What we don't know is that details of this sort were not invented, that Marguerite was not, in fact, a fiction.

On the way back to England, or shortly after he returned, Arnold wrote the first of his so-called 'Marguerite poems' – a lyric addressed not to her but 'To My Friends, who ridiculed a tender Leave-taking'.[24] From this awkward, almost blushing, piece we learn that the poet's loved one is indeed blue-eyed ('those eyes so blue, so kind', 'Those frank eyes, where deep I see/ An angelic gravity'). The poem also speaks of her 'figure's pliant grace', of her 'soft face', its 'pale, sweet-rounded cheek' and of 'a lilac kerchief . . . Tied under the archest chin/Mockery ever ambushed in.'

All in all, we might suppose, not Arnold's type; or, maybe, just the type we might expect him to beware of. In the poem, the two lovers agree to meet again in one year's time. They will rendez-vous in Switzerland, we guess. Meanwhile, the poet will preserve his beloved's likeness, in verse – the verse he is now writing. The poet wonders if this impulse to commemorate suggests that his infatuation is already on the wane. Or does it mean that frozen Art means more to him than vibrant Life? Whatever its signifi-cance, the urge to 'fix' the whole experience is inescapable:

> Time's current strong
> Leaves us fixed to nothing long.
> Yet, if little stays with man,
> Ah, retain we all we can!
> If the clear impression dies,
> Ah, the dim remembrance prize!
> Ere the parting hour go by,
> Quick, thy tablets, Memory!

This first 'Marguerite' poem and another called 'A Modern Sappho' (in which an ardent passion is expected to be overtaken by 'fatigue, discontent and dejection')[25] were added to the manuscript of Arnold's first book of poems, *The Strayed Reveller and Other Poems*, a manuscript which had probably been put together before the September Swiss vacation. The book, covering all of Arnold's work since 1843, apart from 'Cromwell', appeared in February 1849, in a printing of 500 copies. The author was announced as 'A'.

Even in the copies that were sent out to Arnold's friends, his authorship was not specifically acknowledged, but those closest to him of course knew the book was his. His family received it with some puzzlement. It was not at all what was expected from the bantering Matt. For one thing, the poems were unwaveringly *earnest*. For sister Mary, reading *The Strayed Reveller* was, she said, 'a new introduction' to her brother. An enthusiastic Christian Socialist, she was gratified to discover clear signs of 'moral strength' – well, 'moral consciousness'. The book revealed 'knowledge of life and conflict that was strangely like experience'.[26] And, happily, it did not try to make her laugh.

Sister K was, it would appear, more circumspect. She did not respond at once, causing Arnold to write to her, some four weeks after publication: 'I have not heard from you my darling since you got my book, which I hoped to have done, seeing your intimacy with it and me.' Eventually, K did react – but not, apparently, with the wholehearted approval that Arnold surely hoped for. Still, he rallied manfully:

Fret not yourself to make my poems square in all their parts, but like what you can my darling. The true reason why parts suit you while others do not is that my poems are fragments *i.e.* that I am fragments, while you are a whole; the whole effect of my poems is quite vague and indeterminate: this is their weakness: a person therefore who endeavoured to make them accord would only lose his labour: and a person who has any inward completeness can at best like only parts of them: in fact such a person stands firmly and knows what he is about while the poems stagger weakly & are at their wits end. I shall do better some day I hope – meanwhile change nothing, resign nothing that you have in deference to me or my oracles: and do not plague yourself to find a consistent meaning for these last, which in fact they do not possess through my weakness.[27]

'There – ' he concluded, 'I would not be so frank as that with everyone.' Nor, we suspect, would he have been so humble. This was a delicate moment in his relationship with Jane. Her opinion was important to him, and he wanted to avoid any suggestion of a conflict. He might have recalled, though (and so might she), that in his earlier letter to her – the one in which he prodded her for a response – he had written about the book less modestly. *The Strayed Reveller*, he said there, was 'selling very well' (in fact, it wasn't) and 'from a good many quarters I hear interest expressed about it'.[28] Some Oxford wits had found that 'the subjects treated do not interest them' but Arnold claimed that he had welcomed such complaints: 'As I feel rather as a reformer in poetical matters, I am glad of this opposition. If I have health and opportunity to go on, I will shake the present methods until they go down, see if I don't.'

8

The Strayed Reveller, Obermann and Marguerite, Once More

Although Arnold boasted to his sister that he would one day 'shake the present methods until they go down', his first book of poems was not proffered as the work of a 'reformer'. On the contrary, its presentation was almost defiantly reluctant. Arnold declined to put his name to *The Strayed Reveller* but he did attach to it, as epigraph, the following (in Greek; a quotation from one Choerilus of Samos):

> Ah, blessed he who was a servant of the Muses, one skilled in song, during that time when the meadow was yet unmown! But now, when all the spoils have been divided and the arts have reached the goals of perfection, we are left behind, the last of all in the race.

In later years, Arnold would exclude this motto from selections and collections of his poetry. In 1849, though, it seemingly came from the heart. Certainly, it set a tone which many readers said they found repugnant.

John Duke Coleridge, one of Arnold's oldest friends, would publicly deplore the epigraph as the 'utterance of a repining and weary soul' and not at all, said he, 'the keynote we should have desired for the songs of a Christian Englishman of the present day'. Sister Jane had similar misgivings. In October 1848, she wrote to Tom Arnold in New Zealand, telling him that Matthew, when visiting Fox How, had shown her some of his most recent verse (the manuscript, presumably, of *The Strayed Reveller*). She had admired several of the poems and she could see that they might well, if published, 'attract a great deal of attention and do much to improve the poetical taste of the country'. But she had doubts about their general impact. Matthew's work, she feared, would never 'become very popular or deeply impress the mind of the country'. Its 'philosophy', she said, was not what the country, any country, needed at this hour:

> Matt's philosophy holds out no help in the deep questions which are stirring in every heart and in the life & death struggle in which the world is every year engaged more deeply, and poetry which does not do this may charm the taste, excite and gratify the intellect, but not I think, take lasting possession of the heart.[1]

She went on to praise Wordsworth for having 'led men back to nature, and through nature & the natural piety of the heart, to Him who is the source of both'. Nowadays, she said, the route to Him should be made even more direct:

> . . . surrounded by tumults and perplexities without and within, we want to know the spell which shall evoke a righteous and peaceful order from this chaos, and what but our Christian Faith can give us this?[2]

Jane did not, she stressed, want poems to be Christian sermons. She too had taste and intellect. The age *was* out of joint, though, and it was not enough merely to say so. People yearned for the ministrations of some 'Mighty Helper'. What assistance could be found in verse which 'tells them of a dumb, unalterable order of the universe and of the vanity of the labours in which they are vexing'? There was nothing at all inspirational in Matthew's work. Still, maybe this was just a phase that he would soon outgrow:

> . . . he is a dear, dear boy, and I cannot say how much pleasure it gives me to have him at home, so loving as he is, and surely the time will come when he will find that nothing but the faith of the little child in Him who has united together Heaven & Earth, Christ, our Lord and our God, can avail to guide him through the 'waves of this troublesome world' . . .[3]

And this, we can presume, was the main drift of Jane's letter to her brother after publication of his book, the one to which he answered: 'I am fragments, while you are a whole.' Had Dr Arnold lived to read *The Strayed Reveller*, he would have responded as Jane did – and Matthew, of course, knew this.

If he did not, a reminder came in the form of a review by Charles Kingsley in *Fraser's Magazine*. Kingsley, writing anonymously, pretended not to know who 'A' was, but he surely did:

> In sober sadness, here is a man to whom God has given rare faculties and advantages. Let him be assured that he was meant to use them for God. Let him feast himself on all beautiful and graceful thoughts and images; let him educate himself by them, for his capacity for them indicates that in that direction lies his appointed work. Let him rejoice in his youth, as the great Arnold told his Rugby scholars to do, and walk in the sight of his own eyes; but let him remember that for all these things God will bring him into judgement. For every work done in the strength of that youthful genius he must give account, whether it be good or evil. And let him be sure, that if he chooses to trifle with the public by versifying dreamy, transcendental excuses for laziness, for the want of an earnest purpose and a fixed creed, let him know that the day is at hand when he that will not work neither will he eat.[4]

Other notices adopted a similar pious-indignant line. That Arnold in his poems clearly craved an 'earnest purpose', 'a fixed creed', was not held in mitigation. A doubter ought to keep his doubtings to himself. Arnold should have waited until he had a worthwhile function for his gifts – the gifts, Kingsley conceded, 'of a scholar, a gentleman and a true poet'.

Not every critic was ready to acknowledge that 'A' was a 'true poet'. There were grumblings about his less-than-lively rhythms, his echoings of Tennyson, his obsession with Greek forms and subjects. At least one reviewer warned that certain of 'A''s poems – and especially the book's title-piece – could well ('by an unlettered person') be taken for translations.[5]

As might be expected, Arnold gave few outward signs of being troubled by such notices. When writing home, his comments on the book's reviews were smilingly dismissive: 'There is a little notice in the Literary Gazette, it says . . . that the poems show skill rather than feeling: in fact, just the opposite of the Spectator. I think from the page or two they read in order to review the book, they do not well know what to make of it.'[6] But then his usual technique, when dealing with his family – who also did not 'well know what to make of' his first book – was to pretend that *The Strayed Reveller* was but a trifling thing, a collection of uncertain jottings which he already half-regretted. As early as March 1849, he told his mother that he was 'getting quite indifferent about the book. I have given away the only copy I have and never look at them.' By May he was able to report to sister Jane: 'My last volume I have got absolutely to *dislike*.'

With his literary friends, he was much less inclined to self-disparagement. When J. Campbell Shairp expressed the wish that 'Matt would give up all that old Greek form', he got a sharp reply.[7] Matt 'says he despises all the modern ways of going about the art and will stick to his own one'. Shairp was reporting here to Clough. Arnold's own account of the exchange (also to Clough) was slightly different in emphasis: 'Shairp urges me to speak more from myself: which I less and less have the inclination to do: or even the power.'[8]

Shairp, perhaps without intending to, had touched a nerve. Arnold the poet already knew that he was at his best when he 'wrote for himself'. In *The Strayed Reveller*, it was not the Greek 'drapery' that had caused Kingsley and the Arnold clan to sound alarms. The book's real provocation was that it gave haunting public voice to private failures of belief. It recognised those 'deep questions' which were 'stirring in every heart', questions to do with the whole, godless indirection of 'the age', but it refused to offer any balm – apart from solitude, disdain, high-toned estrangement. If poetry amounted to no more than individual lamentation, what – these days – was poetry *for*?

When Arnold, in his epigraph and in several of his poems, suggested that modern poets were the 'last of all in the race', he was half-agreeing with his sister's, and Charles Kingsley's, point of view. This being so, he understandably resented being cast as merely a low-spirited freethinker. He had spent over a year reading widely in the world's philosophers and, although he could no longer accept the Christian orthodoxies, there had been no surrender in his work, or in his life, of what he described as the 'religious mood'. God had, so to speak, *absented* Himself from mid-century Europe, and from England in particular, but He was possibly still reachable. The way to make contact, though, would not be the old Arnold way, church-bound and biblical: it would involve a painful openness to all spiritual possibilities, including the possibility that God's absence would prove permanent.

The predicament was not easy to explain, without offence, to Arnold's family and friends. And yet there seemed to be a call for explanation. The young Arnold was constantly being put in the position of having to distance himself from his own personality and, in the matter of his verses, from the true nature of his talent. His poetic 'credos' in these early years hardly ever tallied with the best of his own practice.

Writing to Jane about his wish to 'reform' English verse, he said: 'More and more I feel bent against the modern English habit (too much encouraged by Wordsworth) of using poetry as a channel for thinking aloud, instead of making anything.'[9] This representing of himself as a high-purposed architect of verse, not just a speaker of his own intense feelings and ideas, was partly for Jane's benefit, of course, but it sprang also from ingrained notions about service, selflessness, the public good. Was it possible to serve – or save – 'the age' and at the same time nurture one's own inner 'line', that 'distinct seeing of my way as far as my own nature is concerned'? Could Obermann be reconciled with Dr Arnold?

Today we value most those moments in *The Strayed Reveller* collection when the poet is most candidly prepared to 'think aloud', to seek his own 'line' in his own poems. We note too, though, that these moments nearly always are embedded in an antique, 'dramatic' structure or are presented as developments of an objective 'argument'. The poet seems to want to speak in his own person but dares not:

> 'Come,' you say, 'opinion trembles,
> Judgment shifts, convictions go:
> Life dries up, the heart dissembles –
> Only, what we feel we know.'

('The New Sirens', ll. 81–4)

> Chief dreamer, own thy dream!
> Thy brother-world stirs at thy feet unknown,
> Who hath a monarch's hath no brother's part;
> Yet doth thine inmost soul with yearning teem.
> – Oh, what a spasm shakes the dreamer's heart!
> *'I, too, but seem.'*

('In Utrumque Paratus', ll. 36–42)

Dr Thomas Arnold, *Oriel College,* Oxford

Mrs Mary Arnold, *Rugby School*

Rugby School from the Close, *Rugby School*

Fox How

A. H. Clough, *National Portrait Gallery, London*

Thomas Arnold, *Dr Mary Moorman Collection*

Jane Arnold, *Dr Mary Moorman Collection*

Matthew Arnold, 1856, *Balliol College, Oxford*

In 1849 Arnold began drafting a long poem which, he surely hoped, would forcefully elucidate his riven state of mind. According to Shairp, this new work would, as before, employ an 'old Greek form' as 'the drapery of his own thoughts'. A poem's length, the scope and ingenuity of its construction, the dignified remoteness of its sources: with Arnold, such as these were offered up almost as guarantees of conscientiousness, of serious, 'impersonal' intent. This time the drapery would be provided by Empedocles, a Sicilian-Greek thinker (*c.* 495–435 BC), famous for having pitched himself head first into the crater of Mount Etna.

In an 1849 note on his projected poem,[10] Arnold attempted a prose sketch of Empedocles, presenting him as one who 'sees things as they are – the world as it is – God as he is'. Empedocles understands 'the mysteries which are communicated to others by fragments, in parables'. In his youth, this sense of having special insights brought him joy; joy he could share with similarly prescient friends. But now his youth is gone, and so too are his friends. 'The world is all against himself.' Other people have 'religious consolation, facile because adapted to their weaknesses'; for them, an orthodox belief in God charges the 'atmosphere they breathe'. Empedocles inhales a purer air: he knows 'the truth of the truth'. But this knowledge no longer 'transports' him as it used to. In middle age, he finds his 'spring and elasticity of mind are gone: he is clouded, oppressed, dispirited, without hope and energy'. Arnold's poem – or might it turn into a play? – would focus on Empedocles at this low point, this nadir of pitch-black depression:

> Before he becomes the victim of depression and overtension of mind, to the utter deadness to joy, grandeur, spirit, and animated life, he desires to die; to be reunited with the universe, before by exaggerating his human side he has become utterly estranged from it.

'It' means 'the universe', presumably. So far as we know, Arnold in 1849 made little progress with the actual writing of 'Empedocles'. In March he told his mother that he was working on 'a tragedy I have long had in mind' but he was probably referring there to his long-standing scheme for a verse-drama on the subject of Lucretius. It is probable that bits of 'Lucretius' – which he never finished – found their way into 'Empedocles'.

In September 1849, Arnold headed back to Switzerland, to Thun. His 1848 Swiss expedition had been part-inspired by *Obermann*, a work which seemed to glamorise his own mysterious unrest. He thrilled to Obermann's despair, his love of nature, his renouncement of 'the main forces by which modern life is and has been impelled'. And the Swiss locations Obermann had fled to must have seemed wondrously grand-scale to a young English melancholic for whom nature largely meant Fox How.

By the time of this second trip Arnold had become a published poet. His inner waverings had been discussed at length in the reviews, and he had not found himself indifferent. He knew he had a taste for worldly recognition. He also had the prospect of a reunion with Marguerite. Passion, or the idea of it, placed further limits on his independence. The spirit of Obermann still lived – 'Yes, Obermann, all speaks of thee/I feel thee near once more' – but there had been a distancing – a distancing that made it possible for Arnold, within days of his arrival, to begin writing an address, in verse, to his dead mentor (Senancour, the author of *Obermann*, had died three years before). 'Stanzas in Memory of the Author of *Obermann*' was not completed at this time but certainly it was begun in Switzerland.

The poem has a strange, excited tone, and Arnold makes no effort to disguise his personal involvement. He is writing both a homage and a farewell. For Obermann, the choice had been quite clear: the serene, unpeopled majesty of nature or the sick hurry of the human round? 'What shelter to grow ripe is ours?' he asked. 'What leisure to grow wise?' He chose the mountain-top and from this elevated station listened in on the 'ground-tone of human agony'. His antennae, he believed, were all the sharper because he had so comprehensively renounced his own, constricting 'human side'.

Arnold was no Obermann, he knew. The hermit-urge was strong in him but intermittent, and a touch theatrical. The high and lonely path still beckoned – but to where? Writing of Obermann, he makes the claim that 'He only lives with the world's life/who hath renounced his own', but he himself had little to renounce. There was his fashionable life in London, his secure fellowship at Oriel, his family, his friends, his loyalty to Dr Arnold's memory, and so on. None of these was he quite ready to relinquish, in spite of his unrest. So far his distressed inner life had been kept separate from the unruffled drift of his 'career'. His poems had raised eyebrows, but no more. Sooner or later, he – like Obermann – would have to choose:

> Ah, two desires toss about
> The poet's feverish blood.
> One drives him to the world without,
> And one to solitude.

On 23 September he wrote to Clough, with urgency, enclosing a few lines from his new poem about *Obermann*. The letter is the most detailed description that survives of Arnold's state of mind at this key moment of his life. He writes from Thun. He has been with Marguerite but the reunion has been a failure. His love has been renounced – by him, it seems – and he will now, with Obermann, stride off into the mountain wastes, for the few days of his vacation that remain. And then he will return to England: a renunciant indeed, but to what end? The letter to Clough begins with a few condescending flourishes, in the old Arnold manner, and then falters:

What I must tell you is that I have never yet succeeded in any one great occasion in consciously mastering myself. I can go thro: the imaginary process of mastering myself and see the whole affair as it would then stand, but at the critical point I am too apt to hoist up the mainsail to the wind and let her drive. However as I get more awake to this it will I hope mend for I find that with me a clear almost palpable intuition (damn the logical senses of the word) is necessary before I get into praxis: unlike many people who set to work at their duty self-denial &c. like furies in the dark hoping to be gradually illuminated as they persist in this course. Who also perhaps may be sheep but not of my fold, whose one natural craving is not for profound thoughts, mighty spiritual workings &c. &c. but a distinct seeing of my way as far as my own nature is concerned: which I believe to be the reason why the mathematics were ever foolishness to me. –

I am here in a curious and not altogether comfortable state: however tomorrow I carry my aching head to the mountains and to my cousin the Blümlis Alp.

> Fast, fast by my window
> The rushing winds go
> Towards the ice-cumber'd gorges,
> The vast fields of snow.
> There the torrents drive upward
> Their rock-strangled hum,
> And the avalanche thunders
> The hoarse torrent dumb.
> I come, O ye mountains –
> Ye torrents, I come!

Yes, I come, but in three or four days I shall be back here, and then I must try how soon I can ferociously turn towards England.

My dearest Clough these are damned times – everything is against one – the height to which knowledge is come, the spread of luxury, our physical enervation, the absence of great *natures*, the unavoidable contact with millions of small ones, newspapers, cities, light profligate friends, moral desperadoes like Carlyle, our own selves, and the sickening consciousness of our difficulties: but for God's sake let us neither be fanatics nor yet chaff blown by the wind but let us be ὡς φρονιμος διαρισειεν ['as the man of practical wisdom would define it'] and not as anyone else διαρισειεν.[11]

'Then I must try how soon I can ferociously turn towards England,' Arnold writes. Why so ferocious? Arnold's rejection of Marguerite is described, lamented, justified in several poems, which he would later group under the heading 'Switzerland'. Most of these Marguerite poems would be written after his return to England but at Thun, in addition to the *Obermann* address, he seems to have sketched out some stanzas of the poem 'Parting' (one of these, beginning 'Fast, fast . . .' he quotes in his letter – see above – to Clough). In 'Parting'[12] the poet registers an anguished wavering between romantic passion, as proposed by Marguerite, and solitary nature-worship, as exemplified by Obermann.

Like the poem in memory of Senancour, of which it bears some echoes, 'Parting' has a frantic, late-night tone. In parts, and in spite of its neat either-or construction, it reads like a private letter. As with the Senancour poem, and the letter to Clough, Arnold can no longer stop himself from 'thinking aloud'.

'Parting' begins with a paean to snowy solitude. The white peaks call: 'How deep is their stillness! Ah, would I were there!' This is, of course, the Way of Obermann: 'vast fields of snow', 'ice-cumber'd gorges', the 'rock-strangled hum' of mountain torrents. The call seems irresistible: 'I come, O ye mountains/ Ye torrents, I come!' But not so fast. 'What voice is this I hear, buoyant as morning, and as morning clear?' The poet finds himself detained by the 'sweet voice' of Marguerite:

> The sweet blue eyes – the soft, ash-coloured hair –
> The cheeks that still their gentle paleness wear –
> The lovely lips, with their arch smile that tells
> The unconquered joy in which her spirit dwells –
>> Ah! they bend nearer –
>> Sweet lips, this way!

At which, the mountain-voices speak again – this time less violently. Nature's seductive turbulence has given way to a more soothing, stable prospect. Nature supports, indeed enhances, the

reflective cast of mind; arch smiles merely distract. Suddenly the
poet is resolved:

> . . . let me go
> To the clear, waning hill-side,
> Unspotted by snow,
> There to watch, o'er the sunk vale,
> The frore mountain-wall,
> Where the niched snow-bed sprays down
> In powdery fall.
> There its dusky blue clusters
> The aconite spreads;
> There the pines slope, the cloud-strips
> Hung soft in their heads.
> No life but, at moments,
> The mountain-bee's hum.
> – I come, O ye mountains!
> Ye pine-woods, I come!

As to the rejected, or transcended Marguerite: 'Forgive me!
Forgive me!' cries the poet, as he speeds away. He would, he
says, like to have stayed locked in her embrace but ''tis in vain':
'. . . a sea rolls between us – Our different past'.

All at once, it is a sea that rolls between them, not a mountain
torrent. During his reunion with Marguerite at Thun, Arnold –
we deduce – has found out more about his loved one's background. Has she, we are led to ask, been unfaithful during their
year's separation? Or is it simply that she had had other lovers
before he came along?

> In the void air, towards thee,
> My stretched arms are cast;
> But a sea rolls between us –
> Our different past!

> To the lips, ah! of others
>> Those lips have been pressed,
> And others, ere I was,
>> Were strained to that breast;
>
> Far, far from each other
>> Our spirits have grown;
> And what heart knows another?
>> Ah! who knows his own?

In another poem – called 'A Farewell'[13] – Arnold recalls the detail of his 1849 reunion with Marguerite. At first, we learn, there was mute passion: 'Locked in each other's arms we stood /In tears, with hearts too full to speak.' As the days passed, though, it became clear to the poet that something important had been lost, or had gone missing. There was 'A trouble in thine altered air!' Her hand 'lay languidly' in his, her 'cheek was grave', her 'speech grew rare'. In this poem, instead of 'Forgive me!' it's 'I blame thee not!':

> I blame thee not! – this heart, I know,
> To be long loved was never framed;
> For something in its depths doth glow
> Too strange, too restless, too untamed.

Women, he says, prefer the men they love to offer 'stern strength and promise of control'. Being themselves susceptible to 'fever of the soul', they are usually drawn less to 'kindness, gentle ways' than to 'a soul which never sways with the blind gusts that shake their own'. The poet has tried to achieve self-mastery, has tried to wish away his 'starting, feverish heart'. 'I too,' he says, 'have longed for trenchant force' and 'praised the keen unscrupulous course/Which knows no doubt, which feels no fear' but he has also longed for Love – which, he contends, is rarer than Strong Will. Marguerite will learn this one day, but not soon enough for their love to succeed. In the meantime they must go their separate

121

ways. And this is terrible, because there is surely a strong bond between them, a spiritual affinity. Who knows? They might meet again, in Heaven:

> Then, in the eternal Father's smile,
> Our soothed, encouraged souls will dare
> To seem as free from pride and guile,
> As good, as generous as they are.
>
> . . .
>
> And we, whose ways were unlike here
> May then more neighbouring courses ply;
> May to each other be brought near,
> And greet across infinity.
>
> How sweet, unreached by earthly jars,
> My sister! to maintain with thee
> The hush among the shining stars,
> The calm upon the moonlit sea!
>
> How sweet to feel, on the boon air,
> All our unquiet pulses cease!
> To feel that nothing can impair
> The gentleness, the thirst for peace –
>
> The gentleness too rudely hurled
> On this wild earth of hate and fear;
> The thirst for peace a raving world
> Would never let us satiate here.

This is Arnold at his most exposed, or so at first it seems, and yet to this day we are puzzled. Was it his pusillanimity, his restlessness, his feebleness of will that caused Marguerite to withdraw from him at Thun? Did she want a more definite commitment? Was it then Arnold who withdrew? Or was the 'raving world' to blame, 'this wild earth of hate and fear'? The suggestion of a blissful afterlife is glib and false – and so too in its way is the ear-wrenching final stanza. The poet scarcely believes what he is saying, and has no deep wish to persuade us – or his beloved – that he does.

In 'A Farewell' there is no reference to Marguerite's 'different past', nor to her former loves. Even so, it does seem that she, in some way, revealed herself in Thun as an 'unsuiting consort'. Certainly the opening lines of 'Isolation: To Marguerite' suggest a lapse of staying power:

> We were apart; yet, day by day,
> I bade my heart more constant be.
> I bade it keep the world away,
> And grow a home for only thee;
> Nor feared but thy love likewise grew.
> Like mine, each day, more tried, more true.
>
> The fault was grave! I might have known,
> What far too soon, alas! I learned –
> The heart can bind itself alone,
> And faith may oft be unreturned.
> Self-swayed our feelings ebb and swell –
> Thou lov'st no more; – Farewell! Farewell![14]

If Marguerite was indeed inconstant, the lesson learned by the regretful Arnold is that 'two human hearts' can never satisfactorily 'Bind/in one'. We are each condemned to 'isolation without end'. Arnold's generalising bent is nowhere more tellingly deployed than in 'To Marguerite – Continued'.[15] In this utterly bleak lyric, the real-life Marguerite has gone, and so too has the ideal of a durable romantic love. The solitary endurer we have met before in Arnold's verse but this time he has something to endure.

> Yes! in the sea of life enisled,
> With echoing straits between us thrown,
> Dotting the shoreless watery wild,
> We mortal millions live *alone*.

But when the moon their hollows lights,
And they are swept by balms of spring,
And in their glens, on starry nights,
The nightingales divinely sing;
And lovely notes, from shore to shore,
Across the sounds and channels pour –

Oh! then a longing like despair
Is to their farthest caverns sent;
For surely once, they feel, we were
Parts of a single continent!
Now round us spreads the watery plain –
Oh might our marges meet again!

Who ordered, that their longing's fire
Should be, as soon as kindled, cooled?
Who renders vain their deep desire? –
A God, a God their severance ruled!
And bade betwixt their shores to be
The unplumbed, salt, estranging sea.

In October 1849 Arnold returned to England, his love renounced, Obermann left to his snowy solitude, all the old English options still intact. Arnold was at his lowest point. He now knew – or in his black mood feared he knew – what he was really like: a spiritual and emotional irresolute, a ditherer. He had neither taken to the mountains with Obermann nor persisted in his love for Marguerite. His pose of superior detachment was exposed as a vain affectation. His hunger for 'experience' was shown to have been hollow and neurotic.

And yet, in sharper moods, he knew that this was by no means the whole story. Part of him still lingered in the realm of Obermann. 'I go, fate drives me; but I leave/Half of my life with you.' Part of him was still with Marguerite:

> But each day brings its petty dust
> Our soon-choked souls to fill,
> And we forget because we must
> And not because we will.
>
>   . . .
>
> I struggle towards the light – but oh,
> While yet the night is chill,
> Upon time's barren, stormy flow,
> Stay with me, Marguerite, still!

During the last months of 1849 – from October to December – Arnold wrote nearly twenty poems, some of them his best work to date by far; poems written with no thought of Grecian draperies or poetic reformations, no thought of how they might be read by sister Jane or by Charles Kingsley. There were the Marguerite love poems, reliving the Thun drama, but there were also half a dozen self-despising lyrics, with grim titles like 'Human Life', 'Courage', 'Destiny' and 'Self-Dependence'.[16] In these, Arnold repeatedly berates himself for having lost his nerve, for having perhaps lost his chance to break free of the 'petty dust'.

In 'Courage', for example, he insists that 'we must tame our rebel will', 'must learn to wait, renounce, withdraw', but the real point of the poem is to envy those 'sterner spirits' – the 'fierce and turbid Byron', the suicidal stoic Cato – who knew how to determine their own destinies. Heroes of this stamp, the poet says, are of the past. The modern sensibility, by comparison, is broken and enfeebled:

> Our bane, disguise it as we may,
> Is weakness, is a faltering course.
> Oh that past times could give our day,
> Joined to its clearness, of their force!

In 'Self-Dependence' there is a similar craving for 'lucidity of soul'. Arnold writes here of the sea-voyage that took him finally away from Obermann, from Marguerite, from the monastic and the passionate:

> Weary of myself, and sick of asking
> What I am and what I ought to be,
> At this vessel's prow I stand, which bears me
> Forwards, forwards, o'er the starlit sea.

He looks up at the stars and begs them to inspire him, as they have before, with dreams of spiritual enlargement: 'Let me, as I gaze upon you,/Feel my soul becoming vast like you!' To which a voice replies: the stars know what their business is: they *shine*, no more, no less; they are 'self-poised', they never 'pine with noting/All the fever of some differing soul'. Would he, Arnold, wish to be like them: 'Unaffrighted by the silence round them/Undistracted by the sights they see'? Well, yes and no. Although he would not wish to surrender his capacity for 'love, amusement, sympathy', he does envy their predestined certainty of aim. To paraphrase Carlyle: *they knew what they couldst work at*. What were the 'tasks' into which he, Arnold, might pour all *his* powers? 'Resolve to be thyself', was his conclusion, 'know that he/Who finds himself, loses his misery.'

Arnold, at mid-century, was back at Lansdowne House, the realm of banter and high-level gossip. He visited his family at Fox How and spent some time at Rugby, where a new headmaster was about to be elected (there were moves afoot, he understood, to dilute Dr Arnold's legacy). At Fox How he heard of William out in India, 'with a whole Ocean of doubts, distances and, it may please God, dangers before me'.[17] William had been soldiering in the Punjab and was now thinking of trying his hand at part-time teaching. And Tom, Arnold discovered, had just been offered an 'Inspectorship of schools in V. Diemen's land [Tasmania] £400 a year and his expenses . . . I shouldn't wonder if he took it. I think I shall emigrate,' Matt wrote to Clough.[18]

Jane, in her letters at this time, was full of family news but gave

126

no hint that Matthew had been going through a crisis. 'Dear old Matt' gets mentioned, but only in connection with the Rugby goings-on. Jane was a great letter-writer and clearly saw it as her job to keep the absent Arnold sons informed about each other. She also wanted to make sure that none of them forgot what he was missing:

> From the valley come rural sounds the ploughman with his team, the hammer in the quarry, the rushing of the Rotha, and the fluttering of the wind in the red leaves which have not yet been pushed off the oak trees by the swelling buds. Within doors there is the same scene of admired confusion which has characterised Fox How ever since it was built – letters, drawings, dictionaries, Bibles, needle-books and daffodils are scattered all about.[19]

Here was a whole complicated world of dependent and dependable affections, a world not easily renounced. And Matthew, whenever he visited Fox How, was always ready to succumb.

Jane was his closest confidante, he used to say, but rarely was he able to confide in her. As she herself regretfully conceded, there was something forbidding – 'stiff and harsh'[20] – in her high-principled goodwill. None of her brothers wanted to disappoint her. The only evidence we have of Arnold's true state of mind in 1849 is in the poems he poured out on his return from Switzerland, and these he was surely keeping to himself: at least for now. Critics of *The Strayed Reveller* – including Jane – would not be greatly heartened by the spiritual progress he had made in this momentous year. He wasn't: why should they be?

9

Marriage to Miss Wightman

A nother well-known Arnold poem was begun in Switzerland in 1849. The idea for 'Tristram and Iseult' came to
him from a French periodical he chanced upon at Thun's
Hotel Bellevue. An essay by Theodore de la Villemarqué (on
French versions of the Arthurian legend) gave an account of the
Tristram/Iseult enchantment and told also of the misery that had
ensued from their great love: how the two lovers were forced to
separate and how Tristram then married a more suitable Iseult,
with whom he lived not very happily for many years. Arnold, in
his anguish of uncertainty at Thun, was struck by this story of
high passion and sensible adjustment, which he had not come
across before. 'It fastened on me,' he remembered later on. 'When
I got back to England, I looked at the Morte d'Arthur and took
what I could, but the poem was in the main formed, and I could
not well disturb it.'[1]

It seems improbable that 'Tristram and Iseult' was actually 'in
the main formed' during Arnold's brief sojourn in Switzerland. At

Thun, as we have seen, he had two other poems on the go and for several days was busy with his mountain-hikes, not to mention his 'reunion' with Marguerite. 'Tristram and Iseult' is a lengthy work, around 800 lines. Also, it shifts its centre halfway through, as if responding to a change of circumstance: the poem turns from the love fevers of a dying Tristram to the more subtle, low-key deprivations of his marriage. In 1849 Arnold had fled from his own Iseult, and within months he was pursuing – with some eagerness – her substitute. The self-lacerating sections of 'Tristram' were probably sketched out at Thun, in the heat of Arnold's grand renunciation, but Section Three, which sees real love as something of a compromise, a 'second best', was surely written later: a year later, we might guess. By the end of 1850, Arnold believed he had won free of 'this fool passion' and could view his fevered Swiss excursion as a danger overcome, a passage of 'diseased unrest', now sturdily becalmed.

Arnold met Frances Lucy Wightman at the Park Crescent home of Sir John Taylor Coleridge, father of John Duke. Sir John, an Oxford contemporary of Dr Arnold, was a prominent barrister and thus a professional associate of Frances Lucy's father, Sir William Wightman, Judge of the Court of Queen's Bench. Arnold had several lawyer-friends and had seemingly observed Frances Lucy at earlier gatherings, without ever managing to fix an introduction. One of his failed attempts to meet her is described in a letter to his friend Wyndham Slade:

Last night for the 5th time the deities interposed: I was asked specially to meet the young lady – my wheels burned the pavement – I mounted the stairs like a wounded quaggha, the pulsations of my heart shook all Park Crescent – my eyes devoured every countenance in the room in a moment of time: she was at the opera, and could not come. At the last moment her mother had had tickets sent her, and sent a note of excuse.

I suffer from great dejection and lassitude this morning – having shown a Spartan fortitude on hearing the news last evening.[2]

When Arnold experienced a London setback, his first instinct was usually to go abroad. In this same letter, he suggests to Slade that the two of them might head off for the Pyrenees or the Italian Lakes. And then he returns to the subject of Miss Wightman:

> How strange about die unerreichbare schöne! ['the unattainable beauty']. To have met her, to have found something abstossend ['something repugnant'], and to have been freed from all disquietude on her account, voilà comment je comprends a matter of this kind. But all the oppositiveness & wilfulness in the human breast is agacée by a succession of these perverse disappointments. farewell. denke mein ['think of me'].[3]

This Slade letter was not dated but it probably belongs to spring or early summer 1850 (since summer vacations are under discussion). The meeting with Miss Wightman was achieved, presumably, soon after. And, as it turned out, she was not at all 'abstossend'. On the contrary, Arnold was instantly beguiled. Indeed, the speed with which he fell was somewhat puzzling to his friends. Miss Wightman, as they saw it, might easily have been dismissed. She was a pious High Anglican, a staunch Tory and – by Arnold's own admission – 'entirely free from the taint of letters'.[4] Her appearance was 'something like a Fairy Queen and something like a Dresden shepherdess'. Still, she was well off, well connected and reckoned to be something of a catch. And, at twenty-five, she was ready to be caught.

So too was Matthew Arnold. Frances Lucy was a woman. She reminded him of Marguerite:

> In this fair stranger's eyes of grey
> Thine eyes, my love! I see.
> I shiver; for the passing day
> Has borne me far from thee.

This is the curse of life! that not
A nobler, calmer train
Of wiser thoughts and feelings blot
Our passions from our brain . . .

Miss Wightman's Toryism, her Tractarian sympathies, her metropolitan 'society ways': all these, Arnold knew, would be severely frowned on by his family, and especially by Jane. In summer 1850, though, he was quite happy to offend his sister. After all, *she* had offended *him*. In May 1850, Jane had announced that she was planning to get married. Her betrothed was William Edward Forster, a Quaker wool manufacturer from Bradford – a man Arnold had never met and did not greatly like the sound of. Forster had not been to public school or university. His family was well known in the north for practical good works, and for supporting liberal causes, but knew little Greek. It was not really Forster's poor credentials, though, that caused Arnold to react to Jane's announcement as he did. On hearing the news he wrote to her in some confusion and distress. The letter survives but is severely damaged: four-fifths of pages three and four have been cut off. Even so, we have the drift:

I must write again before I see Mr Forster – I have been in a kind of spiritual lethargy for some time past, partly from headache partly from other causes which has made it difficult for me to approfondir any matter of feeling – but I feel quite sure my darling that when I can sink myself well down, into the consideration of you and your circumstances as they really are then will you be truly set right in my mind in respect of your engagement. This I say not to please you but because I really feel it to be the truth; at present my objections are not based in *reality*, that I feel.

I am subject to these periods of spiritual eastwind when I can lay hold of the outside of events or words – the material eastwind which now prevails has something to do with it, and also the state of strain and uneasiness in which in these days & in London it is so hard not to live. You my darling have been a refreshing thought to me in my dryest periods: I may say that you have been one of the most faithful witnesses (almost the only one after papa) among those with whom I have lived & spoken of the reality & possibility of that abiding inward life which we all desire most of us talk about & few possess – and I have a confidence in you & in this so great that I know you will never be false to yourself: and everything merely fanciful & romantic should be sacrificed to truth . . .[5]

Is Arnold suggesting here that Jane should renounce the fanciful and the romantic, just as he had? If so, she must have been puzzled by the letter since she almost certainly knew nothing (yet) of his Swiss travails. At the same time, *we* know nothing of the letter's missing paragraphs. Clearly, though, Arnold felt let down by Jane's surprise announcement. For him this was a second deadly wound – delivered this time by his spiritual physician. In many ways, his letter is repugnant: demanding, childish, self-absorbed and falsely pious. Compared with 'Resignation', it is depressingly indifferent to Jane's actual prospects. But then 'Resignation' was written to console her for a broken romance. This time she was planning to defect. Later on, Arnold would be properly ashamed of his response but even so Jane's marriage marked the beginning of a serious estrangement. He would never again turn to her as his most faithful witness. The wedding was in August, with Arnold perhaps in attendance, perhaps not. There are no mentions of him even in quite detailed family descriptions of Jane's wedding day.

A month before Jane's engagement, Wordsworth died, and Arnold was asked to 'dirge' the Poet Laureate in *Fraser's Magazine*. The resulting 'Memorial Verses' do not seem deeply felt but then they were deliberately aiming for a classical 'grand style'. In truth, though, Wordsworth's death was an important severance. With Wordsworth gone, and Jane about to go, Fox How was suddenly less haven-like. At the same time it was less forbidding, its piety less *there* to be lived up to. The presence of

Wordsworth had for years maintained a complicated link to the memory of Dr Arnold, adding – Matthew may have felt – a 'poetical' authority to the headmaster's moral earnestness. And the poems had been all-important, too: both exemplary and intimidating. Jane had always wanted him to be like Wordsworth.

The London society in which Arnold courted Frances Wightman was not at all Wordsworthian. Still less was it Arnoldian. In Eaton Place, the Judge's domicile, the name Arnold was normally not to be mentioned, standing as it did for liberal politics, Broad Church religion and all manner of progressive perils. And the name Lansdowne was not much more acceptable. From Judge Wightman's point of view, Matthew Arnold's credentials as a suitor could hardly have been less appealing: Thomas Arnold's son, a so-called poet, and flunky to a Whig supremo. And Matthew's languidly sophisticated manner did not help. Nor, clinchingly, did his finances. Arnold earned about £300 a year from his Lansdowne House appointment. The Oriel fellowship was worth a further £120, but this of course would not be paid if he got married. The Judge – well known in the courts for his erratic temper – made his opposition clear. Arnold was forbidden access to Miss Wightman until he could show signs of being able to support her.

In August 1850, Arnold made off to Switzerland once more. As Tom said later: 'It was not all prosperous sailing in his love, any more than is the case with ordinary mortals.' It was the Judge's 'counterblast' that drove Matthew 'out of England and towards the Alps'.[6] The counterblast also intensified Arnold's interest in Miss Wightman. Before leaving, he took to dawdling outside the Wightmans' house in hopes of catching sight of her. During August, he wrote or began at least six poems on the subject of his thwarted passion.

In one of these, 'A Summer Night',[7] he finds himself pacing a 'deserted, moon-blanched street' – presumably Eaton Place. The windows of the house he gazes at frown back at him, 'repellent as the world'. He remembers an earlier night, 'a past night, and a far different scene', when he had been forced to experience 'the same restless pacings to and fro/And the same vainly throbbing heart'. He had thought such agonies were past, but here he is – still pacing. And 'the calm moonlight seems to say':

> Hast thou then still the old unquiet breast,
> Which neither deadens into rest,
> Nor ever feels the fiery glow
> That whirls the spirit from itself away,
> But fluctuates to and fro,
> Never by passion quite possessed
> And never quite benumbed by the world's sway?

Should he 'pray still to be what I am', or should he 'yield and be/Like all the other men I see'? These 'other men' tire themselves out with 'barren labour' and 'unmeaning taskwork' and die 'having seen nothing, nothing blest'. He will soon become one of them if he is to win the Judge's daughter. But what is the alternative? To chuck up everything and just clear off? To set sail on the stormy sea of life, 'with anguished face and flying hair/Grasping the rudder hard', 'still bent to make some port he knows not where', and end up as a wreck?

> Is there no life, but these alone?
> Madman or slave, must man be one?

The poem ends with one of Arnold's characteristic visions of celestial fulfilment, of 'a world above man's head': 'Plainness and clearness without shadow of stain! Clearness divine!' If man could understand 'how boundless might his soul's horizons be/How vast', he might yet be able to transcend the madman/slave antithesis, and once again 'breathe free'.

The same sense of being locked into a false and cruelly limiting dilemma surges through 'The Buried Life', in which the hope of 'breathing free' achieves more down-to-earth expression.[8] 'The Buried Life' is perhaps Arnold's most urgently intimate attempt to pinpoint the true source of his unceasing disaffection, his sense of being out of tune and out of touch. The poem hauntingly elaborates the theme of his 1849 unburdening to Clough, his wish for 'a distinct seeing of my way as far as my own nature is concerned'. Arnold's way of thinking aloud now is to think in the first-person-plural. In 'The Buried Life', our 'thirst' is for a 'knowledge of our buried life', 'our true original course'.

> But deep enough, alas! none ever mines,
> And we have been on many thousand lines,
> And we have shown, on each, spirit and power;
> But hardly have we, for one little hour,
> Been on our own line, have we been ourselves –
> Hardly had skill to utter one of all
> The nameless feelings that course through our breast,
> But they course on for ever unexpressed.
> And long we try in vain to speak and act
> Our hidden self, and what we say and do
> Is eloquent, is well – but 'tis not true!

There are moments when a loved one's touch, or voice, can seem to animate our numbed or stupefied true selves, or so we like to think. But over-animation is a danger too. Our aim now is, or should be, not for passion but for 'calm':

> Only – but this is rare –
> When a beloved hand is laid in ours,
> When, jaded with the rush and glare
> Of the interminable hours,
> Our eyes can in another's eyes read clear,
> When our world-deafened ear
> Is by the tones of a loved voice caressed –
> A bolt is shot back somewhere in our breast,

And a lost pulse of feeling stirs again.
The eye sinks inward, and the heart lies plain,
And what we mean, we say, and what we would, we know.
A man becomes aware of his life's flow,
And hears its winding murmur; and he sees
The meadows where it glides, the sun, the breeze.

And there arrives a lull in the hot race
Wherein he doth for ever chase
That flying and elusive shadow, rest.
An air of coolness plays upon his face,
And an unwonted calm pervades his breast.
And then he thinks he knows
The hills where his life rose,
And the sea where it goes.

Arnold's other 'love poems' of summer 1850 focus more specifically on Frances Lucy – or attempt to. In 'The River', the poet
describes a farewell meeting with his love.[9] Like Arnold's
Marguerite in 'A Farewell', the loved one is preoccupied, she
turns away when he addresses her, she fiddles with her shawl. In
one stanza, she even has 'arch eyes' and a 'mocking mouth'.

Much later on, Arnold would feel obliged to separate his
'Marguerite' poems from his 'Frances Lucy' poems. Marguerite's
would eventually appear under the heading 'Switzerland' and
Frances Lucy's under 'Faded Leaves'. In practice, and not at all
surprisingly, the boundaries are blurred. After all, the Swiss
poems were written in late 1849; the 'Faded Leaves' in 1850.
There was, at most, a six-month interval between them. Hence
the 'arch eyes' lapse. In 'Separation', the beloved's eyes are 'grey'.
In 'On the Rhine' they turn into a 'soft, lucent blue' – or, rather,
'eyes too expressive to be blue/Too lovely to be grey', which
seems a reasonable compromise. Frances Lucy's eyes, we know,
were grey.

It could be argued that Judge Wightman's opposition helped

Arnold by affording him a pretext for recovering his self-esteem. This time, he could tell himself, the prohibitions were external. It was not Arnold who could not make up his mind. For a period at least, he could recast himself as a rejected swain. Heading for the Alps in August 1850, he lingered for a spell at Calais, knowing that the Wightman family would soon be stopping off there too, en route for their summer vacation. Musing on Calais' medieval past, the poet yearns to have 'Thy lovely presence at my side'. Arnold did not include the poem 'Calais Sands' in 'Faded Leaves'. Indeed, he did not publish it for many years, although – or should we say 'because'? – it is the one 'Frances Lucy' poem that does seem to have been unequivocally hers:

> Thou comest! Yes! the vessel's cloud
> Hangs dark upon the rolling sea.
> Oh, that yon sea-bird's wings were mine,
> To win one instant's glimpse of thee!

> I must not spring to grasp thy hand,
> To woo thy smile, to seek thine eye;
> But I may stand far off, and gaze,
> And watch thee pass unconscious by,

> And spell thy looks, and guess thy thoughts,
> Mixed with the idlers on the pier.
> Ah, might I always rest unseen,
> So I might have thee always near![10]

Arnold was indeed anxious to be married. This had been a year of family weddings. Jane's was the one that really mattered, but both Tom and William also got married in 1850. At Fox How in December for his birthday – then for Christmas and New Year – Arnold wrote to Frances Lucy, with whom he had been corresponding throughout the Judge's ban. He told her that he would soon have a new job: a real job, an Inspectorship of Schools, at

£700 a year. Lord Lansdowne's influence would help to fix it, he was certain, but in any case the path seemed fairly smooth. Ralph Lingen, the Education Secretary, had been one of his Balliol tutors. The actual appointment would not be made until the spring and he would not start work until October 1851, but without doubt he was now a man of prospects. By spring of the next year, the Judge was reassured. Matthew and Frances Lucy were allowed to be engaged.

Their announcement caused a small flurry of excitement at Fox How. Arnold had said nothing much about his marriage hopes, although it was known that he had been pursuing a 'serious flirtation with Miss Wightman'. Sisters Mary and Frances, writing to Tom in New Zealand, each expressed some apprehension. Mary feared that 'dearest Matt' would find it difficult to bear the 'hard work' of an inspectorship, although she was sure that he would rather like the travel.[11] Also, his 'quiet effectiveness' and his refusal to 'make troubles of what he undertakes' would help to see him through.[12] Frances was more concerned about her brother's bride-to-be, to whom she and the other Arnolds had not yet, it seems, been introduced: 'I like what we know of Fanny Lucy who I hope is simple and loving and unworldly though she has lived in the great London world and must have breathed so much of an artificial atmosphere.'[13] (With Jane married, Frances Arnold − now eighteen − became her mother's close companion at Fox How and co-custodian of Arnold 'values'. She herself did not get married.)

Jane's response to Matt's attachment to Miss Wightman is not known, although at Fox How over Christmas she did sketch out one drawing-room still life. It seems to speak of an uneasy truce: 'Matt is stretched at full length on one sofa, reading a Christmas tale of Mrs Gaskell's [*Moorland Cottage*], which moves him to tears, and the tears to complacent admiration of his own sensibility − and on the other sofa, also exceedingly at his ease, is stretched my respected spouse reading a newspaper −'[14] Her own dealings with Matthew were presumably a little tentative. During

the few months since her marriage, she had been unwell –
afflicted, so it seems, with a form of nephritis (she was being
treated by Richard Bright, of Bright's Disease, which is an
inflammation of the kidneys). Arnold already felt guilty about
his egotistical response to her engagement. Her illness – and now
of course his own imminent engagement – made things worse.
Returning from Fox How to London in mid-January 1851, he
wrote to her, hoping to make peace. The letter's awkward
formality is a measure, rather touching, of his loss. He can no
longer be certain that she will read his words with total sympathy:

My dearest K,

Since you do not write to me, I must be the first – so long as I was
at Fox How I heard your letters, but in town, unless we write to each
other I shall almost lose sight of you, which must not be.

How strong the tendency is, though, as characters take their bent,
and lives their separate courses, to submit oneself gradually to the
silent influence that attaches us more and more to those whose
characters are like ours, and whose lives are running the same way
with our own, and that detaches us from everything besides – as if we
could only acquire any solidity of shape and power of acting by
narrowing and narrowing our sphere, and diminishing the number of
affections and interests which continually distract us while young,
and hold us unfixed and without energy to mark our place in the
world: which we thus succeed in marking only by making it a very
confined and joyless one. The aimless and unsettled but also open
and liberal state of our youth we *must* perhaps all leave and take
refuge in our morality and character: but with most of us it is a
melancholy passage from which we emerge shorn of so many beams
that we are almost tempted to quarrel with the law of nature which
imposes it on us.

I feel this in my own case, and in no respect more strongly than in
my relations to all of you. I am by nature so very different from you,
the worldly element enters so much more largely into my composition, that as I become *formed* there seems to grow a gulf between us,

which tends to widen till we can hardly hold any intercourse across it. But as Thomas à Kempis recommended – frequenter tibi ipsi violentiam fac ['frequently do violence to yourself'] – and as some philosopher advised to consort with our enemies because by them we were most surely apprised of our faults, so I intend not to give myself the rein in following my natural tendency, but to make war against it till it ceases to isolate me from you and leaves me with the power to discern and adopt the good which you have & I have not.

This is a general preface to saying that I mean to write about the end of every month – as I can at the time – and I hope you, my dearest K, will do the same.[15]

This is a prickly olive branch. Has Jane become an enemy whose chief function is to censure Arnold's faults? There is a thin line here between the bantering and the aggrieved. But Arnold's habit these days is to present himself as 'worldly' and mature. The Thomas à Kempis quotation reads in full: 'The patient man has a great and wholesome cleansing who frequently does violence to himself and who strives in every way to subjugate flesh to spirit.' Most of Arnold's reading at this time – in Goethe and Spinoza, chiefly – was in the direction of a 'reconciling calm', 'a sedative for my passions', a way forward from the 'perturbing activity' of his mid-twenties.

It is, as he admits to Jane, a 'melancholy passage' – from the open and liberal to the confined and joyless – and his pocket diary for the early months of 1851, the months building up to his engagement, suggest an intermittent sense of flatness and defeat. He is exchanging letters almost every day with Frances Lucy (or 'Flu' as he nicknames her), he is seeing London friends like Clough and Coleridge, but repeatedly he complains of feeling anxious, tired, unsettled. It may have been the strain of waiting for Judge Wightman to relent. It may have been a toothache, or the weather. The diary is in terse note form: 24 February: a 'wretched nervous day'; 26 February: 'a wretched day'; 1 March: 'very anxious still'; 13 March: 'very restless and unsettled'; 23

March: 'Languid and unwell . . . very bad night.'[16] After his engagement was announced, in early April, he found himself church-going with the Wightmans every Sunday (sometimes twice) and on weekdays often dining *en famille* at Eaton Place. In May Clough grumbled to Tom Arnold that he, and other friends of Matt, had had to make 'a gracious withdrawal' from his life. He wrote: 'I consider Miss Wightman as a sort of natural enemy. How could it be otherwise? – shall I any longer breakfast with Matt twice a week?' Miss Wightman, he grudgingly supposed, would 'suit well enough' as Matthew's bride. After all, she had 'seen lots of company and can't be stupid'.[17]

As Arnold's wedding day approached, he wrote once more to Jane, requesting her to deal kindly with his bride: 'Neither Flu nor my much maligned and adamantine Self could feel anything but love to you in return for loving her: and she is so loveable: I am more inclined sometimes to cry over her than anything else: it is almost impossible to be soft and kind enough with her.'[18] In the same letter he refers to Jane's still-fragile health:

> I cannot tell you how grieved I was to read that passage in your letter in which you account for your spoiled handwriting by saying that you have so often to write on the sofa: for I know my darling would not willingly be there – and it shews me that she is still far from strong. Seldom as I write to her and cold as my tone often is I never think of my K in weakness or suffering without remembering that she has been to me what no one else ever was, what no one else ever will exactly be again; unless indeed we were both to lose what we have dearest, and then we should be drawn together again, I think, as in old times.[19]

It is a troubling fantasy: that he, the newly affianced, and she, the recent bride, might one day come together in bereavement, having each lost 'what we have dearest'. Arnold's letter ends with the wish that he might visit K in Yorkshire and 'fish the Wharfe for a week or so'. It was well known that her husband was a vehement opponent of field sports, angling included.

'Nothing,' it was said, 'appeared to arouse him to more intense indignation than any persecution of the animal kingdom.'[20]

'It's very difficult to fancy the Emperor married,' was Tom Arnold's response when he got word of Matthew's wedding plans,[21] and brother William agreed: 'I own that Matt is to me the last man in the world I can fancy happily married.' From Matt himself the brothers-in-exile heard nothing until after the event, and then only (to Tom) the throwaway 'They will have told you from Fox How who she is.'[22] It was left to Mary to fill in the background. She told the brothers that Matthew 'loved and delighted in' his bride and that there was something 'quite affecting' in the way he treated her. The day before the wedding, Matt wrote to Francis Palgrave: 'If you listen attentively towards 12 tomorrow you will hear heaven and earth tremble in attestation of my vows.'[23]

The ceremony took place at Teddington, close to the Wightmans' country home. Arnold's relatives and friends turned out in force. Clough wrote: 'I, Walrond, Slade, Blackett [John Blackett, like Slade a lawyer-friend from Oxford days], Edward and some Bucklands were here. Nobody cried; Matt was admirably dressed and perfectly at his ease. It rained but we did well enough – they went off before the breakfast – where old Croker sat cum Judice. She seems, as Matt calls her, a charming companion.'[24] ('Old Croker' was John William Croker, the fierce *Quarterly Review* critic who – said Byron – 'killed John Keats'. Croker was also a fierce Tory, and a close friend of Judge Wightman.)

Arnold's diary entry on his wedding day reads: 'June 10. Married. To Alver.'[25] By 'Alver' he meant Alverstoke in Hampshire. After a week there, the couple were in London, where they took temporary rooms in Hampstead. Their plan was for a European honeymoon in late summer, between Matthew leaving Lansdowne House and taking up his new inspectorship. On 1 September they took the night ferry from Dover to Calais and were in Paris the following day. Flu described the crossing in some detail. The boat was noisy, she told her mother, and crowded –

mostly with foreigners – but the night was very warm, the sea 'calm as a mill-pond'.[26] The calmness of the sea she mentions twice. (Was 'Dover Beach' – 'the sea is calm to-night' – begun on 1 September, or did Arnold already have a draft of it? His diary records a visit three months earlier to Dover and he and his wife stayed there on the last night of their honeymoon.)

From 'dear old Paris', as Flu called it, the couple travelled across France to Chambéry, by way of Dijon, Lyons and Grenoble. En route, Flu learned that her new husband liked to wander off alone, that he actively enjoyed cold weather (which she loathed) and that music and painting were not central to his concept of high culture. Nor did he care much for shopping or late nights. And when the newly-weds visited the Alpine monastery of the Grande Chartreuse, she was surprised to find herself required to sleep alone:

> The Grande Chartreuse I was not going to turn my back upon: as women are not admitted I was lodged in a small house not far from the monastery where I spent rather an uncomfortable time as it was bitterly cold. Matt was allowed to have supper with me, but at ½ past 7 he was turned out & went into the monastery where he had a cell to sleep in. He got up at 11 & went to the Chapel & heard midnight mass, which he said was very striking, the monks chaunting the service in a low monotonous tone, each holding a taper: indeed every man had one and the Chapel was lighted in that way. In the morning I went to a small chapel: also for ladies, where I heard mass, the Père Superieur of the Chartreuse officiating. The situation of the monastery is very fine & the size immense, but it looked dreadfully gloomy. The weather was bad as there was a fog the whole time we were there & it was raw cold.[27]

Arnold's reaction to this Carthusian overnight can be discovered in his 'Stanzas from the Grande Chartreuse'.[28] In these, he thrills to the monastery's ambience of rigour and abstention – but as much from habit as conviction. His response is more aesthetic than religious, rather like the thrill of listening to Newman. In God's absence, what religious value can be placed on the aesthetic? The Romantic poets who believed that poetry might take over from religion were surely as misguided as these enviably ardent monks. Or so it seems to their immediate inheritors. The sons of the Romantic Movement wander now 'between two worlds, one dead/The other powerless to be born'. Is 'life lighter now' because of Byron's 'bleeding heart' or Shelley's 'lovely wail'? Surely 'the pangs which troubled them remain'? And even Obermann had nothing much to teach us, except how to hide our heads. Things might change for the better, although – as viewed by Arnold – the prospect could scarcely be more vague: 'Years hence, perhaps, may dawn an age/More fortunate, alas! than we.' In the meantime, though, posterity is merely asked to 'heed our tears', to 'leave our desert to its peace'.

What was it about monks and mountains that plunged Arnold into such pits of cultural despair? And how much of this despair was known to his new wife? In letters to her mother and her sister, Flu says very little about Arnold, and nothing at all about her own changed status. She is factual, chatty and touristic, and her only grumbles are to do with the vile Alpine weather. When she arrives in Italy, her mood noticeably lightens. The couple reached Milan around mid-September and from there proceeded to Venice, where they stayed for a week – Matt, she says, 'delighted in the gondolas' – before returning, via Switzerland, to Paris. They were back at Dover on 8 October. Arnold was scheduled to start his inspectorship three days later.

In other words, he was at last about to take his place in the real world. Religion, solitude, romantic love: all these were now outgrown, or had been stabilised as attitudes. And he was not yet thirty. 'Leave our desert to its peace,' he says in 'Stanzas from the Grande Chartreuse'. In 'Dover Beach', the desert turns into a dimly apprehended field of battle. At Rugby, one of Dr Arnold's favourite Thucydidian conflicts was the Battle of Epipolae, where – in a night encounter – the two sides could not distinguish friend from foe. He took this as a fitting image of the modern world's confusion and perplexity: 'The Athenians were trying to find their own comrades, and regarded as hostile what came from the opposite direction, even though it might be a party of friends belonging to the troops already in flight . . . coming into collision with their own comrades in many different parts of the army . . . they not only became panic-stricken but came to blows with one another.'

'Ah, love, let us be true/To one another.' In 'Dover Beach', a deeply felt lament for lost belief gives way to a strained, anxious pledge of faith – or of fidelity: fidelity to what might happen next. The poem marks the closing scene, the closing sigh – it could be said – of Arnold's youth, a sigh of part-relief, part-resignation:

> The sea is calm to-night.
> The tide is full, the moon lies fair
> Upon the straits; on the French coast the light
> Gleams and is gone; the cliffs of England stand,
> Glimmering and vast, out in the tranquil bay.
> Come to the window, sweet is the night-air!
> Only, from the long line of spray
> Where the sea meets the moon-blanched land,
> Listen! you hear the grating roar
> Of pebbles which the waves draw back, and fling,
> At their return, up the high strand,
> Begin and cease, and then again begin,
> With tremulous cadence slow, and bring
> The eternal note of sadness in.
>
> Sophocles long ago
> Heard it on the Aegean, and it brought
> Into his mind the turbid ebb and flow
> Of human misery; we
> Find also in the sound a thought,
> Hearing it by this distant northern sea.

The Sea of Faith
Was once, too, at the full, and round earth's shore
Lay like the folds of a bright girdle furled.
But now I only hear
Its melancholy, long, withdrawing roar,
Retreating, to the breath
Of the night-wind, down the vast edges drear
And naked shingles of the world.

Ah, love, let us be true
To one another! for the world, which seems
To lie before us like a land of dreams,
So various, so beautiful, so new,
Hath really neither joy, nor love, nor light,
Nor certitude, nor peace, nor help for pain;
And we are here as on a darkling plain
Swept with confused alarms of struggle and flight,
Where ignorant armies clash by night.[29]

In 1849, before sailing to New Zealand, brother Tom had found himself 'as on a darkling plain'. He had witnessed the 'human degradation' of London's labouring masses and felt miserably powerless to help. For a man of conscience, a son of Dr Arnold, this feeling of paralysis in the face of a clear social wrong had been impossible to bear. If such a man could find no way to 'stem the stream' of human suffering, the only course was to take flight, to join 'the great company of just men throughout all past time', to be a pure and proud renunciant: 'I am fed and clothed,' Tom had said, 'by the labour of the poor, and do nothing for them in return.'

Matthew, in his different way, had also attempted to withdraw. His flight had not, like Tom's, been spurred by an uneasy social conscience. At the same time, his personal distress had always seemed to have its social aspect: it was, he often said, a symptom of the age, the general state of things. And his fantasies of isolation and escape were usually shot through with social guilt. By 1851 he had – he might have said – renounced renunciation. True enough, he had been forced to, in order to get married. On the other hand, he knew that his free time had more or less run out, that now a different kind of battle must be joined. He had no strategy, could not distinguish friend from foe, and certainly could entertain no hopes of a heroic triumph. He was simply ready to bear arms, and prepared also to concede that his young dream of the poetic life might have to be among the early casualties:

> Au reste, a great career is barely possible any longer – can hardly now be purchased even by the sacrifice of repose dignity and inward clearness – so I call no man unfortunate. I am more and more convinced that the world tends to become more comfortable for the mass, and more uncomfortable for those of any natural gift or distinction – and it is as well perhaps that it should be so – for hitherto the gifted have astonished and delighted the world, but not trained or inspired or in any real way changed it – and the world might do worse than to dismiss the high pretensions, and settle down on what it can see and handle and appreciate.[30]

10

Empedocles Renounced

'Seek not that the things which happen should happen as you wish, but wish the things which happen to be as they are, and you will have a tranquil flow of life.'[1] This advice from the Greek Stoic Epictetus is echoed many times in Arnold's 'Empedocles on Etna'.[2] Before he kills himself, Empedocles delivers a lengthy homily to his acolyte Pausanias, urging him to settle for whatever second best might come his way, to settle and endure. 'Thou hast no *right* to bliss,' he tells him. The wise man knows his limitations, knows the limitations of the age in which he lives, and tries to work within them, to some modest purpose. Such a man may not feel happy or fulfilled but 'gets what cure he can'. Empedocles concludes:

> I say, Fear not! Life still
> Leaves human effort scope.
> But, since life teems with ill,
> Nurse no extravagant hope;
> Because thou must not dream, thou need'st not then despair.

Empedocles himself, though, does despair. Before throwing himself into the volcano, he makes it evident that Stoic verities are not much use to *him*. His disaffection runs too deep:

> He is too scornful, too high-wrought, too bitter.
> 'Tis not the times, 'tis not the sophists vex him:
> There is some root of suffering in himself,
> Some secret and unfollowed vein of woe.

We are left in no doubt that Empedocles, for all his talk of moderation and acceptance, continues to believe in the superior distinctiveness of his own plight. His exaltations are felt with more intensity than other people's:

> Oh, that I could glow like this mountain!
> Oh, that my heart bounded with the swell of the sea!
> Oh, that my soul were full of light as the stars!
> Oh, that it brooded over the world like the air!

And so too are his depressions. Recalling Arnold's star-struck 'Self-Dependence', Empedocles looks to the heavens:

> No, no ye stars! there is no death with you,
> No languor, no decay! languor and death,
> They are with me, not you! ye are alive –
> Yes, and the pure dark ether where ye ride
> Brilliant above me! And thou, fiery world,
> That sapp'st the vitals of this terrible mount
> Upon whose charred and quaking crust I stand –
> Thou, too, brimmest with life!
> . . .
> I only,
> Whose spring of hope is dried, whose spirit has failed,
> I, who have not, like these, in solitude
> Maintained courage and force, and in myself

149

Nursed an immortal vigour – I alone
Am dead to life and joy, therefore I read
In all things my own deadness.

When Empedocles finally does take the plunge, he hopes that he will thus, in death, 'breathe free', transmute into the elemental, rid himself at last of 'mind' and 'thought'. 'Receive me, save me!' is his cry as he jumps into the deep 'sea of fire'.

We do not know the exact stages of this poem's composition. 'Empedocles on Etna' was conceived, as we have seen, in 1849. Arnold set it to one side but probably returned to it early in 1850 and wrote the bulk of it between then and, we would guess, mid-1852. It was presumably 'in progress' throughout the period of the Marguerite poems, 'Faded Leaves' and 'Dover Beach'. As with 'Tristram and Iseult', the work's mood alters in response to events in Arnold's life, as these unfold. Thus we might surmise that Empedocles's terminal soliloquy predates the grin-and-bear-it wisdom he dispenses to Pausanias. By the time Arnold came to prepare his final version of 'Empedocles on Etna', he had already moved back from the crater's edge and was heading, resignedly, towards the 'darkling plain'.

Four days after beginning work as an inspector, Arnold wrote to his wife from Manchester: 'I think I shall get interested in the schools after a little time.'[3] He hoped that Flu would accompany him on his tours of inspection, at any rate during the first months, but he would shortly learn that she was pregnant. As yet, the couple had no London home. Flu lodged at her parents' house in Eaton Place and Arnold joined her there at weekends.

What he thought of this arrangement we can only guess: he says nothing much about it in his letters – although Judge Wightman is more than once referred to as 'the Judge' – and post-1851 his diary is routinely used for train schedules and cash calculations. Less than six months before, this bachelor-poet had had a home in Mount Street, an office in Grosvenor Square, rooms at Oriel College, Oxford and regular weekends at Lord

Lansdowne's stately Bowood House. His social life was often interestingly tied in with his job – diplomatic receptions and the like – and he could cut a dash among his friends with his insider's gossip. He was somewhat short of money but could afford to keep pace with his fabled dress-sense, take holidays abroad, dine out, go to the theatre, and so on. And he had plenty of free time.

All this had changed. His new life was both hectic and obscure, his home a succession of shabbily provincial stop-offs, or – at weekends – the well-mannered Wightman residence, with lots of church-worship on Sunday. He rarely saw his Oxford friends, although in 1851 he did take a renewed interest in Clough's continuing misfortunes (Clough had lost his job at Doubting Castle and would soon emigrate to the United States). The consolation was that he now had a task, a line, a clear sense of direction.

The destination he was not so sure of. Looking over the poems he had written since *The Strayed Reveller*, Arnold would have noted their habitual polarities: energy/languor; turbulence/calm; lunacy/slavery; art/social duty; mountains/darkling plains. He would have noted too their steady drift towards conditions of numbed stasis, or capitulation. Habitually, his poems seemed to speak against themselves, to question their own right to have been written. When not bemoaning the hostile temper of the age, they were exploring some mysterious authorial malaise: the poet's spiritual irresolution, his arid intellectualism, his terror in the face of real-life passions. These were 'thinking aloud' poems, even when they posed as narratives or dramas. They were subjective and exposed, and not at all the sort of work that Arnold wanted to be known for – especially nowadays, in his new, earnest situation. But what of the work he *did* want to be known for? In the year of *In Memoriam*, no English poet was quite safe from humbled self-assessment, no poet could feel wholly *fluent*. And the debate about 'modernity' raged on. The most highly praised new voices of the day were held to be dynamic, up to date, in tune with the new, expansive spirit of the age. The Great Exhibition was held in 1851 and poets were expected to take part in the celebrations. Arnold not only felt out of tune with the age; he also felt out of tune with his own work – which he could see was neither celebratory nor even very *helpful*. But what if this was what his gift amounted to: all diagnosis and no cure? And what, in any case, could now be hoped for – poetically – in his unpoetical new life? Does second best in life, he asked himself, mean second best in art – and if so, which comes first, which causes which?

In spite of his father's great reputation as an educationist, Arnold knew little about how things worked in England's schools. And the schools he was hired to inspect were elementary schools – with pupils aged from four to nine: of schools like these he probably knew nothing. In 1851 England had no system of state education. Most schools were run privately for profit or were Anglican foundations, staffed and administered by clergy. These the state left well alone: too well alone, some said. Only the nonconformist schools were open to inspection by the HMIs. These schools charged fees – two pence a week or thereabouts, from parents who could ill afford them – but were none the less dependent on a measure of state subsidy. And this, of course, put them in line for a measure of state regulation. It was Arnold's job to tour these nonconformist schools and file reports on their endeavours – from classroom performance to the condition of their roofs and drains. He was also expected to take an interest in the matter of so-called 'pupil-teachers': schoolchildren of thirteen or over who doubled as trainees. After five years of such 'training', these children would be reckoned to have qualified as teachers.

Arnold was one of twenty HMIs. Between them, the twenty had responsibility for some 4,000 elementary schools throughout the land. In his first year, Arnold's personal domain included Lancashire, the Midlands, East Anglia, and parts of Wales and the West Country: a vast territory – covering it meant almost constant travel and, of course, mountains of bureaucracy. Arnold was not a habitual complainer – at any rate not in his life and letters – but he could not disguise the gruelling dreariness of his new daily round: 'A hard day,' he would murmur, 'I am often in bad spirits,' or 'I have been sore put to it today.' These grumbles would often be accompanied by rather lengthier despondencies about the loss of youth, the swift passage of time, the lack of any real sense of achievement: 'How life rushes away – and youth,' he wrote to Clough in 1852. 'One has dawdled and scrupled and fiddle-faddled – and it is all over.'[4] 'What a difference there is between reading in poems and novels of the loss of youth, and experiencing it.'[5] 'We are growing old and advancing towards the deviceless darkness: it would be well not to reach it till we had at least tried *some* of the things men consider desirable.'[6]

It was not in Arnold's nature merely to serve time as an inspector. From the very first week of his employment, he was seeking to *interpret* his new work. Was it an enslavement or could it be a mission? What would his father have advised? After all, even the headmastership of Rugby had involved long stretches of low-level tedium. Arnold's first letter to his wife, from Manchester, sounds – or tries to sound – like Dr Arnold:

> I think I shall get interested in the schools after a little time; their effects on the children are so immense, and their future effects in civilising the next generation of the lower classes, who, as things are going, will have most of the political power of the country in their hands, may be so important.

Over the next thirty or so years, Arnold would ponder these 'future effects' with deepening urgency: they would become the subject of his 'mission'. In 1852, though, he was more concerned with his own immediate effects, with the management of his diminished self-esteem. In July Flu gave birth to their first child: a boy named Thomas. 'I think,' wrote Arnold to his mother, 'he will be a dear little boy – sweet and patient I fancy his little countenance is already.'[7] The new child was worryingly delicate and sickly – the doctors said he had inherited the 'Arnold heart' – and his infancy would prove to be precarious, with 'everybody', Arnold said, 'prophesying that we should not rear him', even to full boyhood. (Thomas in fact survived for sixteen years.) Arnold would turn out to be a conscientious parent but these early weeks of fatherhood were taxing. Eaton Place, he said, had turned into 'a howling wilderness'. Of babies he half-joked to Clough: 'The plague of their nursing and rearing is more than the pleasure of their society can ever repay me for.'

A married man, an elementary educationist and now a father, living with his in-laws: there were indeed moments when Arnold felt 'like my own Empedocles'. Unlike Empedocles, however, he knew that he had work to do. Between inspections he was putting together a new book of poems, with 'Empedocles on Etna' as its centrepiece. The volume – to be called *Empedocles on Etna and Other Poems* – would also include the Marguerite poems, 'A Summer Night', 'The Buried Life' and 'Tristram and Iseult'. 'The River' and 'On the Rhine' (which later on were grouped as 'Faded Leaves', the poems to his wife) would in this presentation sit alongside verses quite explicitly addressed to Marguerite. 'Dover Beach' and 'Calais Sands' were not included.

Arnold once again called himself 'A' on the title-page, and again the printing was 500 copies. But Arnold was not at all happy with the book. Its 'strain of thought generally', he said, was 'much too doleful and monotonous. I had no notion *how* monotonous till I had the volume printed before me.' He had hoped 'they would possess a more general attraction than their predecessors: I now see they will not'.[8] In the month of the book's publication – October 1852 – he wrote somewhat perplexingly to Clough about the difference between a 'mature age of the world', such as the present, and earlier, more 'youthful' epochs, such as those of Keats, Shelley, Shakespeare, the Elizabethans.[9] A poet in a youthful age could afford to dabble in luxuriant poetic diction. In a post-Christian epoch, though, such flights of individual creativity were not enough. Poetry nowadays had an 'immense task to perform'. In the absence of religion, the poet's duty was to respond to humanity's continuing 'religious wants'. This was no time for 'fiddle-faddling', no time for 'ornament', diverting mini-narratives, 'exquisite bits and pieces'.

Arnold found his own work 'doleful'. Maybe he also found it insufficiently 'exquisite': closer to reflective prose than to the feelingful linguistic richness of a Keats or Shelley. He may also have dolefully remarked its scatter-gun display of exclamation marks, a sure sign of fake vigour, the repeated sighs of 'Ah!' with which he padded out weak lines, the over-dependence on a small stock of recurring images: star, sea, moon, mountain. In 'Dover Beach', of course, all of Arnold's most typical effects had come together in a single masterpiece, but 'Dover Beach' was missing from the book. In 1852 life for Arnold would, he may have thought, be easier to handle if he could decide that his poetic gifts were, so to speak, not altogether *natural*.

Within a few months of its publication, *Empedocles on Etna* was withdrawn from circulation, on the instructions of its author. Few of the 500 copies had been sold and there had been only a handful of reviews. In December, Arnold wrote again to Clough, enclosing an 'oracular quatrain':

As for my poems, they have weight, I think, but little or no charm.

> What poets feel not, when they make,
> A pleasure in creating,
> The world in *its* turn, will not take
> Pleasure in contemplating.

. . . I feel now that my poems (this set) are all wrong, which I did not a year ago: but I doubt whether I shall ever have heat and radiance enough to pierce the clouds that are massed over me.[10]

But could any poet – *should* any poet – be hot and radiant in times like these? Even the most ardent and spontaneous of talents would/should be dampened by this 'modern situation in its true *blankness* and *barrenness* and unpoetrylessness'.

As Arnold saw it, the year 1853 – his thirtieth – was one of purposeful beginnings. The decision to annul *Empedocles* was not, in his view, timorous or retrograde. For him, it advertised a healthy new self-confidence, and a grownupness. Altogether, it was as if Arnold – having, so to speak, demoted his own talent – could finally, with certitude, declare himself to be a working poet. He was no longer a strayed reveller, no longer an Empedocles or Obermann. He was no longer, even, 'A'. In August 1853, he wrote to the publisher Thomas Longman offering a new volume to replace the now-withdrawn *Empedocles on Etna*. The new book would, he said, include 'those poems of the previous volumes which have been the most liked, together with a new poem which I think more likely to be popular than any of those which I have hitherto published.'[11] And the title-page would read: 'By Matthew Arnold.'

The likely-to-be-popular new poem was 'Sohrab and Rustum', which Arnold had completed in the spring. The writing of 'Sohrab' was Arnold's first adventure in maturity and he seems to have found it a relief. Here was a subject both heroic and impersonal, or so he thought: an oriental tale, with battles, feasts and an abundance of drawn-out Homeric similes. And the actual composition was *enjoyable*: for Arnold, a quite new sensation. He told Clough that 'Sohrab' 'pleases me better than anything I have yet done'. And to his mother he enthused, in May: 'All my spare time has been spent on a poem which I have just finished, and which I think by far the best thing I have yet done.'[12] In the projected new collection, 'Sohrab' would replace 'Empedocles'. A shrill, fragmented suicide note would be supplanted by an epic narrative of bold deeds and noble aspirations. 'Sohrab' was a learned poem: a poem to be learned from.

Longman agreed to publish and the new book, *Poems* (1853), appeared in October. 'Empedocles' was not the only intense, subjective piece from Arnold's youth to be excised. Gone too were 'The Buried Life', 'A Summer Night' and 'Stanzas in Memory of the Author of *Obermann*'. Slight early works were kept, such as the cutely juvenile 'Forsaken Merman' (the one poem of Arnold's that *everybody* liked). Also preserved were most of his stiff sonnets from the 1840s. Here at last was a book that he could put his name to. It would do no harm: 'not advance me and not pull me down'.

Appended to the 1853 book was a *Preface* in which Arnold attempted to outline the rudiments of his new, purposeful self-image. The poem 'Empedocles on Etna', he said, had been left out because it was too 'morbid' and 'monotonous'. It was a poem in which 'a continuous state of mental distress is prolonged, unrelieved by incident, hope or resistance', in which 'everything is to be endured, nothing to be done'. It was neither instructive nor enjoyable. It had been crippled from the outset by its subjectivity. Great poetry should speak of great events. Great poets should be cheerful, calm, invisible. They should be like ancient Greeks. And since the modern world was unlikely to afford sufficiently heroic subjects, the beginning poet nowadays could do much worse than set himself to imitate the classics. To keep the past alive might well turn out to be the modern writer's most trustworthy function. It might turn out to be his *only* function. During the course of his long *Preface*, Arnold's tone becomes both weightier and loftier; the troubled poet steadily gives way to the prescriptive sage:

The confusion of the present times is great, the multitude of voices counselling different things bewildering, the number of existing works capable of attracting a young writer's attention and of becoming his models, immense. What he wants is a hand to guide him through the confusion, a voice to prescribe to him the aim which he should keep in view, and to explain to him that the value of the literary works which offer themselves to his attention is relative to their power of helping him forward on his road towards this aim. Such a guide the English writer at the present day will nowhere find.

Failing this, all that can be looked for, all indeed that can be desired, is, that his attention should be fixed on excellent models; that he may reproduce, at any rate, something of their excellence, by penetrating himself with their works and by catching their spirit, if he cannot be taught to produce what is excellent independently.[13]

This was indeed a wan prospectus, aimed in part to rile the fashionable moderns but aimed also to map out the path for a new sort of English poetry: the sort which knows itself to have been permanently overshadowed. On the one hand, Arnold could speak of poetry offering a substitute for religion; on the other, he was able to direct young poets (and he too was a young poet) to settle for their true inheritance: the second best. And of course there was no contradiction. As Arnold saw it, the poetry that might actually supply 'religious wants' had already been achieved. It was already in the world: why add to it? What was needed now was not more poetry but more awareness of what existing poetry could offer. To this end, the requirement was for a sagacious guiding hand, a helpful voice, a teacher who could keep alive some vital 'commerce with the ancients'.

Such commerce would, he said, have more than merely literary value. A deep knowledge of the classics would bring with it 'a steadying and composing effect upon men's judgement, not of literary works only, but of men and events in general'. It would also bring with it a deep and deeply needed modesty. Beneficiaries of ancient excellence do not inflate themselves with 'a belief in the pre-eminent importance and greatness of their own times':

They do not talk of their mission, nor of interpreting their age, nor of the coming poet; all this, they know, is the mere delirium of vanity; their business is not to praise their age, but to afford to the men who live in it the highest pleasure which they are capable of feeling. If asked to afford this by means of subjects drawn from the age itself, they ask what special fitness the present age has for supplying them. They are told that it is an era of progress, an age commissioned to carry out the great ideas of industrial development and social amelioration. They reply that with all this they can do nothing: that the elements they need for the exercise of their art are great actions, calculated powerfully and delightfully to affect what is permanent in the human soul; that so far as the present age can supply such actions, they will gladly make use of them; but that an age wanting in moral grandeur can with difficulty supply such, and an age of spiritual discomfort with difficulty be powerfully and delightfully affected by them.[14]

'Sohrab and Rustum' was quite clearly the centrepiece of *Poems* (1853) – a carefully constructed Homer for beginners and yet also, Arnold felt, a story of 'incomparable beauty and nobleness', 'a very human story'. In his *Preface*, he attacked those modern poets who would use old tales as 'allegories' of their private states of mind but he seems not to have recognised the allegorical susceptibilities of his own 'objective' epic; or if he did, he certainly downplayed them. A father and son destined to meet face to face in mortal combat; a son's death at his father's hand; a hero brought low by his hero: the poem these days makes its mark not as an exercise in classical severity but as a study of severities much closer to the poet's own experience. Arnold was, he knew, beginning to turn into something like his father's son and, as 'Sohrab' seems to intimate, there was an element of welcome easefulness in the capitulation:

> His head drooped low,
> His limbs grew slack; motionless, white, he lay –
> White, with eyes closed; only when heavy gasps,
> Deep heavy gasps quivering through all his frame,
> Convulsed him back to life, he opened them,
> And fixed them feebly on his father's face;
> Till now all strength was ebbed, and from his limbs
> Unwillingly the spirit fled away,
> Regretting the warm mansion which it left,
> And youth, and bloom, and this delightful world.[15]

Another important Arnold poem appeared for the first time in *Poems* (1853) – a poem unignorably 'subjective'; or, rather, a poem unignorably to do with Arnold's flight from his own subjectivity. 'The Scholar-Gipsy'[16] is a touching valediction, a farewell to the 'poetic life' that Arnold now believed himself to be forsaking. It is also a farewell to youthfulness: to Balliol, to Lélia, to mountain-tops, to Obermann and Marguerite. Old landmarks, old intensities are wistfully recalled: the Cumnor fields where Arnold, the full-of-life young poet, used to roam are represented here as other-worldly, lost.

The scholar-gipsy of the poem's title was a creature of myth: a two-centuries-old college truant whose blithe spirit was reckoned still to haunt the Oxford countryside to which he had originally fled: in search, the legend said, of wisdom more instinctual and profound than was on offer at the university. 'Tired of knocking at preferment's door', he had 'one summer morn' simply dropped out; he 'forsook his friends, and went to learn the gipsy-lore'. He never returned to the university and, in men's eyes, 'came . . . to little good'. But the idea of him lived on, in rumour, and over the years he had been sighted more than once: on river-banks or hanging on garden gates; picking flowers or sitting in the corner of some local hostelry. There were reports of his 'outlandish garb', his 'dark vague eyes and self-abstracted air'. Once he had been spotted idling in a punt:

> And leaning backward in a pensive dream,
> And fostering in thy lap a heap of flowers
> Plucked in shy fields and distant Wychwood bowers,
> And thine eyes resting on the moonlit stream.

According to the myth, the gipsy was perpetually on the move, intent on some lone romantic quest. 'Pensive', 'shy', he never spoke: a stray but not a reveller, he was enviably self-sufficient. We learn nothing much about his aims but we are none the less expected to accord him a rich spiritual significance. Like Keats's nightingale, to which we are referred, this creature was not born for death.

And yet his immortality, we should take note, was surely earned. The vague-eyed nomad had been brave enough to quit the social world, the world of books, of family, work and duty. He had had the courage also to stay fixed to his own disaffected line, to wait believingly for some eventual 'spark from heaven'. Such a spark would, he was confident, make wondrous sense of his whole enterprise. The narrator of Arnold's poem had, we learn, similarly made himself available for heavenly encouragements. He too had opted out. But he had never matched the scholar-gipsy's steadfast resolution. And in this he typified the age. The gipsy had '*one* aim, *one* business, *one* desire'. By quitting early, and so absolutely, he had kept his powers 'Fresh/undiverted to the world without/Firm to their mark/not spent on other things.' He knew nothing of our 'sick fatigue', our 'languid doubt'. 'O life unlike to ours!' Should the scholar-gipsy ever encounter one of us, in his phantasmal wanderings, he would be well advised to look the other way; for he is not like us, and we are not at all like him:

> O born in days when wits were fresh and clear,
>   And life ran gaily as the sparkling Thames;
>   Before this strange disease of modern life,
>   With its sick hurry, its divided aims,
>   Its heads o'ertaxed, its palsied hearts, was rife –
>   Fly hence, our contact fear!

>   . . .

> But fly our paths, our feverish contact fly!
>   For strong the infection of our mental strife,
>   Which, though it gives no bliss, yet spoils for rest;
>   And we should win thee from thy own fair life,
>   Like us distracted, and like us unblest.
>   Soon, soon thy cheer would die,

Thy hopes grow timorous, and unfixed thy powers,
  And thy clear aims be cross and shifting made;
  And then thy glad perennial youth would fade,
Fade, and grow old at last, and die like ours.

'The Scholar-Gipsy' ends with two of Arnold's most compelling, and most mystifying, stanzas. Advised to shun the shallow company of moderns, the gipsy is compared to a 'grave Tyrian trader' who journeys across oceans in search of a fit destination for his wares:

Then fly our greetings, fly our speech and smiles!
  – As some grave Tyrian trader, from the sea,
    Descried at sunrise an emerging prow
  Lifting the cool-haired creepers stealthily,
    The fringes of a southward-facing brow
      Among the Aegean isles;
  And saw the merry Grecian coaster come,
    Freighted with amber grapes, and Chian wine,
    Green, bursting figs, and tunnies steeped in brine –
  And knew the intruders on his ancient home,

The young light-hearted masters of the waves –
  And snatched his rudder, and shook out more sail;
    And day and night held on indignantly
  O'er the blue Midland waters with the gale,
    Betwixt the Syrtes and soft Sicily,
      To where the Atlantic raves
  Outside the western straits; and unbent sails
    There, where down cloudy cliffs, through sheets of foam,
    Shy traffickers, the dark Iberians come;
  And on the beach undid his corded bales.

These haunting lines have caused much puzzlement over the years. George Saintsbury once claimed that 'no ingenuity can work out the parallel between the "uncloudedly joyous" scholar who is bid avoid the palsied, diseased *enfants du siècle*, and the grave Tyrian who was indignant at the competition of the merry Greek, and shook out more sail to seek fresh markets'. Arnold's attitude towards the 'merry Greek' has been the crux. But these Greeks are not ancients of the type revered by Arnold in his *Preface*. These are *modern* ancient Greeks: debasers of a proud inheritance. Even so, we have to ask, do they deserve the Tyrian's disdain? Do they not in many ways remind us of the scholar-gipsy: light-hearted, close to nature, not too good at making money? And as for the Tyrian: is he not more like a school inspector than a college drop-out? Are we perhaps meant to find a pathos in his indignation?

And what about those 'corded bales'? What cargo does this merchant carry? Certainly not grapes, or wine, or bursting figs. Perhaps he bears a consignment of high culture, or of poetry composed in imitation of the ancients. Who then are his 'shy' customers, these dark Iberians who steal down from the 'cloudy cliffs' to check the merchandise? Arnold was part-Cornish and, according to his father's *History of Rome*, some gipsy-like Iberians once settled on the coast of Cornwall. Did the swarthy Arnold suspect that he had gipsy blood, Iberian blood? Dwight Culler, one of his best critics, thinks he did.[17] The gipsy way of life, in Arnold's verse, invariably stands for the poetic way of life: the life that Arnold, in 'real life', believes he has abandoned. 'The Scholar-Gipsy' ends with the Tyrian about to 'undo' – no pun intended, we feel sure – his 'corded bales'. Will the Iberians do business? Will the dark, gipsy-like, 'poetic' side of Arnold's nature ever be able to have fruitful dealings with his grave, indignant 'teaching' side? The poem leaves us in the dark – or, to put the matter differently, it leaves us wondering: would Arnold's scholar-gipsy really have preferred 'Sohrab and Rustum' to 'Empedocles'?

II

'This for our wisest!'

Halfway through 'The Scholar-Gipsy', Arnold permits himself a curious digression, or aside. Lamenting in his usual way the 'unpoetical' condition of the modern age, he all at once shifts his attention to the current literary scene – a scene depressingly ungipsy-like in its wan hesitations, its half-beliefs, its 'casual creeds', its 'vague resolves'. The scholar-gipsy, it has been proposed, waits for a 'spark from heaven'; he is confident that such a spark will come. Arnold and his contemporaries wait too, but not with any real conviction. And while they wait, they suffer; they make poetry from their suffering. Rather like Empedocles, they wallow in 'a continuous state of mental distress . . . unrelieved by incident, hope and resistance, in which there is everything to be endured, nothing to be done':

> . . . and amongst us one,
>   Who most has suffered, takes dejectedly
> His seat upon the intellectual throne;
>   And all his store of sad experience he

Lays bare of wretched days;
Tells us his misery's birth and growth and signs,
    And how the dying spark of hope was fed,
    And how the breast was soothed, and how the head,
And all his hourly varied anodynes.

This for our wisest! and we others pine,
    And wish the long unhappy dream would end,
        And waive all claim to bliss, and try to bear;
    With close-lipped patience for our only friend,
        Sad patience, too near neighbour to despair . . .

'This for our wisest!' Of whom does Arnold speak here? Who is this downcast monarch? Much later on, when asked, Arnold would say that it was Goethe, but nobody believed him: after all, in every one of Goethe's named appearances in Arnold, the great German is presented as heroic and exemplary. The likeliest candidate is Tennyson. *In Memoriam* appeared in 1850, the same year that Tennyson became Poet Laureate, in succession to Arnold's revered Wordsworth. And 'This for our wisest!' pretty well sums up Arnold's attitude towards the senior – indeed dominant – poetic presence of his day.

Although Arnold shrank from writing publicly about Tennyson, in private he rarely missed a chance to snipe at him. Several factors may have been at work here. Tennyson was universally praised as a 'born' poet, whereas Arnold – it was often said – had 'made' himself write poems. At the same time, Arnold was frequently accused of being over-influenced by Tennyson: the plangent melancholia, the fondness for antique or mythic subjects, the gloomily foot-shuffling approach to God – all these, some critics said, were Tennysonian.

Such accusations hit a nerve, not least because there was some truth in them. As Arnold once confided, when the last two lines of 'Sohrab' were called Tennysonian: 'One has him so in one's head one cannot help imitating him sometimes.'[1] The overall effect, though, was to make Arnold ever more determined to seek differences between his methods and the Laureate's. Thus, much of his railing against 'thinking-aloud' poetry was done with Tennyson in mind. The *In Memoriam* lyrics (which surely Arnold *should* have liked, and maybe did) he offhandedly dismissed as 'holdings forth in verse which, for anything in the nature of the composition itself, may perfectly well go on for ever'.

Tennyson, Arnold had told Clough in 1847, was decorative rather than penetrative (dawdling in the universe's 'painted shell'): he had a certain facility but was 'deficient in intellectual power'. Was there a trace of Balliol snobbery in such disparagements? Well, yes, perhaps. Certainly Arnold – when Tennyson was on his mind, as he so often was – tended to play up his own 'objective', scholarly persona at the expense of whatever might have seemed too 'natural', or Tennysonian, in his poetic make-up. After all, compared to Tennyson, Arnold could never be natural enough. This Tennyson-phobia, we might easily conclude, was at least partly to blame for the repudiation of *Empedocles*.

It was never Arnold's practice to speak out against (or for) his immediate contemporaries. 'No man,' he once opined, 'can trust himself to speak of his own time and of his own contemporaries with the same sureness of judgement and the same proportion as of times and men gone by.'[2] Arnold could scarcely have believed this, since 'his own time' was – repeatedly – his subject, and he always kept a watchful eye on current reputations. He knew the dangers, though, of present-tense polemics, especially in the field of poetry. Good manners could be deadlier than indignation and Arnold took pride in his good manners. He liked to see himself as the unrufflable promoter of 'sweet reason'. In 1853 sweet reason told him that a critique of Tennyson would be ill-advised: 'inevitably', it would be 'attributed to odious motives'.

So too would a critique of the up-and-coming Alexander Smith. If Tennyson in the mid-1850s was English poetry's reigning king, Smith was the most glittering pretender. On all sides, the

23 year old's long poem, *A Life-Drama*, was being lauded as the new great thing: exuberant, impassioned, up to date. Arnold knew that his own verse was most unlikely to appeal to Smith's admirers, and the younger man's publicity got on his nerves, but he was careful to disguise his irritation, at any rate in print. The closest Arnold came to speaking against Smith was in his *Preface*, in which Smith – not named – is an important background presence. Almost certainly, *A Life-Drama* was chief among those disapproved-of modern works which 'seem to exist merely for the sake of single lines and passages'. And when Arnold derided a modern critic for proposing that 'allegories' of the inner life were modern poetry's highest aim, he was speaking of the critic David Masson, who had put this view in an admiring piece on Smith.

Still, *Poems* (1853) did cause its own gratifying stir. Most of the reviews concentrated on the *Preface* and took issue with its neo-classical prescriptions. Why did a Christian English poet need to look to ancient Greece and Rome for heroes worthy of the epic manner? This question Arnold deflected with some ease in a note attached to the second edition of his book: 'It has been said that I wish to limit the poet in his choice of subjects, to the period of Greek and Roman antiquity; but it is not so. I only counsel him to choose for his subjects great actions, without regarding to what time they belong.'[3] He was somewhat less composed, though, in his rebuttal of the charge (levelled by G.H. Lewes) that imitation of the Ancients was not quite the same as emulation.[4] Arnold made 'no objection' to Lewes's point: 'All I say is, let us study them.' Again, the suggestion was that Arnold now cared more for modern reading than for modern writing. Better to study well than to write poorly. The Ancients – even though, as poets, we could never hope to rival them – had much to teach us about how to live:

They can help to cure us of what is, it seems to me, the great vice of our intellect, manifesting itself in our incredible vagaries in literature, in art, in religion, in morals: namely, that it is *fantastic*, and wants *sanity*. Sanity, – that is the great virtue of the ancient literature . . .[5]

'Classical' meant 'sane'; 'romantic' meant 'unstable' – or, as Goethe put it, 'sickly'. Arnold had come to fear his own tendency to sickliness – to that disruptive restlessness from which the best of his own poems had been made.

Even so, he was still touchy about the reception of his works, the sickly and non-sickly. Two reviews, in particular, upset him – and quite understandably, since they issued from two of his best friends. One was by Clough, who compared Arnold unfavourably with – of all people – Alexander Smith.[6] The other was by John Duke Coleridge, who set out to expose him as a pasticheur of Tennyson.[7] If the intention was to wound, or to repay Arnold for some bygone act of lordliness, the aim – in each case – could not have been more deadly. And Coleridge carried his assault a venomous stage further, by making out that 'Sohrab and Rustum' was lifted from an essay by Sainte-Beuve. Arnold had privately told Coleridge that the Sainte-Beuve essay had been one of his sources for the poem and was astonished by this 'vicious' comeback.[8]

Again, he kept his temper – with Coleridge and with Clough. With Coleridge, he took the trouble to append a note to the second edition of his book in which he explained the true extent of his debt to Sainte-Beuve: 'It would have been more charitable,' he commented, 'had the reviewer, before making his good-natured suggestion, ascertained . . . how far it was confirmed by the fact.'[9] (Coleridge's attack, it should perhaps be said, appeared in an obscure Christian magazine and might have gone unnoticed but for Arnold's mild response; but mutual friends – like Shairp and Stanley – were shocked by what they saw as a betrayal, and may have encouraged Arnold to reply.) To Clough, Arnold wrote directly – but again with stunning calm: 'There is no one to whose aperçus I attach the value I do to yours – but I think you are sometimes – with regard to *me* especially – a little cross and wilful.'[10]

The evidence is sparse but what we have suggests that Arnold's farewell to the intense poetic life was not as painlessly sagacious as he made it sound in his public pronouncements. His letters of 1853–5 are heavy with a sense of premature aridity: 'I am past thirty and three parts iced over,' he wrote to Clough in February 1853, 'and my pen, it seems to me, is even stiffer and more cramped than my feeling.'[11] And again in May: 'I feel immensely – more and more clearly . . . what I have (I believe) lost and choked by my treatment of myself and the studies to which I have addicted myself. But what ought I to have done in preference to what I have done? This is the question.'[12]

Arnold's school-inspecting he usually depicts as a life-sapping grind. Day after day he finds himself 'too utterly tired out to write', oppressed, bored, harassed by the constant travel, the dull company, the repetitive, low-level schoolroom chores. Whenever he complains, though, he invariably adds: 'but I must tackle to'; 'it would not do to let the feeling get too strong'; 'it will wear off in a few days'. However bad things got, he was resolved to 'do my duty, whatever that might be'.[13] To give way to his unhappiness would be, well, sickly, self-indulgent.

Vacations at Fox How are now viewed as paradisal interludes: 'In the discomforts of the present I find myself perpetually looking forward to being there again, and to the best and pleasantest peace I ever obtain.'[14] These Fox How holidays were, of course, school holidays. Arnold thought often of his father, comparing his own dispirited surrender to the call of duty with Dr Arnold's vehement idealism. His father had not merely acquiesced; he was a leader. 'He was not only a good man saving his own soul by righteousness . . . he carried so many others along with him in his hand, if they would let him, along with himself.'[15] For Matthew, on the other hand, it was effort enough these days to carry himself from one schoolroom to another.

By the mid-1850s, four of Dr Arnold's sons had jobs in education. Tom was a school inspector in Tasmania; Edward a school inspector in Cornwall and the South West counties (in spite of being an ordained priest and a Fellow of All Souls). Even William, the military man, was now in charge of Public Instruction in the Punjab (he had also just published a fervently Rugbeian novel, *Oakfield*). In Matthew's view, these brothers were more temperamentally suited to the work than he was: more earnest, more Christian, more instinctively egalitarian. Writing to William, on the occasion of his younger brother's appointment to the school-inspecting fold, Matthew ruefully remarked upon the 'absurdity and disadvantages' of the Arnold inheritance. Everybody, he said, expected an Arnold to care deeply about education. He often felt tempted to reply: 'My good friends, this is a matter for which my father certainly had a specialité but for which I have none whatever.'[16]

All the same, he continued, William would surely succeed as an educationist, if only because he would throw himself into it with such wholeheartedness. As for himself, he 'half cannot' and 'half will not' make such a commitment to the work, and must therefore expect to feel 'the weight of it doubly in consequence'. But then:

> I am inclined to think it would have been the same with any active line of life on which I had found myself engaged – even with politics. So I am glad my sphere is a humble one and must try more and more to do something worth doing in my own way, since I cannot bring myself to do more than a halting sort of half work in other people's way.[17]

And, late in life, Arnold would describe his own early inspecting years as follows:

> . . . though I am a schoolmaster's son . . . school teaching or school inspecting is not the line of life I should naturally have chosen . . . the irksomeness of my new duties was what I felt most, and during the first year or so this was sometimes almost insupportable. But I met daily in the schools with men and women discharging duties akin to

mine, duties as irksome as mine, duties less well paid than mine, and I asked myself, Are they on roses? Would they not by nature prefer, many of them, to go where they liked and do what they liked instead of being shut up in school? I saw them making the best of it; I saw the cheerfulness and efficiency with which they did their work, and I asked myself again, How do they do it? Gradually it grew into a habit with me to put myself into their places, to try to enter into their feelings, to represent to myself their life, and . . . I got many lessons from them.[18]

The softening described here was, as Arnold says, a gradual process and did not take root until he had developed his own line of interest in the field of education – an interest not so much in the schools he was obliged to tour but in the types of school which did not then exist: state-aided schools for secondary pupils. In the schools Arnold actually inspected, the highest aim was to ensure some very basic education for children who would almost certainly be leaving school and set to work before they had reached adolescence. Arnold was fond enough of his own infants (his own 'plague of babies', as he called them) but – at the age of thirty-plus – he was not greatly concerned about whether or not working-class ten year olds knew how to do their sums. Nor had he begun to give much thought to his own children's further education. Again, he slightingly compared himself to Dr Arnold. Writing to his mother, who had sent him a newly discovered (but now lost) letter from her husband, he observed:

I ought before this to have thanked you for sending the letter, which is ennobling and refreshing as everything which proceeds from him always is . . . I think he was 35 when that letter was written – and how he had forecast and resolved, even then, the serious interests and welfare of his children – at a time when to many men their children are still little more than playthings. He might well hope to bring up children, when he made that bringing up so distinctly his thought beforehand – and we who treat the matter so carelessly and lazily –

we can hardly expect ours to do more than *grow up* at hazard – not be *brought up* at all. But this is just what makes him great . . .[19]

This 'greatness' of Dr Arnold would shortly be commemorated in Matthew's 'Rugby Chapel', a poem which tells us more about the son's low sense of his own worth than it does about the father's excellence:

> And through thee I believe
> In the noble and great who are gone;
> Pure souls honoured and blest
> By former ages – . . .
> Yes! I believe that there lived
> Others like thee in the past,
> Not like the men of the crowd
> Who all round me today
> Bluster or cringe, and make life
> Hideous, and arid, and vile;
> But souls tempered with fire,
> Fervent, heroic, and good,
> Helpers and friends of mankind.

This is Carlylean hero-worship – the notion of the 'great man' who leads and helps his fellows rise above themselves. If Matthew Arnold were to continue as a poet, he would have to aim for a 'great-man' kind of poem. But, these days, what could even a great poem *do*? And, in any case, did Arnold have the stuff of greatness? He doubted that he did. Compared even with Clough – who, for all his faults, had always been straightforwardly *impassioned* – Arnold believed himself to be a pallid soul: languid, fickle, insincere, cold, arid. '*Arid* – that is what the times are!'[20] On occasions, as we have seen, he was quite ready to scold Clough for not settling to a single task or 'line' – 'you would never take your assiette as something determined, final and unchangeable for you and proceed to work away on the basis of that' – but what of his own assiette, his own determined and unchangeable life-plan? In May 1853, he wrote to Clough:

> I catch myself desiring now at times political life, and this and that; and I say to myself – you do not desire these things because you are really adapted to them, and therefore the desire for them is merely contemptible – and it is so. I am nothing and very probably never shall be anything – but there are characters who are truest to themselves by never being anything . . .[21]

No doubt, in these 'almost insupportable' first years of his inspectorship, Arnold sometimes thought of breaking free, of opting out, but he was stuck: to *be* stuck was his 'line' now. When, in 1856, he was offered a job as a 'Colonial Secretary' in Mauritius, he swiftly turned it down: 'I should have sate all day on a coral rock, bathing my legs in the Southern ocean.'[22] The best that could realistically be yearned for was early retirement. 'We can always look forward to retiring to Italy on £200 a year,' he told his wife in 1851, on the first day of his new job. Over the years, this became a regular refrain: 'How I should like to live quietly in Switzerland with you and the boys.'

Such wistfulness intensified after the appearance of his book: 'I should like, now, to go abroad,' he wrote, 'above all – to Rome – to live for some months quite quietly there – to see no English, and to hear nothing more about my Poems. It does me no good hearing the discussion of them . . .' In the summer of 1854, he and his wife did manage to escape across the Channel, but not to Switzerland or Rome. For £15, which Arnold could not easily afford, they were able to see Brussels, Ghent and Antwerp. 'But we have both recorded a solemn vow, if we live, to spend at least seven weeks abroad next year.' When, in October of this year, he heard from K that she and her husband had been journeying in the Italian Alps, he wrote to her in some excitement:

> I have so much to say to you, you dear soul. It was odd – as your letter about the country you went through on the Italian side of the

Alps was being read it brought to my mind delightfully just what had
been present to it when many of the poems of mine which are nearest
to me were composed – and then came your sentence saying that
what you had seen had brought these Poems to your mind. That was
a *correspondence* to give one real pleasure – but there is no one and
never will be any one who enters into what I have done as you have
entered into it, dearest K, – and to whom I so want to communicate
what I do.[23]

He signed himself 'your faithless and most affectionate brother'.
The loss of K still hurt but it was on the mend – or rather, the
relationship was settling into a viable new shape, with Arnold
now able to send his kind regards to Mr Forster with some show
of sincerity: 'I should like to know what William thinks of [X],'
he wrote, or 'I feel sure William would be interested in [Y].' So far
as we can judge, K was still keen to serve as his best critic – 'No
one ever writes so pleasantly about my poems as you do,' said
Arnold – and perhaps she too had learned to be more tactful.
What did K really think of her brother's new direction as a poet?
'The preface I think will stand,' he wrote, 'I am anxious for
William to read that' – but we do not know how she, or indeed
William, responded to that all-determining pronouncement. K
seems to have liked 'Sohrab and Rustum' – but then Arnold from
the start had made it clear how much this poem meant to him –
and her remarks on his Swiss verses seem to have been kindly. She
also followed his reviews with loyal interest.

However, a gulf between them was still evident. Arnold, for all
his protestations ('My love to William: he knows how truly, by
this time, he has made relations of us all'), never really warmed to
William Forster, and K had little time for Flu Wightman: 'I
cannot say,' she wrote in 1855, 'that I think life in London and the
constant intercourse with Judge Wightman are very good for
dearest Matt – for I think both he and Fanny Lucy are quite
enough inclined to value the externals and proprieties of life.'[24]
Flu, she believed, encouraged Arnold's 'artificial' side.

Certainly, Arnold was spending more time with the Wight-mans than he did with his own family at Fox How, but this 'constant intercourse' was largely unavoidable. In London, it was natural enough for Flu – when Arnold was away – to gravitate to Eaton Place. (Pregnant again in 1855, she moved in with her parents for the birth of her third child – 'that business', Arnold called it – and afterwards she and her husband found a house to rent in nearby Lower Belgrave Street.) Also, Arnold himself had a professional association with his father-in-law. When Judge Wightman travelled the Circuit, Arnold – for £75 a year – went with him as his marshal: a sinecure but time-consuming – two or three weeks out of the school holidays – and none too entertaining, it would seem. Sometimes, the Circuit took Arnold to congenial locations – the Cotswolds, the Welsh borders – but he rarely spoke about life in the courts and seems to have found scant 'human interest' in their goings-on.

His closeness to the Wightmans, then, had much to do with money and with day-to-day convenience. K was perhaps right, though, to be troubled. Arnold was troubled too. His discomfi-ture, however, had nothing much to do with 'artificial London life', for which he had a well-developed taste. On the few occasions when he dropped his guard on the subject of his home-life, he spoke of noisy, ailing infants, in-laws to be humoured, lack of privacy, and so on. On the whole, his London situation was a good deal more enticing than the provincial lodgings he was usually condemned to. He rarely missed a chance to get back to the capital whenever he could find an opening in his timetable. Even so, the provinces at least provided opportunities for solitude and steady concentration. When, in 1856, Arnold found himself elected to the Athenaeum, he was overjoyed:

I am elected at the Athenaeum . . . and look forward with rapture to the use of that library in London. It is really as good as having the books of one's own – one can use them at a club in such perfect quiet and comfort. (To K, February 1856)[25]

I was elected here in February [at the Athenaeum] and could not have got to a place more perfectly to my mind. I am sitting now, at ½ past 12 in the day, writing at a window in the great Drawing Room with only two other people in the room – every side of this magnificent room covered with books and the room opening into others also full of books – it is a cloudless day . . . (To William Arnold, March 1856)[26]

(Arnold was a member of the Athenaeum for a further thirty years and his love of the place remained undimmed. To this day his portrait can be found hanging near the club's main entrance.)

Ironically enough, it was William Forster (soon to be an MP and, much later on, a Minister for Education – and thus Arnold's boss) who helped to get Matthew elected to the Athenaeum. The ironies were several: Forster was an ill-educated Northerner, of Quaker business stock, whose wife deplored the artificiality of city life: yet here he was, facilitating Arnold's entry to a prestigious London club.

Despite the Athenaeum, though, Arnold in 1856 was not sure what his next step, as a writer, ought to be. Thanks to his *Preface*, he was now in some demand as a prose writer for the periodicals – but he was 'so dead sick of criticism' and either refused suggestions from editors or failed to deliver pieces he had promised. He was also under some pressure from his mother to develop what she saw as his Arnoldian inheritance. Now that he was in his thirties and something of a public figure, Mrs Arnold reckoned it was time for him to take up some of Dr Arnold's social causes. His poetry meant little to her; he always felt that her praise of his verses, when she offered it, was hurtfully lukewarm. She still saw her eldest son as something of a ditherer. Having finally made a professional commitment, why didn't he do *more*?

In 1854, it seems, Arnold's mother expressed some dissatisfaction with Matt's progress to her Lake District neighbour, the 'radical' journalist Harriet Martineau. Martineau reported to a friend:

Speaking of Poems, I am throbbing all through with Matt Arnold's. *Have* you read his Preface? & Rustum? To think that his father underrated, even insulted, his quality of mind – setting his soft, pious younger brother over him, – (a mere girl in comparison) & here is Matt: absorbing all the Arnolds that ever were & ever will be! How amazed she wd be to know how his good, earnest, narrow father shrivels up before his torch! But I suppose it would kill her. '*Do* write to Matt,' she says to me. But I dare not. It wd be an impertinence.[27]

Martineau would have done well to say these things in print. Nobody ever told Matthew Arnold that the memory of his good father 'shrivels up before his torch'. What Harriet Martineau *did* say – in the *Daily News* – could not have been more damning. Reviewing the very book which she is here 'throbbing all through with', she brutally dismissed it:

Finally, we take leave of Mr Arnold, with his cleverness and his scholarship, his somewhat superciliously announced theories of poetry, his attachment to ancient models, and his echoes (for all that) of the Tennysonian cadences, in the conviction that, although he has written no common verses – nay, better than some men today of celebrity as 'poets' – he was not born a poet, and therefore never can be one. Many claim the rank; few show claims as plausible as his, because of the superiority of his general talents and culture; but his claims also want the genuine stamp. We say so, not without pain, but distinctly.[28]

Arnold was indeed unfortunate in his admirers. Clough, Coleridge, Harriet Martineau – these for our loyalest! (In the case of Martineau, however, Arnold's views were inconsistent, though he largely kept them to himself. When he did write about her publicly – in 'Haworth Churchyard' – it was to praise, ironically enough, her 'steadfast soul'. At the time of writing that stiff poem, though, he understood that she was ill and had not long to live. And perhaps he had not read the *Daily News*. Harriet

Martineau lived on for a further twenty years, causing Arnold to withdraw his elegiac lines from circulation.)

Such was the literary world, and – in 1854–5 – Arnold had good reason to feel disaffected. At the same time, though, he still nursed the hope that he could somehow fashion a poetic life that would support and be supported by a life of duty. If he could write the kind of poem which K and his mother would *enthusiastically* acknowledge as worthy of his father's legacy, perhaps a way forward could be found. In his 1853 *Preface*, he had outlined his master-plan. Now all he had to do was put it into practice.

12

A Professor of Poetry

At least one of Arnold's friends was able to approach his *Poems* (1853) without damaging intent. One of the book's most sympathetic reviewers was James Froude, shunned by Oxford on account of *The Nemesis of Faith* and now a professional historian and journalist. 'I only half like him,' Arnold had said of Froude a few years earlier, 'he comes and hangs about people.'[1] This time, however, Froude's hovering had some effect. Preferring 'Sohrab' to 'Empedocles', he agreed with Arnold's *Preface* that 'the relentless craving after novelty, so characteristic of all modern writing . . . is mere disease'. 'It is indeed nonsense,' he went on, 'to speak, as some critics speak, of the "present" as alone making claims upon the poet.' But why, Froude had to ask, did Arnold dwell exclusively on ancient Greece and Rome?

We do not dream of prescribing to Mr Arnold what subject he should choose. Let him choose what interests himself if he will interest his readers: and if he chooses what is really human, let it come from what age it will, human hearts will answer to it. And yet it seems as if Teutonic tradition, Teutonic feeling, and Teutonic thought had the first claim on English and German poets. And those among them will deserve best of the modern world, and will receive the warmest welcome from it, who will follow Shakespeare in modelling into forms of beauty the inheritance which has come down to them of the actions of their own race.[2]

Arnold was by instinct drawn to think of history in terms of racial lines and strains, and he took note of Froude's remarks. It so happened that he had lately been reading P.H. Mallet's *Northern Antiquities*, with its renditions of 'La mythologie . . . des anciens Scandinaves', and he was familiar too with Carlyle's *Heroes and Hero-Worship*, which makes much of the Norse sagas. He was aware also of Thomas Gray's poetic dabblings in Norseland ('The Descent of Odin'). Altogether, Froude's suggestion was well timed. Arnold decided to take as his first post-*Preface* subject not some noble episode from Greek or Roman myth but an obscure tale from the *Norse Edda*, as recounted in Mallet and briefly mentioned in Carlyle.

'Balder Dead',[3] a work of some 500 lines, tells of the Nordic gods' refusal to accept the death of the thought-to-be-immortal Balder, who was a kind of minstrel sun-god (in Clough's words, 'a Scandinavian Apollo'). Although Odin and his co-gods bury Balder, with lengthy and elaborate Norse-Graeco-Roman cere-monial, they still have hopes that they might save him, or retrieve him, from the Kingdom of the Dead. With this in mind, Hermod – Balder's brother – is sent off on a nine-day horse ride, through many a black labyrinth and grim valley. His mission is to locate 'death's abode' and there to strike a deal with the chief death-god, Hela. A deal is indeed struck, but there are strings attached: Balder will be returned to life, Hela decrees, provided that 'all things in the world, both living and lifeless, weep for him . . . if any one or thing speak against him or refuse to weep, he shall remain in hell'. Odin, hearing this, arranges for 'everything to weep'. He is not able, though, to coax a tear from a certain 'old hag' named Thaukt. This Thaukt, we learn, is actually Loki, Balder's arch-enemy and the original cause of his demise. Thanks to the dry eyes of Thaukt, poor Balder must stay dead.

This, then, was the 'great subject' chosen by Arnold to exemplify his new pursuit of 'sanity' in verse, his new hostility to the 'fantastic'. Admittedly, some of the Norse legend's more comical imaginings do not appear in Arnold's version and in general he does incline to 'Homerise' his source, playing down what Carlyle called a 'Hyper-Brobdingnagian' element in the original. Even so, the tale *is* absurdly tall, and seems all the taller in Arnold's profoundly unamused retelling. T.S. Eliot was right to describe 'Balder Dead' as high-class academic verse: it carries more than a whiff of the Rugby classroom. The good student Arnold, we suspect, is resolved first of all to cover what he knows to be the set requirements, as if for an end-of-term prize poem: the high-flown rhetorical address, the magnificent-ceremony episode, the heroic-action sequence, the hair-raising Hades evocation, and so on. With similar earnestness, he works through all the set emotions, injecting equal measures of pity, terror and rage. But Arnold had no gift for magniloquence: between the lines, there is a constant sense of steady effort. Steeped as he was in Homer, Virgil, Milton and now Mallet, he could conjure a passable pastiche of epic grandeur. At the same time, his mighty line is always on the edge of falling flat:

> So spake the King of Gods, and straightway rose,
> And mounted the horse Sleipner, whom he rode;
> And from the hall of Heaven he rode away
> To Lidskialf, and sate upon his throne,
> The mount, from whence his eye surveys the world,
> And far from Heaven he turned his shining orbs
> To look on Midgard, and the earth, and men.

And on the conjuring Lapps he bent his gaze
Whom antlered reindeer pull over the snow;
And on the Finns, the gentlest of mankind,
Fair men, who live in holes under the ground . . .

Arnold's heroic posture is at best a grim-jawed, pumped-up thing. Sky-high apostrophes, big brazen adjectives, mechanically strummed pentameters, gratuitous inversions – all the epic style-aids are deployed, but with no real story-telling drive. Throughout there is an air of laboured fabrication, of poetry toilsomely got up to demonstrate what poetry ought to be.

'Balder Dead' is now the least read of Arnold's longer works. It is often omitted from selections of his verse. And so it should be. But the poem does happen to have buried in it a few true and haunting passages, and these remind us of what Arnold was here trying to suppress, to purge from his poetic make-up. The passages are framed as similes: those 'luxurious comparisons' insisted on by epic precedent. As was the way with Milton and with Homer, Arnold's similes don't always take their orders from the central narrative. And yet, as Johnson said of Milton's strayings from the purpose: who would wish away such superfluities? Arnold's superfluities in 'Balder Dead' we welcome as breathing-space, off-duty moments of forgetfulness in which the author's natural poetic self blinks through to us between long, tiring bouts of 'epic' mimicry:

Nor yet could Hermod see his brother's face,
For it grew dark; but Hoder touched his arm,
And as a spray of honeysuckle flowers
Brushes across a tired traveller's face
Who shuffles through the deep dew-moistened dust,
On a May evening, in the darkened lanes,
And starts him, that he thinks a ghost went by –
So Hoder brushed by Hermod's side, and said: –

The setting is more Cumbria than Asgard, to be sure. And the delicacy of the perception – the spray of honeysuckle flowers, the tired traveller – is also out of place. But we don't mind.

There are other such 'intervals' in 'Balder Dead', and they deserve to be rescued from the context they are trapped in. In one of these, Arnold compares Hell's hordes of dead with swallows that 'crowd the bulrush-beds of some clear river':

> And from the dark flocked up the shadowy tribes
> And as the swallows crowd the bulrush-beds
> Of some clear river, issuing from a lake
> On autumn-days, before they cross the sea;
> And to each bulrush-crest a swallow hangs
> Quivering, and others skim the river-streams,
> And their quick twittering fills the banks and shores –
> So around Hermod swarmed the twittering *ghosts* . . .

They *did*? And this will be most readers' first response to the description. Just for a few moments, though, Arnold seems 'at home' with his materials – and thus, of course, wildly out of tune with his main purpose. And there is a similarly welcome faltering when he compares Hermod's attempt to cross the river Giall with a cowherd's attempt to steer his cattle through a narrow mountain-pass. In the Norse tale, Hermod's path is blocked by a fearsome female named Modgruder. The cowherd's obstacles are – shall we say? – more homely:

> And on the bridge a damsel watching armed,
> In the straight passage, at the farther end,
> Where the road issues between wailing rocks,
> Scant space that warder left for passers-by;
> But as when cowherds in October drive
> Their kine across the snowy mountain-pass
> To winter pasture on the southern side,
> And on the ridge a wagon chokes the way,

Wedged in the snow; then painfully the hinds
With goad and shouting urge their cattle past,
Plunging through deep untrodden banks of snow
To right and left, and warm steam fills the air –
So on the bridge that damsel blocked the way . . .

Arnold completed 'Balder Dead' towards the end of 1854. In December of that year it appeared as the leading item in *Poems: Second Series*, a collection largely made up of works excluded from the 1853 book (which had itself been reissued in 1854, by Longmans, and was now to be called *Poems: First Series*). 'Empedocles on Etna' was, of course, missing from both *First* and *Second Series*, although in *Second Series* Arnold did print from it four of the Callicles songs – under the heading 'The Harp Player on Etna' – as well as a fragment from the main body of the text, entitled here 'The Philosopher and the Stars'. Arnold also in his 'Balder Dead' volume (i.e. *Poems: Second Series*) grouped together his 1850 'love poems' – 'The River', 'On the Rhine', 'Separation', 'Leaving' and 'Too Late'. These had hitherto appeared as separate poems and been mixed up somewhat confusingly with pieces specifically to do with Marguerite. Now they were printed as a batch, under the title 'Faded Leaves', and were clearly intended to refer to Arnold's courtship of his wife. In addition, *Second Series* restored to favour works like 'Resignation' and 'The Buried Life'. In the space of three years, then, the poet formerly known as 'A' had put out three books of verse under his full name. Most of the work in them had already been printed in book form, as by 'A', but each of the early, unsigned (or 'A') books was now withdrawn from circulation.

Matthew Arnold the poet is a bibliographer's nightmare. To sum up, though: a reader new to Arnold's work who purchased, in 1854, the two new Longmans books (*First Series* and *Second Series*) would in effect be getting the collected poems: with the exception of 'Empedocles on Etna'. Such a reader would also get the text of Arnold's famous *Preface*, explaining why 'Empedocles' (of which the new reader would presumably know nothing) had been left out. This new reader might as a result have problems fitting Arnold's *Preface* theories to his practice. Which poems, he might ask, are meant to exemplify the precepts of the *Preface*; which are not? Apart from 'Sohrab' and 'Balder Dead' and an omnipresence of Greek drapery, there were few signs that Arnold had been following his own prescriptions – or knew how to.

In December 1854, Arnold wrote to K: 'I think Balder will consolidate the peculiar sort of reputation that I have got by Sohrab and Rustum – and many will complain that I am settling myself permanently in the field of antiquity, as if there was no other. But I have in fact done with this field in completing Balder – and what I do next will be, if I can do it, wholly different.'[4]

Over the next year, Arnold's pursuit of a 'wholly different' line involved plans for a 'tragedy at the end of the Roman Republic – one of the most colossal times of the world, I think . . . It won't see the light, however, before 1857',[5] and for a resumption of labour on his on-and-off Lucretius epic. Neither of these designs was ever carried out, but Arnold evidently felt the need to set himself poetic goals that would at least *sound* arduous and worthy: courses of writing that could also be justified as courses of study. The last thing he really needed was an increase in his daily workload: his letters during 1855–7 repeatedly complain about the difficulty of finding space and time in which to attend to his own private intellectual pursuits. This being so, hours spent writing poetry had to be hours verifiably well spent. His poems, or schemes for poems, had to bear the appearance of hard, selfless graft.

Arnold's family life at this time was becoming ever more cramped and congested. He and his wife still had no settled home in London. By the summer of 1856, he, Flu and their three often-ailing little boys, aged four, three and one (a girl, Lucy, would be born in 1858), were lodging once again at Eaton Place. Arnold still had the Athenaeum ('a place at which I enjoy something resembling beatitude') but he had nowhere to base himself for a sustained literary effort. Also, he was short of money. 'The longer I live,' he wrote in August 1856, 'the more I see that marriage with a narrow income and precarious future is a sort of gambling state which can only be supported by those of firm nerves and strong ready wits: the feeble sink under the anxiety of it.'[6]

In December 1856 he briefly gained access to his old bachelor rooms in Mount Street (now occupied by his friend Wyndham Slade, a barrister, who was out at work during the day). He wrote to K:

> I fly and hide myself here from the everlasting going in and coming out of Eaton Place, in the profoundest secrecy, no one but Wyndham Slade knowing where I am. 'Hide thy life' – said Epictetus – and the exquisite zest there is in doing so can only be appreciated by those who, desiring to introduce some method into their lives, have suffered from the malicious pleasure the world takes in trying to distract them till they are as shatter-brained as the world itself.[7]

'I think I shall be able to do something more in time,' Arnold had written to his sister earlier in this same year, 'but am sadly bothered and hindered at present – and that puts one in *deprimirter Stimmung* [a mood of dejection], which is a fatal thing. To make a habitual war on depression and low spirits which in one's early youth one is apt to indulge and be somewhat interested in is one of the things one learns as one gets older – they are noxious alike to body and mind, and already partake of the nature of death.'[8]

When Arnold wrote this, his Oxford friend John Blackett had just died – 'his being cut short . . . seems a sort of intimation to *me* . . . This is indeed "one's own generation falling also" ' – and he was in the mood for taking stock, however gloomily. On the surface, there had been improvements in his situation. His money worries were easing ('I am fast getting entirely free of debt . . . for

the first time these I don't know how many years')[9] and there was a
good chance that he might shortly be elected to the Professorship
of Poetry at Oxford: an official acknowledgement, as he would see
it, of his prestige as a man of learning (the Professorship in those
days was meant to enhance interest in 'ancient poetry'). People
who met him around this time remarked upon his self-assurance,
his 'grand manner' and his dandiacal dress-sense ('a regular swell,
in brilliant kid gloves, glittering boots, and costume cut in most
perfect fashion').[10] To K, though, he continued to express feelings
of confinement and malaise. He longed to go abroad, he said, to
'disappear', if just for a few weeks: 'Next year I shall make an
urgent appeal to my family and friends to adopt my dear little boys
for six weeks, and disappear for that time – which I long to do.'[11]
And later, when this plan did not work:

> We talk of going abroad for three weeks – but I sometimes have
> doubts whether we shall manage it – What to do with the three
> children is too embarrassing. Else I have a positive thirst to see the
> Alps again, and two or three things which I cannot finish till I have
> again breathed and smelt Swiss air. I shall be baffled, I dare say, as
> one continually is in so much – but I remember Goethe – 'Homer and
> Polygnotus daily teach me more and more that our life is a Hell,
> through which one must struggle as one best can.'[12]

Arnold wrote this in May 1857 – a few days before learning that
he had indeed triumphed in the Oxford Poetry Professorship
election, defeating one John Ernest Bode, author of *Ballads from
Herodotus*. He was delighted by his victory. He had discreetly
canvassed for it, among his Balliol friends, but had expected the
decision to be tight. In the event, he romped home with a majority
of eighty-five ('It was an immense victory,' he told his mother,
'some 200 more voted than ever before').[13]

Arnold had several reasons to be pleased by the prospect of a
five-year attachment to Oxford University. It would afford him
the opportunity of reliving, without too deep a sense of loss, his

own student years – 'the *freest* and most delightful part, perhaps of my life':

> . . . the sentiment of the place is overpowering to me when I have leisure to feel it and can shake off the interruptions which it is not so easy to shake off now as it was when we were young.[14]

His election was also, he felt, an Oxford tribute to his father ('I was supported by people of all opinions – the great bond of union being, I believe, the affectionate interest felt in papa's memory'). On this subject, he wrote proudly to his mother:

> I am never tired of thinking how he would have rejoiced in his son's thus obtaining a share in the permanence and grandeur of that *august* place which he loved so much and to which he so gladly attached himself – how there could hardly perhaps have been conferred on me a distinction, of those conferred by men, which he would have so much prized. This doubles the worth of the distinction in my eyes – although it is in itself very pleasant to me, from the way in which it has been bestowed, and from its finding me in a profession which admits of no rise and no distinction.[15]

The Oxford Professorship paid '£130 a year, or thereabouts', which would be useful, and in return Arnold would be required to give 'three Latin lectures on ancient poetry in the course of the year. These lectures I hope to give in English.' In securing this concession (thus becoming the first Oxford Poetry Professor *not* to lecture in Latin), the Professor-elect had put it to the university's Vice-Chancellor that 'in late years learned men have more & more abandoned the use of the Latin language even in treating subjects of pure learning, while the indisposition on the part of students to receive instruction conveyed by a modern Teacher in a dead language, has become even greater, perhaps, than the indisposition of the learned to convey it'.[16] At the same time, he affirmed that the purpose of his lectures would be to 'promote and animate the study of the Poetical literature of classical Antiquity'.

For two years Arnold had been reading Shakespeare, Plutarch and Macaulay and for a few months had set himself to write a sub-Shakespearean historical drama: or so we can deduce from his various jottings. There was the Roman tragedy he alluded to in 1856 and he almost certainly renewed his efforts with 'Lucretius', perhaps hoping to bend this project to his 'wholly different' purpose. Much of 'Lucretius', though, had probably already gone into the now-banished 'Empedocles on Etna', and in any case Arnold no longer wished to identify himself with a 'gloom-weighted, morbid' Roman poet. Lucretius, he had come to think, was unacceptably Empedoclean. And so he was. The few fragments of 'Lucretius' that remain are full of the old, pre-*Preface* Arnold. They are full too of significance for students of Arnold's curtailed poetic life. Among the fragments, for example, we find seventeen lines of rather bad blank verse based on the following prose paragraph by Arnold. It is the prose paragraph that moves us now:

> It is a sad thing to see a man who has been frittered away piecemeal by petty distractions, and who has never done his best. But it is still sadder to see a man who has done his best, who has reached his utmost limits – and finds his work a failure, and himself far less than he had imagined himself.[17]

For Arnold, in 1856–7, this was not a line of thinking that he dared pursue. It was, he feared, no longer safe for him to dwell for long on 'pangs which place the mind in hell':[18] pangs, finally, of second-rateness, or the fear of second-rateness. Lucretius was abandoned and almost at once Sophocles was called to take his place. Sophocles, Arnold had come to think, represented the perfect example of an artist 'adequate' to the age in which he lived. In Arnold's rosy view, Athens in the 5th century BC was an age of near-perfection: 'There was the utmost energy of life there,

189

public and private, the most entire freedom, the most unpreju-
diced and intelligent observation of human affairs.'[19] In Sophocles he found 'the same energy, the same freedom, the same
intelligent observation; but all these idealised and glorified by the
grace and light shed over them from the noblest poetic feeling'.[20]
(And it is from this time that we can date the beginnings of
Arnold's promiscuous use of words like 'light', 'grace' and 'noble'
to signify the highest-of-high cultural apotheoses.)

Of course, Victorian England is not Athens, presenting as it
does an altogether more complex and confusing spectacle. How
much the more sharply, therefore, does it yearn for some
Sophoclean 'comprehension', for an 'intellectual deliverance'
of the kind that can only be looked for in great art. If living
artists are unable to offer such deliverance, it makes sense for
Victorians, in their thwartedness, to take heed of the most
excellent among the ancients:

> The literature of ancient Greece is, even for modern times, a mighty
> agent of intellectual deliverance; even for modern times, therefore, an
> object of indestructible interest. But first let us ask ourselves why the
> demand for an intellectual deliverance arises in such an age as the
> present, and in what the deliverance itself consists? The demand
> arises, because our present age has around it a copious and complex
> present, and behind it a copious and complex past; it arises, because
> the present age exhibits to the individual man who contemplates it
> the spectacle of a vast multitude of facts awaiting and inviting his
> comprehension. The deliverance consists in man's comprehension of
> this present and past. It begins when our mind begins to enter into
> possession of the general ideas which are the law of this vast
> multitude of facts. It is perfect when we have acquired that
> harmonious acquiescence of mind which we feel in contemplating
> a grand spectacle that is intelligible to us; when we have lost that
> impatient irritation of mind which we feel in presence of an immense,
> moving, confused spectacle which, while it perpetually excites our
> curiosity, perpetually baffles our comprehension.

This, then, is what distinguishes certain epochs in the history of the human race, and our own amongst the number; – on the one hand, the presence of a significant spectacle to contemplate; on the other hand, the desire to find the true point of view from which to contemplate this spectacle. He who has found that point of view, he who adequately comprehends this spectacle, has risen to the comprehension of his age: he who communicates that point of view to his age, he who interprets to it that spectacle, is one of his age's intellectual deliverers.[21]

And this – high-sounding, deeply vague and straining for a non-impatient, non-irritated point of view from which to make forward-looking sense out of an age that Arnold once called 'damned' – would form the drift of his first Oxford lecture as Poetry Professor. Before delivering that lecture, though, Arnold had already completed his own bid to be seen as a 'deliverer'. For several months he had been working on a Sophoclean verse-drama called *Merope*, an attempt – he later said – 'to come to closer quarters with the form which produces such grand effects in the hands of the Greek masters'.[22] This, then, was the 'wholly different' project he had promised in his letter to Wyndham Slade: *Merope*– the story of a son called home by his mother to honour the memory of his dead father (although this is perhaps not quite how Arnold would have paraphrased the plot).

With 'Sohrab and Rustum' and 'Balder Dead', Arnold had rendered homage, as he thought, to Homer and the epic form. Now, with *Merope*, he paid tribute to Sophocles and the Greek drama, a form which he now viewed as more 'modern' than the epic. Each of the three works was meant to be regarded as exemplary: texts to accompany the urgings of his 1853 *Preface*. And *Merope*, it so happened, had the added advantage of lending weight to his new academic status. In 1858 Arnold said of his Greek play that it was 'calculated rather to inaugurate my Professorship with dignity than to move deeply the present race of *humans*'. Its publication, he planned, would swiftly follow his first lecture.

The lecture, called 'The Modern Element in Literature', was delivered in Oxford's Sheldonian Theatre on 14 November 1857, and was received with condescension by his new academic colleagues. 'Tutors who heard him,' says Park Honan, 'were very unimpressed; they told students to avoid his talks.' And Wordsworth's grandson reported to Crabb Robinson: 'As a composition it was pointed & telling: tho' the matter was little to my taste: he seems to lust after a system of his own: and systems are not made in a day: or if they are – like a hastily built fort, the stronger they are at one point, so much the weaker are they at another.'[23] Looking back on his first lecture (which was never reprinted in book form), Arnold himself, ten years after the event, called it 'sketchy and generalising'.

Arnold's original intention had been to make this first lecture an introduction to a linked series, which would eventually become a book, but his second performance, in May 1858, seems to have been something of a flop. Flu did not like it and the audience was thin. Very few undergraduates attended, and the Sheldonian seemed depressingly large for the occasion. It was much the same with his third lecture, given later that month. Neither lecture (two and three) survives: indeed, we are not even certain of their subjects.

After this shaky start, Arnold's Oxford performances steadily improved and in 1860 he would score a notable success with his combative 'On Translating Homer', which turned into a series of three lectures: delivered 'to a full audience', he said, and 'cheered, which is very uncommon at Oxford'.[24] His career as a dramatist, however, did not proceed beyond *Merope*. At first, Arnold had high hopes for his play. It was, he said to Jane, 'above all calculated for the stage – a sort of *opera-stage*',[25] and to this end he sent a copy of the text to Helena Faucit, perhaps the most celebrated actress of the day, 'with a view to ascertain whether it would be possible to induce you, were it brought upon the stage, to undertake the principal character'.[26] Faucit, in response, warned him against subjecting *Merope* to 'the more than doubt-ful test of a public representation'.[27]

The published text of *Merope* appeared in 1858 and was received with, shall we say, luke-warmth – both by the critics and by Arnold's friends. Even the usually supportive Froude felt bound to argue that 'to exhibit Greek poetry exhaustively you ought to have been a Greek and to have been without experience of two thousand years'.[28] There was also a witty letter from Max Müller. 'A poet,' Müller wrote, 'no doubt has the right of choosing his own path, and if he wishes to imitate rather than to create new forms of poetry, he has a very good excuse at this present time of the world's history. But may not a poet be classical, and yet modern and English?'[29] It was doubtful, Müller reckoned, that *Merope* would find much favour with 'John Bull' or with the average 'London cockney'. The play's appeal was to 'a few carefully educated men' whose taste for Greek poetry had not been drowned by Greek and Latin scholarship. But the sympathy of such as these would not be 'strong or warm enough to keep a poet alive'. Müller ended by thanking Arnold for 'a breeze of fresh pure Greek air' but at the same time wishing him 'some English clouds – nay some London fog – on the blue sky of your classical soul'.

The reviews of the play sounded a similar note. *Merope* was admirable enough as an experiment, but in the end it seemed a little pointless and too 'theory-bound'. 'Mr Arnold's theory upon poesy is much better than his practice,' said the *Athenaeum*. Arnold was sorely disappointed but he put on a brave face. Of one hostile critic, he said that 'the comparison of the rhythm of one of the choruses in *Merope* to the noise of a stick drawn along a railing was . . . one of the happiest things I ever read.' When the *Dublin University Review* described *Merope* as 'clever, systematic rubbish', Arnold wrote to his mother: 'Tell me if you have seen the Dublin University? It is clever and I will send it to you if you have not.'[30] He also promised to send a 'very interesting article on *Merope* in the new number of the *National* [*Review*]'. This article, by W.R. Roscoe, spoke of Arnold's Attic enterprise as follows:

He thinks he can dig up the dusky olive from the plains of Attica, and plant it in our English wheat-fields; that he can take in its fullest development the most purely indigenous and the most intensely and narrowly national literature the world ever saw, and bid it find new springs of life some two thousand years later in a nation which has already found its expression in a dramatic literature evolved by itself. Did such an attempt ever succeed?[31]

Merope is, in truth, a lifeless piece of work. It follows the Sophoclean blueprint with plodding respectfulness but has little in it that Arnold could genuinely call his own. The play has certain themes which meant a lot to him – the fated, unrefusable inheritance, the thin line that separates leadership from tyranny, the mother–son entrancement – and the character of Polyphontes is given a certain anachronistic depth: his troubled self-inspection seems more English–Victorian than ancient Greek. Altogether, though, Arnold is too preoccupied with getting the Greek form right, and too studied in his striving for an appropriately 'elevated' diction.

And yet, for all his pro-Hellenic theory, Arnold was not at all in tune with certain stock features of Greek drama. The chorus, for example, is treated as something of an inconvenience. It stands around listening to long speeches from the principals, with not much more to offer in response than the occasional: 'And I too say, *Ah me!*' The Greek gods are a problem, also. Like the chorus, they have to be there even though Arnold does not quite know what to do with them. But then he is generally uncertain when it comes to fathoming Greek moral values. In the Merope legend, as in Sophocles' *Electra* (which Arnold followed fairly closely), there is an absolute, not-to-be-questioned commitment to the concept of revenge. Arnold in his blood may well have found such strictness rather thrilling. As a Victorian thinker, though, he was obliged to question it. Polyphontes, twenty years ago, murdered the husband of Merope and usurped his throne. For twenty years, Merope has plotted her revenge: her son, Aepytus, will do the deed as soon as he grows up. But what if Polyphontes has for these twenty years shown himself to be a worthy king and genuinely remorseful? Should he still be put to death? Arnold gives Polyphontes an opportunity to state the case for the defence. A Sophoclean Polyphontes would have known that, by Greek rules, only the gods can grant reprieves.

It is easy enough now to mock *Merope* and over the years it has come in for quite a mauling. Surely, though, there is a sadness in contemplating the whole enterprise: so diligent, so well intentioned and so wrong! Arnold, we feel, must have known that he was on a barren track. Indeed he admitted as much – in a letter to K, written in September 1858:

> People do not understand what a temptation there is, if you cannot bear anything not *very good*, to transfer your operations to a region where form is everything: perfection of a certain kind may there be attained, or at least approached, without knocking yourself to pieces: but to attain or approach perfection in the region of thought and feeling, and to unite this with perfection of form, demands not merely an effort and a labour, but an actual tearing of oneself to pieces, which one does not readily consent to (although one is sometimes forced to it) unless one can devote one's whole life to poetry.[32]

Arnold had, it seems, received from Froude a further response to *Merope*, begging him to discontinue his Greek line and (presumably: we do not have the letter) urging him to devote himself to his own poems. Arnold was flattered, as he always was when people praised his verse, but wished that 'the opinion of the general public about my poems were the same as that of the leading literary men'. He might then 'make more money by them than I do':

> But, more than this, I should gain the stimulus necessary to enable me to produce my best – all that I have in me, whatever that may be – to

195

produce which is no light matter with an existence so hampered as mine is.[33]

He knew now that he would never be able to devote his 'whole life to poetry'. Wordsworth had been able to; so too Shelley and Byron, although these two 'were besides driven by their demons to do so'. And of course Tennyson, a bestseller and 'a far inferior natural power to either of the three', could also function as a full-time poet. Of the near-moderns only Goethe had been able to throw himself 'with great result into poetry' in spite of having had an '*existence assujetie*' ['a life ruled by obligations']:

> And even he felt what I say: for he could no doubt have done more, *poetically*, had he been freer: but it is not so light a matter, when you have other grave claims on your powers, to submit voluntarily to the exhaustion of the best poetical production in a time like this: Goethe speaks somewhere of the endless matters on which he had employed himself, and says that with the labour he had given to them he might have produced half a dozen more good tragedies: but to produce these he says, I must have been *sehr zerrissen* [torn to pieces]. It is only in the best poetical epochs (such as the Elizabethan) that you can descend into yourself and produce the best of your thought and feeling naturally, and without an overwhelming and in some degree morbid effort: for then all the people around you are more or less doing the same thing: it is natural, it is the bent of the time to do it: its being the bent of the time, indeed, is what makes the time a *poetical* one. But enough of this . . .[34]

Arnold wrote this – his letter of resignation, one might say – from France. He was on a walking holiday with Theodore Walrond, his old Oxford friend, and had revisited some of the Swiss haunts of his youth. But he experienced nothing of the old excitement. Indeed, he could now 'feel with Papa about the time lost of mere mountain and lake hunting (though everyone should see the Alps once to know what they are)'.[35]

13

Last Poems

In January 1858, Arnold wrote to his mother, enclosing further reviews of *Merope* ('none of them exactly favourable') and assuring her that he had 'no intention of producing, like Euripides, 70 dramas in this style' – the style, that is, of *Merope* – but would 'now turn to something wholly different'.[1]

Again, that 'wholly different'. This time, however, it seems to have been understood that any new or different work by him would almost certainly be in the field of drama. Perhaps Arnold's professorial performances – notable, by all accounts, for their drab presentation – had something to do with this new taste for the theatrical. Or maybe it was just that, as he saw it, his first play had not been given a fair chance. *Merope*, he complained to brother Tom, was 'nothing without the stage'. If he had the time and the means he would, he said, 'establish a school of actors' and 'provide a stage'[2] for plays like his: by which he meant, presumably, uncommercial works of literary interest. In such circumstances, he might well think of writing 'a series of works, I do not say like Merope, but belonging to the same sphere of imagination'. As things stood, though, he would probably give up his playwriting for the moment: 'Although there are one or two other old Greek stories on which I *must* try my hand some day!'

In this same letter to Tom, Arnold reflected with maturity on the reception of *Merope* and on his own new attitude to criticism. When criticised these days, he found himself, he said, 'more curious than sensitive':

> I mean I listen to it more with reference to the testimony it gives me of the state of public feeling and public taste about literature, and of what can and cannot be done to influence or change that taste and feeling, than with reference to its praise or blame of me myself; though of course I am not without the natural liking for praise and dislike of blame. But the personal matter grows less and less important for me, and the general matter more and more.[3]

And this, from now on, will be Arnold's public stance: the observer, the analyst, the cultural physician. A tendency to symptomatise has, of course, been there all along: henceforth, though, he will have no personal creative axe to grind – and, by the same token, no hopes that his own poetry might prove to be an instrument of England's cultural 'deliverance'.

By an apt coincidence, the failure of *Merope* coincided with the publication, and the huge popular success, of Thomas Hughes's Rugby novel, *Tom Brown's Schooldays* – a work which not only revived his father's fame in intellectual and academic circles but enormously extended it, so that Dr Arnold – fifteen years after his death – was all at once a figure of great national renown: 'a man whom we felt to be with all his heart and soul and strength striving against whatever was mean and unmanly and unrighteous in our little world'. If mid-Victorian England had reason to be proud of herself, as many thought she did, then Thomas Arnold clearly deserved much of the credit: the country was now ruled by his former pupils, or by near-imitations of them.

Arnold admired *Tom Brown's Schooldays* and was much incensed by a review of it (by Fitzjames Stephen) in the *Edinburgh Review*. Stephen used his review to mount a savage and comprehensive attack on Dr Arnold and his moral legatees, portraying the headmaster as a humourless fanatic who had turned lively schoolboys into earnest prigs ('boys into men before their time'). Later on, Matthew Arnold would say that Stephen's article impelled him to write what was probably his first post-*Merope* poem: 'Rugby Chapel', a fulsome and determined tribute to his father's memory.[4] The poem is dated 'November 1857' but may well have been written rather later (Stephen's piece did not appear until January 1858). It does seem fitting, though, that Arnold should begin this new 'poetryless' phase of his career with an attempt to measure his own poor achievements against the illustrious example of his father. Dr Arnold, says the poem, was not 'like the men of the crowd/Who all round me today/Bluster or cringe, and make life/Hideous, and arid, and vile', men who 'eat and drink,/Chatter and love and hate/Gather and squander, are raised/Aloft, are hurled in the dust/Striving blindly, achieving/Nothing . . .' The great headmaster was always 'fervent, heroic and good', a helper and friend of mankind:

> Languor is not in your heart,
> Weakness is not in your word,
> Weariness not on your brow,
> Ye alight in our van! at your voice,
> Panic, despair, flee away . . .
> Ye fill up the gaps in our files,
> Strengthen the wavering line,
> Stablish, continue our march,
> On, to the bound of the waste,
> On, to the City of God.

The 'City of God' was, as Kenneth Allott says, 'not much more than a poetical way of saying "righteousness" '. But what level of mankind-helping righteousness could be aspired to by a humble inspector of elementary schools, or even by a Professor of Poetry at Oxford? Arnold does not, of course, directly raise such questions in his poem but they were surely on his mind. 'Marcus Aurelius,' he later wrote, 'saved his own soul by his righteousness, and he could do no more. Happy they who could do this: but still happier, who can do more!' Dr Arnold had done more. What Matthew finally envies in his father is his moral *power*:

> But thou would'st not *alone*
> Be saved, my father! *alone*
> Conquer and come to thy goal,
> Leaving the rest in the wild.
> We were weary, and we
> Fearful, and we in our march
> Fain to drop down and to die.
> Still thou turnedst, and still
> Beckonedst the trembler, and still
> Gavest the weary thy hand.

Having resolved at last to follow his father, Arnold now needed his father's guidance – or at any rate some turn of circumstance which would determine his next step on the long march to selfless virtue. And in 1859 he did indeed receive what must have seemed to him a fateful summons. Arnold was invited to join a fact-finding tour of Europe on behalf of the Newcastle Commission on Elementary Education. For six months, he would tour France, Holland and Switzerland as the Commission's foreign agent. Oddly enough, the invitation to serve came from none other than Fitzjames Stephen, scourge of his father's memory (Stephen was Secretary to the Commission). At first, Arnold hesitated. He and his family had just moved into a new house in Chester Square (able to 'unpack one's portmanteau for the first time since I was married, now nearly seven years ago') and there had lately been 'a very serious alarm' with his son Tom, whose health was a perpetual worry. Also, as he told his mother, 'I have no special interest in the subject of public education.'[5] Still, remembering his father, he decided that 'a mission like this appeals even to the general interest which every educated man cannot help feeling in such a subject'. He took the job, and by March 1859 he was in Paris.

Arnold would return from his tour one of England's leading experts on European methods of public education, and with a new passion for European politics. Shortly afterwards he published a soon-dated anti-Austrian pamphlet on *England and the Italian Question*. Also, somewhat bizarrely, he joined the Queen's Volunteers (or Pimlico Rifles) for twice-weekly drill sessions in Westminster Hall – 'learning the goose-step', as Clough commented. 'I like the drilling very much,' said Arnold, 'it braces one's muscles and does one the world of good' (also, 'It seems to me that the establishment of these Rifle Corps will more than ever throw the power into the hands of the upper and middle classes, as it is of these that they are mainly composed – and those classes will thus have over the lower classes the superiority, not only of wealth and intelligence, which they have now, but of physical force').[6]

Armed, so to speak, for the good fight and with a new commitment to educational reform which would result in several books, essays and reports, Arnold by the age of forty had become a public presence to be reckoned with. 'How the years fly,' he wrote to K when she reached forty, 'at 20, what would one have thought of the twenty years between 40 and 60, even supposing them to be secured to one!'

The twenty years from 20 to 40 seemed all life to one then – the very heart of one's time here, the period within which all that was interesting and successful and decisive in one's life was to fall. And now, at 40, how undecided and unfinished and immature everything seems still – and will seem so, I suppose, to the end.[7]

201

Early on in Arnold's European trip there had been a family tragedy. In April 1859, it was learned that brother William had died, aged thirty-one. William had been returning home on leave from India, where – a month earlier – his wife had died, leaving him with four small children. It had been agreed that K and William Forster would take care of the children, and later on adopt them (hence the Arnold–Forster line). But William Arnold did not live to see this happen. During his ship's stop in Egypt he fell ill with a fever and should probably have stayed put until he had recovered. He pressed on, though – as far as Gibraltar, where he died. Had Matthew, in Paris, known about his brother's illness, he might have been able to get to him before the end. On 14 April Matthew wrote to his mother:

> I like to imagine, even now that it is so entirely vain, the arriving at Gibraltar – the standing by his bedside – the taking his poor hand – I whom he would hardly perhaps have expected to see there – I of whom he thought so far more than I deserved – and who showed him, poor boy, so far less tenderness than *he* deserved.
>
> How strange it seems that he should have overlived his first terrible illness [William had been seriously ill, with some kind of liver disease, in 1852] when his wife was alive to nurse him and he had but one child to suffer by his loss, to die now alone with only a chance acquaintance to attend him, and leaving those four poor little orphans to whom no tenderness can ever quite replace a father and a mother – And then that he should have overlived the misery of his poor wife's death, to struggle through a year's loneliness, and then to die, too. Poor Fanny [William's dead wife]: – she at Dharmsala, and he by the Rock of Gibraltar – God bless you – what I *can* be to you and to all of them, I will be.[8]

William, according to his wife, had been 'more like his Father than any of his four brothers'.[9] Although he had originally gone to India as an army officer, he had, as we have seen, been swiftly drawn into the educational arena. As Director of Public Instruction for the Punjab, he had agonised for months over the rights and wrongs of compulsory Bible study for the natives (his conclusion was that such an imposition would be 'utterly opposed to the spirit of Christianity'). When in doubt on such matters, he invariably asked himself: what would Papa have done? William's 1853 novel, *Oakfield*, was a forerunner, we might now say, of *Tom Brown's Schooldays*, though more sombrely soul-searching. 'If Tom Brown's Christianity is muscular,' wrote Frances Woodward, 'Oakfield's is musclebound.'[10]

Matthew had always treated William with some condescension, when he had noticed him at all. It was typical of the way of things between them that when William got married, his eldest brother was the only family member who failed to send congratulations (said William: 'dear old Matt . . . might have uncoiled himself on this one occasion'). William's death at such a young age, and coming when it did – just as Matthew was at last steeling himself to assume the Arnold mission – had the effect, it seems, of confirming, and elevating, his resolve. William was a Rugby man who had, it could be said, died for the cause. And with his death, Matthew could find in his brother near-heroic strengths which, a few years earlier, he would surely have been blind to.

In May 1859, Arnold began a poem, called 'A Southern Night', which was an elegy both for William and for Matthew's younger self.[11] Once upon a time, the poem says, the poet Matthew Arnold might have considered the lives of such as William and his wife not 'romantic' enough to have deserved the splendid and exotic foreign graves which each of them had ended up in: he in Gibraltar, she in India –

> Strange irony of fate, alas,
> Which, for two jaded English, saves,
> When from their dusty lives they pass,
> Such peaceful graves!

The new Matthew Arnold, though, will not take such a line. The truth, he now concedes, is that the 'high-souled' William and his selfless bride had fully earned their final settings. People like them, people who *did* things for the sake of others, should not be condescended to by dreamy poets:

> That comely face, that clustered brow,
>   That cordial hand, that bearing free,
> I see them still, I see them now,
>   Shall always see!
>
> And what but gentleness untired,
>   And what but noble feeling warm,
> Whatever shown, howe'er inspired,
>   Is grace, is charm?
>
> What else is all these waters are,
>   What else is steeped in lucid sheen,
> What else is bright, what else is fair,
>   What else serene!
>
> Mild o'er her grave, ye mountains, shine!
>   Gently by his, ye waters, glide!
> To that in you which is divine
>   They were allied.

In the few poems Arnold managed to complete, post-1859, poets and the poetic way of life are regularly targeted as irresponsible. In 'Heine's Grave',[12] for instance, the German poet is rebuked for his bitter, mocking attitude to what Arnold himself used to call 'the general life', for lacking 'Love, without which the tongue/Even of angels sounds amiss'. Heine also – or therefore – lacked 'charm', a favourite word in Arnold's 1860s lexicon:

> Charm is the glory which makes
> Song of the poet divine,
> Love is the fountain of charm.
> How without charm wilt thou draw,
> Poet! the world to thy way?
> Not by the lightnings of wit –
> Not by the thunder of scorn!

'Charm' was also mentioned in 'A Southern Night' ('And what but gentleness untired . . . is grace, is charm?') and had become a vital ingredient of Arnold's new, high-toned self-image. In the early 1860s, he wrote to his mother:

> It is very animating to think that one at last has the chance of *getting at* the English public. Such a public as it is, and such a work as one wants to do with it! Partly nature, partly time and study, have also by this time taught me thoroughly the precious truth that everything turns upon one's exercising the power of *persuasion*, of *charm*; that without this all fury, energy, reasoning power, acquirement, are thrown away and only render their owner more miserable. Even in one's ridicule one must preserve a sweetness and good-humour.[13]

In Arnold's first Oxford lecture he had spoken of the modern age with a new optimism. What the age chiefly lacked, he seemed to say, was a poetic art which would be 'adequate' to its complexities but which would also be in tune with its revitalised religious sense, its sense of hopefulness. No longer was it the 'poetrylessness' of these 'damned times' that was at fault. During the 1860s, Arnold was more inclined to blame the poets: or to blame rather that post-romantic self-absorption which the poets, himself included, had allowed themselves to be lured into. Poetry once offered a hope of refuge to Christian believers who had lost their faith. What Arnold looked for now was a revived and reconstructed Christianity which would have poetry, or some real sense of the poetic, at its centre: a faith, in other words, which could be thought of as a thing of beauty. Arnold found it difficult to describe just what he meant by this. It was easier for him to speak of what he wanted to get rid of: that philosophy which set poetry and religion in opposition to each other. The 'religious mood' and the 'aesthetic mood', he would now say, belonged 'eternally' to 'the deepest being of man, the ground of all joy & greatness for him'.

In the 1840s Arnold had closely identified himself with the poet-figure, Obermann. He had seen Obermann as a spiritual exile, one who could find no outlet in the modern world for his profound 'religious sense'. For Senancour, the author of *Obermann*, as for so many, the French Revolution had marked the end of the old Christendom and 'when the world consolidated itself again after the Revolution without a new religion but with a patching up of the old in which he saw no permanence and no sincerity, "his heart within him", as the Psalmist says, "became desolate" '.[14] It was this desolation that rendered him, and others like him, useless to society and to the human world at large: 'wandering between two worlds, one dead/The other powerless to be born'. Arnold in the 1860s wanted to shake off this feeling of being trapped between two styles of impotence. He wanted now to say, and did say: 'That Christ is alive is language far truer to my own feeling and observation of what is passing in the world, than that Christ is dead.'

Arnold's eagerness to renounce the despairing agnosticism of Obermann, and of his own younger self, is dramatised in 'Obermann Once More' – a poem written some time in the mid-1860s.[15] Here we find the mature Arnold returning to Switzerland and there encountering the shade of his one-time spiritual hero. In 1849 Arnold had addressed Obermann as a kindred soul, a brother poet for whom the world had not much use. In the 1860s, he approaches him as a keen, forward-looking public man, a Christian, a professor, a husband, a prose-essayist, a social prophet, a would-be educational reformer, a son – finally

– of Dr Arnold. Not surprisingly, the ghost of Obermann finds it hard to recognise his former acolyte. Even so, he welcomes and endorses his new sense of purpose:

> Though more than half thy years be past,
> And spent thy youthful prime;
> Though, round thy firmer manhood cast,
> Hang weeds of our sad time,
>
> Whereof thy youth felt all the spell,
> And traversed all the shade –
> Though late, though dimmed, though weak, yet tell
> Hope to a world new-made!
>
> Help it to fill that deep desire,
> The want which racked our brain,
> Consumed our heart with thirst like fire,
> Immedicable pain;
>
> Which to the wilderness drove out
> Our life, to Alpine snow,
> And palsied all our word with doubt,
> And all our work with woe –
>
> What still of strength is left, employ
> That end to help attain:
> *Our common wave of thought and joy*
> *Lifting mankind again!*

In this jaunty, hymn-book manner, then, Obermann is finally accounted for, settled with, and laid to smiling rest. And in another poem, 'The Terrace at Berne',[16] Arnold in much the same way makes a final peace with Marguerite. On his 1859 visit to Switzerland, he finds himself thinking: 'Is my Marguerite there?'

> Ah, shall I see thee, while a flush
> Of startled pleasure floods thy brow,
> Quick through the oleanders brush,
> And clap thy hands, and cry: *'Tis thou!*

Or has she long since 'wandered back . . . to France, thy home', and there 'flitted down the flowery track' to coarseness:

> Doth riotous laughter now replace
> Thy smile; and rouge, with stony glare,
> Thy cheek's soft hue; and fluttering lace
> The kerchief that enwound thy hair?

Or is she dead? Surely, if she were, he would have known. But 'no warning shiver ran/Across my heart, to say thy thread/Of life was cut'. Most likely she is still alive but with her 'spirit vanished, beauty waned', no longer 'the Marguerite of thy prime'. So far as Arnold is concerned, she's of the past: why try to call her back? In the process of making this cool point, Arnold's syntax stiffens into an agonised pomposity:

> I will not know! For wherefore try,
> To things by mortal course that live,
> A shadowy durability,
> For which they were not meant, to give?

The poem ends with a farewell that could as easily be read as an expression of puritanical resolve:

> Like driftwood spars, which meet and pass
> Upon the boundless ocean-plain,
> So on the sea of life, alas!
> Man meets man – meets, and quits again.
>
> I knew it when my life was young;
> I feel it still, now youth is o'er.
> – The mists are on the mountain hung,
> And Marguerite I shall see no more.

Obermann and Marguerite, two lights of Arnold's youth, have been renounced, it may be thought, with some relief. Each of them represented, as Arnold saw it now, a turbulent, misguided chapter. It was different, though, when, in November 1861, he heard that Clough had died, aged forty-two. This death was not entirely unexpected, since Clough's health had been precarious for several years. So too had his way of life, in Arnold's terms. After two years in America, where he scraped a living giving private lessons in Latin and Greek, Clough in 1854 had returned to England, married Blanche Smith, and taken work in education – as an examiner in the Education Office, a job fixed up for him by friends (though not decisively by Arnold).

When Clough died, he and Arnold had not been close for years. There had been a cooling between them around the time of the 'Empedocles' *Preface*. Arnold, though, continued to think of Clough as one of his best critics. Sending him a copy of *Merope* in 1857, he appended a quotation from Goethe: 'With truly like-minded people one cannot in the long run be at outs, one finds oneself always eventually together again.'[17] And as late as 1859, he wrote to K: 'You and Clough are, I believe, the two people I in my heart care most to please by what I write.' The last letter Arnold wrote to Clough was in July 1861, after what seems to have been a fairly lengthy silence on both sides. In it, he advised Clough to stick with his job in education, however uncongenial it sometimes seemed: 'A life of literary tasks and chance jobs', he said, would surely be much worse. 'The mental harass of an uncertain life must be far more extreme than the ennui of the most monotonous employment.'

A week after hearing of Clough's death, Arnold wrote to his mother:

First of all, you will expect me to say something about poor Clough. That is a loss which I shall feel more and more as time goes on, for he is one of the few people who ever made a deep impression upon me, and as time goes on, and one finds no one else who makes such an impression, one's feeling about those who did make it gets to be something more and more distinct and unique. Besides, the object of it no longer survives to wear itself out by becoming ordinary and different from what he was. People were beginning to say about Clough that he would never do anything now, and, in short, to pass him over. I foresee that there will now be a change, and attention will be fixed on what there was of extraordinary promise and interest in him when young, and of unique and imposing even as he grew older without fulfilling people's expectations. I have been asked to write a Memoir of him for the *Daily News*, but that I cannot do. I could not write about him in a newspaper now, nor can, I think, at length in a review, but I shall some day in some way or other relieve myself of what I think about him.[18]

Two weeks after this, he wrote also to Clough's widow:

Probably you hardly know how very intimate we once were; our friendship was, from my age at the time when it was closest, more important to me than it was to him, and no one will ever again be to me what he was.[19]

And in January 1862, planning a professorial visit to Oxford, he wrote to her again. She, it appears, had sent him some fragments of Clough's verse:

I cannot tell you how glad I am to have the lines you have sent me. I shall take them with me to Oxford, where I shall go alone after Easter; – and there, among the Cumnor hills where we have so often rambled, I shall be able to think him over as I could wish. Here, all impressions are half impressions, and every thought is interrupted.[20]

It was not until November or December 1863 – almost a year later – that Arnold began writing 'a new poem about the Cumnor hillside, and Clough in connexion with it'. 'Thyrsis' is an elegy for a dead friend, but it is also an elegy for Arnold's own aspirations as a poet.[21] Unlike 'The Scholar-Gipsy', though, 'Thyrsis' is full of hopefulness: Arnold may no longer be able to write poems but instead he can speak out persuasively on behalf of the illuminating potency of the 'poetic sense', the life of the imagination. Clough, on the other hand, cannot. 'Here came I often, often, in old days –/Thyrsis and I; we still had Thyrsis then.'

But Thyrsis had always gone his own way, right from the start: 'It irked him to be here, he could not rest.' There was always a disruptive instability in Clough's make-up, a 'loose screw in his whole organisation', Arnold felt, and 'Thyrsis', although it touchingly remembers the early Oxford days, their setting and their spirit, is fundamentally a condescending, not to say complacent piece of work. Clough, the poem says, did not fulfil his promise; in truth, he threw his gifts away, through pressing them too hard, expecting too much, or the wrong things of them. Arnold does not feel that he has similarly failed. For one thing, Clough has died and he, Arnold, has lately been reborn. Clough may have been Dr Arnold's best pupil and the most ardent of his acolytes, but Matthew had turned out to be his father's most dependable, real-world descendant. 'Thyrsis' ends with Clough's spirit urging his surviving friend and one-time rival to continue the good work:

> Why faintest thou? I wandered till I died.
>   Roam on! The light we sought is shining still.
>   Dost thou ask proof? Our tree yet crowns the hill,
> Our Scholar travels yet the loved hill-side.

A chin-forward missionary striving tends to be the order of the day in these last Arnold poems – and with it comes an all-too-easy dependence on what we might now object to as the 'sweetness and light' school of adjectival uplift. Later on, in Arnold's literary criticism and social theory, this dependence will become irksomely mechanical, with whole arguments pivoting on undefined concepts of 'perfection', 'the glow of life and light', 'real thought and real beauty', 'the best knowledge and thought of the time', and so on. The more Arnold neglected his own gifts as a poet, the more extravagantly nebulous became his protestations on behalf of poetry's transformatively civilising powers.

It may now be clear to us that Arnold's poetic life ended in the 1860s. Arnold himself, though, had no such sense of finality. He continued to believe that someday he would clear the time in which to resurrect, or liberate, his gift. In 1861 he wrote to his mother: 'I must finish off for the present my critical writings between this and fifty, and give the next ten years earnestly to poetry. It is my last chance. It is not a bad ten years of one's life for poetry if one resolutely uses it, but it is a time in which, if one does not use it, one dries up and becomes prosaic altogether.'[22] And in 1863 he told her: 'After the summer I mean to lie fallow again for some time, or to busy myself with poetry only.'[23] As late as 1886, two years before his death, he was still wondering 'if I shall ever get anything more done in poetry'.[24]

But only once, in Arnold's final two decades, did he recapture the distressed and unaffected eloquence, the heartfelt directness of address, that so urgently impels his best work of the late 1840s and early 1850s. Aptly enough, the poem was called 'Growing Old', and was Arnold's bitter response to Browning's 'Grow old along with me/The best is yet to be':

> What is it to grow old?
> Is it to lose the glory of the form,
> The lustre of the eye?
> Is it for beauty to forgo her wreath?
> – Yes, but not this alone.
>
> Is it to feel our strength –
> Not our bloom only, but our strength – decay?
> Is it to feel each limb
> Grow stiffer, every function less exact,
> Each nerve more loosely strung?

Yes, this, and more; but not
Ah, 'tis not what in youth we dreamed 'twould be!
'Tis not to have our life
Mellowed and softened as with sunset-glow,
A golden day's decline.

'Tis not to see the world
As from a height, with rapt prophetic eyes,
And heart profoundly stirred;
And weep, and feel the fullness of the past,
The years that are no more.

It is to spend long days
And not once feel that we were ever young;
It is to add, immured
In the hot prison of the present, month
To month with weary pain.

It is to suffer this,
And feel but half, and feebly, what we feel.
Deep in our hidden heart
Festers the dull remembrance of a change,
But no emotion – none.

It is – last stage of all –
When we are frozen up within, and quite
The phantom of ourselves,
To hear the world applaud the hollow ghost
Which blamed the living man.[25]

Not quite the 'Thyrsis'-spirit, one might say – but none the worse
for that.

Even as Arnold spoke of clearing time for poetry, he was busily
piling up his prose commitments, and in the early 1860s he
developed a taste for the give and take of public controversy.
Arnold took pride in his powers of rebuttal – his insouciance, his

kindliness, his pinpoint deadliness of aim – and some of his most vigorous prose-writing over the ensuing years would be in response to a response to one or another of his essays. He always liked to put himself on the good-natured side of any argument and it soon became a habit of his smilingly to *anticipate* rejoinders – and, of course, by this means, offer his opponents irresistible come-ons. In the early 1860s, he was learning his prose-trade, but learning it at speed, against the clock: via his professorship, he initiated a long-running, and widely noticed, debate on how Homer ought to be translated; via the inspectorate, he campaigned against a proposed New Code governing state grants to schools and colleges. His February 1863 letter to his mother affords a daunting glimpse of his new, self-imposed work schedule:

> I hope before I come to Fox How (if I come there) this summer, to have printed 6 articles – one on Spinoza, in the Times, one on Dante and one on the Emperor Marcus Aurelius, in Fraser: one on 'A French Eton' and one on 'Academies' (like the French Institute) in Macmillan – and one on Eugénie de Guérin, in the Cornhill. Perhaps I may add to these one on Joubert, an exquisite French critic, a friend of Chateaubriand. Besides all this I must write two lectures for Oxford, and I hope to compose one or two short poems besides. And then there is inspecting. So I have plenty to do.[26]

In part it was money-fear that drove him. He would soon be having to think of his sons' education. An article in *Fraser's* or the *Cornhill* might net him about £30 a time, and in the 1860s he was writing five or six such articles a year. This writing income made a significant difference to his calculations. (Nearly all of Arnold's prose books were actually collections of work which had appeared first in periodicals.)

Of course, it is by no means certain that Arnold would have written more – or better – poems if he had cut down on the prose. His domestic life was often demanding. There were regular crises to do with his children's health – particularly Tom's. More than once during the early to mid-1860s, his parents feared that they had 'lost' him. And Arnold himself was frequently unwell: colds, sore throats, influenzas, dental flare-ups, and the like. There may well have been early-warning chest pains too, but if so he did not mention them in letters. Also, in spite of everything, he retained his boyish 'love of ease'. He liked fishing, playing croquet, discovering obscure wild flowers, visiting grand houses at weekends. He liked to travel, give dinner parties, keep up with the latest gossip. He also seems to have read most of the periodicals he wrote for.

In 1868 the Arnolds would move to Harrow, and then later on to Cobham, in the Surrey countryside, but it was in the early 1860s that Arnold built up his reputation as a metropolitan savant. Such was this reputation that by 1867, when his *New Poems* appeared, there was a tendency for critics to view it in the light of his prose fame. The poems, after all, came out in the same year as his essay 'Culture and its Enemies' (soon to be the first chapter of *Culture and Anarchy*), so it is not surprising that reviewers scrutinised the new verses for evidence of 'sweetness and light', or – worse still – of 'perfection' – that 'harmonious expression of *all* the powers which make the beauty and worth of human nature'.

Arnold's *New Poems* (1867) was his last book of poems: there would be collections and selections in the years to come, but no new work of any substance. And indeed *New Poems* was itself a mixture of the old and new. 'Thyrsis' took pride of place, but seven poems were reprinted from earlier books and a few of the 'new' pieces had been written many years before. 'Dover Beach' appeared in print for the first time but no one apart from Swinburne (who spoke of its 'grand choral cadence') acknowledged that here was one of the century's great poems. Nor was much made of Arnold's decision to reinstate the whole of 'Empedocles on Etna'. The poet's explanatory note read as follows:

I cannot deny myself the pleasure of saying that I reprint (I cannot say *republish*, for it was withdrawn from circulation before fifty copies were sold) this poem at the request of a man of genius, whom it had the honour and the good fortune to interest, – Mr Robert Browning.[27]

It is intensely saddening to contrast this urbane social murmur with Arnold's 1853 *Preface*. That *Preface* may have been misguided, and the original decision to jettison 'Empedocles' was surely wrong, but in 1853 there was a sense that for Arnold these were lofty, all-important matters. In 1867, on the other hand, there is a distinct feeling of: who cares? If Mr Browning wants me to print the thing, I'll print it.

There is also a feeling that with *New Poems* (1867) Arnold is putting his poetic affairs in order. Two years later there would be a two-volume collected edition of his poems, and Arnold would never stop tinkering with his texts, altering titles, dropping poems, reinstating them, and so on, but we are here left in little doubt that the whole enterprise has ended. Certainly reviewers at the time got this impression. 'The poet is dead,' pronounced the *Athenaeum*, 'we have lost a poet.' Arnold was 'aged before his time'. And Arnold himself, although he would always monitor the ups and downs of his poetic reputation with keen interest, was clearly in the mood to look back on the whole body of his work so far as if it formed a chapter of his life that was now closed.

And he was still in his mid-forties. In fact, in 1869, the year of his collected poems, he was forty-six, the same age as Dr Arnold was in 1842, the year he died. And yet, compared to Dr Arnold's life ('how much he seems to have put into it!'), Matthew believed that his own was shamingly lightweight. Two volumes of uneven, unapplauded verse was *not enough*. There had to be a 'new beginning', a new 'poetryless' beginning. But how much time was left?

It may well be that I am at my end, as papa was at my age, but without papa's ripeness, and that there will be little time to carry far the new beginning. But that is all the more reason for carrying it as far as one can, and as earnestly as one can, while one lives.[28]

Arnold's 'second life', so to call it, lasted for some twenty years, the years of *Culture and Anarchy*, *Essays in Criticism* and *Discourses in America*, the works on which his prose reputation now securely rests. In 1888 he died of a heart attack, aged sixty-six. His 'poetic life', though, if we have to put a final date on such a deeply preordained demise, ended in 1869: the year of his two-volume *Poems*, and the year too in which Matthew Arnold became older than Papa.

Chronology

1822   MA born, Laleham-on-Thames (24 December)

1828   Thomas Arnold appointed headmaster of Rugby

1834   Fox How built

1836   MA enrolled at Winchester

1837   MA enrolled at Rugby

1840   MA wins scholarship to Balliol College, Oxford

1841   Thomas Arnold appointed Regius Professor of Modern History at Oxford

1842   Thomas Arnold dies, aged forty-six

1844   MA takes BA, Oxford

1845   MA elected Fellow, Oriel College, Oxford

1846   MA in France (meets George Sand)

1847   MA appointed Private Secretary to Lord Lansdowne

1848   MA in Switzerland (meets Marguerite)

1849   MA's first book of poems, *The Strayed Reveller and Other Poems*

1850   'K' marries

1851   MA appointed Inspector of Schools (April). MA marries Frances Lucy Wightman (June)

Chronology

1852　*Empedocles on Etna and Other Poems*. Thomas Arnold (son) born

1853　*Poems*, with 'Empedocles' *Preface*. Trevenen William Arnold (son) born

1854　*Poems: Second Series*

1855　Richard Penrose Arnold (son) born

1858　*Merope*. MA elected Professor of Poetry at Oxford. Lucy Charlotte Arnold (daughter) born

1859　Newcastle Commission

1861　Clough dies. *On Translating Homer*. Eleanor Mary Caroline Arnold (daughter) born

1864　*A French Eton*

1865　*Essays in Criticism: First Series*

1866　'Thyrsis'. Basil Francis (son) born

1867　*New Poems*.

1868　Arnolds move to Harrow. Basil (son) dies, aged one (January). Thomas (son) dies, aged sixteen (November)

1869　*Poems* (two volumes); *Culture and Anarchy*

1870　MA promoted to Senior Inspector of Schools. *St Paul and Protestantism*

1871　*Friendship's Garland*

1872　William (son) dies, aged eighteen

1873　Arnolds move to Cobham, Surrey. *Literature and Dogma*

1875　*God and the Bible*

1879　*Mixed Essays*

1882　*Irish Essays*

1883　MA in USA on lecture tour

1885　*Discourses in America*

1886　MA in USA on lecture tour

1887　MA retires as Inspector of Schools

1888　MA dies, of heart attack, in Liverpool

Notes

1 Dr Arnold of Rugby

1 Thomas Hughes, *Tom Brown's Schooldays*, World's Classics, Oxford University Press, 1989, p. 162.
2 *Edinburgh Review*, January 1858, p. 190. Quoted from Thomas Arnold by Fitzjames Stephen, in a review of *Tom Brown's Schooldays*.
3 Arthur Penrhyn Stanley, *Life of Thomas Arnold*, London, 1844, Vol. 1, p. 106.
4 Stephen, op. cit., p. 185.
5 Stanley, op. cit., Vol. 1, p. 115.
6 Ibid., p. 119.
7 Stephen, op. cit., p. 185.
8 Stanley, op. cit., Vol. 1, p. 118.
9 See Charles R. Meyer, 'The Idea of History in Thomas and Matthew Arnold', in *Modern Philology*, 67, 1969, pp. 160–7.
10 Stanley, op. cit., Vol. 1, p. 86.
11 Lytton Strachey, *Eminent Victorians* by Michael Holroyd (with an introduction), Penguin Books, 1986, p. 165. First published 1918.
12 Thomas Arnold to Rev. J. Tucker, 2 March 1827. Quoted in Stanley, op. cit., Vol. 1, p. 73.

Notes

13 Stanley, op. cit., Vol. 1, p. 100.
14 See Michael McCrum, *Thomas Arnold, Headmaster: A Reassessment*, Oxford University Press, 1989, p. 75.
15 *Tom Brown's Schooldays*, op. cit., p. 141.
16 See John O. Waller, 'Dr Arnold's Sermons and Matthew Arnold's "Rugby Chapel" ', *Studies in English Literature*, 9, 1969, pp. 633–46.
17 Stanley, op. cit., Vol. 1, p. 33.
18 Ibid., pp. 51–2.

2 'Crabby' in Childhood

1 Stanley, op. cit., Vol. 1, p. 35.
2 Ibid., p. 36.
3 Oswald R. Adamson, *Our Dear Laleham*, Ian Allen Ltd for the Laleham Society, 1989, p. 61.
4 Thomas Arnold to G. Cornish, 4 April 1823, Brotherton Library, Leeds.
5 Ibid.
6 Thomas Arnold to G. Cornish, 23 September 1824, Brotherton Library, Leeds.
7 Mary Arnold, Journal 1 (1822–33), June 1826, Brotherton Library, Leeds.
8 Ibid.
9 Ibid.
10 Norman Wymer, *Dr Arnold of Rugby*, Robert Hale, 1953, p. 138.
11 *Tom Brown's Schooldays*, op. cit., p. 108.
12 Thomas Arnold the Younger, 'Matthew Arnold, By One Who Knew Him Well', *Manchester Guardian*, 18 May 1888, p. 8.
13 'Pimgrim's Progress' by Matthew Arnold, Balliol College MS.
14 Wymer, op. cit., p. 139.
15 Ibid.
16 MA to his mother, 11 February 1863. See Cecil Y. Lang (ed.), *The Letters of Matthew Arnold*, Vol. 2, Virginia University Press, 1997, p. 189.
17 Thomas Arnold to MA, 18 October 1831, Brotherton Library MS.
18 Mrs Mary Arnold to MA, 29 February 1832, Balliol College MS.
19 Thomas Arnold to MA, 20 September 1831, Brotherton Library MS.
20 Thomas Arnold to Frances Buckland, 3 July 1832, Brotherton Library MS.
21 Thomas Arnold to MA, 21 March 1832, Brotherton Library MS.
22 Thomas Arnold to Frances Buckland, 3 July 1832, Brotherton Library MS.
23 Thomas Arnold the Younger, *Passages in a Wandering Life*, Edward Arnold, 1900, p. 10.
24 Wymer, op. cit., p. 139.

Notes

25 Thomas Arnold to Archbishop Whately, 1 February 1833. Quoted in Stanley, op. cit., Vol. 1, p. 306.

26 Thomas Arnold to G. Cornish, 23 December 1831. Quoted in Wymer, op. cit., p. 147.

27 Wymer, op. cit., p. 148.

28 Mary Moorman, *William Wordsworth: A Biography*, Oxford University Press, 1968, Vol. 2, p. 485.

29 Thomas Arnold to Mr Serjeant Coleridge, 12 June 1833. Quoted in Stanley, op. cit., Vol. 1, p. 322.

30 Thomas Arnold to Frances Buckland, 20 December 1831, Brotherton Library MS.

31 Mary Arnold, 1836 Journal, Brotherton Library, Leeds.

32 Wymer, op. cit., pp. 150–1.

33 Thomas Arnold the Younger, op. cit., p. 9.

34 Ibid.

35 Mr Justice Coleridge to A.P. Stanley, September 1843. Quoted in Stanley, op. cit., Vol. 1, pp. 18–19.

36 MA to Jane Arnold (K), 6 September 1858. Quoted in Lang, op. cit., Vol. 1, p. 403.

37 Thomas Arnold to Susannah Arnold (his sister), 2 April 1830, Brotherton Library MS.

38 Copied out in Mary Arnold's Journal, Brotherton Library MS. See Kenneth Allott (ed.), *The Poems of Matthew Arnold*, Longman, 1979, second edition revised by Miriam Allott, Appendix B, pp. 674–5.

3 Schooldays

1 Wymer, op. cit., p. 186.

2 Mary Arnold to Lydia Penrose, 17 September 1838, Brotherton Library MS.

3 Mary Arnold to her Penrose sisters, 8 December 1838, Brotherton Library MS.

4 Mary Arnold to her Penrose sisters, 19 December 1839, Brotherton Library MS.

5 See Park Honan, *Matthew Arnold, A Life*, Weidenfeld and Nicolson, 1981, p. 38.

6 Wymer, op. cit., p. 140.

7 Thomas Arnold the Younger, op. cit., p. 14.

8 Mary Arnold, Journal 2, April 1837, Brotherton Library MS.

9 Honan, op. cit., p. 6.

10 Allott, op. cit., p. 618.

Notes

11 Ibid., p. 621.

12 Ibid., pp. 621–2.

13 Mary Arnold to her Penrose sisters, 24 December 1838, Brotherton Library MS.

14 Allott, op. cit., pp. 622–3.

15 Wymer, op. cit., p. 141.

16 Mary Arnold, Journal, July 1837, Brotherton Library MS: 'The circle was not completed till the 12th when you my two eldest sons came from Winchester.'

17 Moorman transcript, notes on Thomas Arnold letter to D.H.A. Greenhill (one-time Rugby master, married to Dr Arnold's niece), Balliol College MS.

18 Wymer, op. cit., p. 51.

19 Matthew Arnold's Travel Journal, 1837, Balliol College MS. See Lang, op. cit., Vol. 1, pp. 22–32.

20 Thomas Arnold to Rev. A.B. Clough, 19 October 1837. Quoted in Howard Foster Lowry (ed.), *The Letters of Matthew Arnold to Arthur Hugh Clough*, Oxford University Press, 1932, p. 13.

21 Lowry, op. cit., p. 1.

22 Thomas Arnold the Younger, 'Arthur Hugh Clough – A Sketch', *Nineteenth Century*, 43, 1898, p. 106.

23 MA to Arthur Hugh Clough, 12 February 1853. See Lowry, op. cit., p. 129; Lang, op. cit., Vol 1, pp. 252–5.

24 Thomas Arnold the Younger, 'Arthur Hugh Clough – A Sketch', *Nineteenth Century*, op. cit., p. 103.

25 Arthur Hugh Clough to Anne Clough, 10 October 1835. See Frederick L. Mulhauser (ed.), *The Correspondence of Arthur Hugh Clough*, Clarendon Press, 1957, Vol. 1, p. 19.

26 Arthur Hugh Clough to John N. Simpkinson, 18 January 1836. Quoted in Lowry, op. cit., p. 2.

27 Lowry, op. cit., p. 12.

28 Arthur Hugh Clough to his mother, July 1835. Quoted in David Williams, *Too Quick Despairer*, Hart-Davis, 1969, pp. 23–4.

29 Thomas Arnold the Younger, *Passages in a Wandering Life*, op. cit., p. 41.

30 Honan, op. cit., p. 5.

31 Mrs Humphry Ward, *A Writer's Recollections*, London, 1918, p. 52.

32 See Edith J. Morley (ed.), *Correspondence of Henry Crabb Robinson with the Wordsworth Circle*, Oxford, 1927, 2 vols, p. 743.

33 MA to Arthur Hugh Clough, 23 September 1849. See Lowry, op. cit., p. 110; Lang, op. cit., Vol. 1, pp. 155–7.

34 Allott, op. cit., pp. 630–2.

35 Ibid., p. 632.

Notes

36 Ibid., pp. 3–12.
37 Honan, op. cit., p. 45.
38 Katherine Lake, *Memorials of William Charles Lake*, London, 1901, p. 161.
39 Wymer, op. cit., p. 186.

4 Oxford

1 E.G. Sandford (ed.), *Memoirs of Archbishop Temple*, London, 1906, Vol. 2, p. 457.
2 Frances J. Woodward, *The Doctor's Disciples*, Oxford University Press, 1954, p. 34.
3 Arthur Hugh Clough to J.N. Simpkinson, in Mulhauser, op. cit., Vol. 1, p. 66.
4 Lowry, op. cit., p. 16.
5 Quoted in Anthony Kenny (ed.), *The Oxford Diaries of Arthur Hugh Clough*, Clarendon Press, 1990, p. xix.
6 Ibid.
7 Woodward, op. cit., p. 36.
8 Thomas Arnold the Younger, 'Arthur Hugh Clough – A Sketch', *Nineteenth Century*, op. cit., pp. 105–16.
9 R.H. Super (ed.), *The Complete Prose Works of Matthew Arnold*, University of Michigan Press, 1960, Vol. X, p. 165.
10 Thomas Arnold the Younger, *Passages in a Wandering Life*, op. cit., p. 57.
11 'The Voice'. See Allott, op. cit., p. 57.
12 Wymer, op. cit., p. 189.
13 Ibid.
14 Alan Harris, 'Matthew Arnold: The Unknown Years', *Nineteenth Century*, April 1933, p. 501.
15 Master's Examination Register, Balliol College MS.
16 Ernest Hartley Coleridge, *Life and Correspondence of John Duke Coleridge*, London, 1904, Vol. 1, pp. 76–7.
17 Thomas Arnold the Younger, *Passages in a Wandering Life*, op. cit., p. 58.
18 Stanley, op. cit., pp. 288–9.
19 'The Incursion'. See Allott, op. cit., p. 634.
20 Thomas Arnold the Younger, *Passages in a Wandering Life*, op. cit., p. 55.
21 Thomas Arnold to Frances Buckland, 7 December 1841, Brotherton Library MS; see Lang, op. cit., Vol. 1, p. 46.
22 Wymer, op. cit., p. 191.
23 Ibid., p. 192.
24 Stanley, op. cit., p. 317.
25 See Honan, op. cit., p. 62.

Notes

5 First Poems

1 Simon Heffer, *Moral Desperado: A Life of Thomas Carlyle*, Weidenfeld, 1995, p. 220.
2 Wymer, op. cit., p. 179.
3 Ibid., p. 180.
4 Heffer, op. cit., p. 220.
5 Thomas Hughes, *Tom Brown at Oxford*, London, 1861, Ch. 35.
6 David Masson, *Carlyle Personally and in his Writings*, London, 1885, p. 7.
7 See Kathleen Tillotson, 'Matthew Arnold and Carlyle', in *Mid-Victorian Studies* by A. and K. Tillotson, Athlone Press, 1965, p. 219.
8 Ibid.
9 Thomas Carlyle, 'The Hero as Man of Letters', Thomas Carlyle, *Selected Writings*, Edited by Alan Shelston, Penguin, 1971, p. 236.
10 Thomas Carlyle, 'The Hero as Divinity'. Ibid., p. 20.
11 Tillotson, op. cit., p. 218.
12 Allott, op. cit., p. 13.
13 Ibid., p. 26.
14 Thomas Arnold the Younger, *Manchester Guardian* obituary, 18 May 1888.
15 Ibid.
16 Max Müller, *Auld Lang Syne*, London, 1895, p. 124.
17 See Tinker and Lowry, *The Poetry of Matthew Arnold: A Commentary*, Oxford University Press, 1940, pp. 325–6.
18 MA to John Duke Coleridge, 2 March 1843. See Coleridge, op. cit., Vol. 1, pp. 123–4; Lang, op. cit., Vol. 1, pp. 53–5 (dated 11 April).
19 MA to his mother, June 1844. See Lang, op. cit., Vol. 1, pp. 58–60.
20 MA to John Duke Coleridge, 2 March 1843. See Coleridge, op. cit., Vol. 1, pp. 123–4; Lang, op. cit., Vol. 1, pp. 53–5 (dated 11 April).
21 MA to John Duke Coleridge, August 1843. See Coleridge, op. cit., Vol. 1, p. 132; Lang, op. cit., Vol. 1, pp. 56–8.
22 MA to John Duke Coleridge, 28 July 1844. See Coleridge, op. cit., Vol. 1, pp. 145–6; Lang, op. cit., Vol. 1, pp. 60–2.
23 John Manley Hawker to John Duke Coleridge, 11 March 1843. See Coleridge, op. cit., Vol. 1, pp. 125–6; Lang, op. cit., Vol. 1, p. 56.
24 'We arrived on Friday evening . . .': John Manley Hawker to John Duke Coleridge, 3 July 1843. See Coleridge, op. cit., p. 129; Lang, op. cit., Vol. 1, p. 56.
25 Arthur Hugh Clough to Thomas Burbridge, 21 June 1844. See Lowry, op. cit., p. 28.
26 Arthur Hugh Clough to Thomas Burbridge, 11 November 1844. Ibid., p. 29.

Notes

27 MA to Uncle Trevenen (Thomas Trevenen Penrose), 8 April 1845. See Lang, op. cit., Vol. 1, pp. 66–8.

28 Arthur Hugh Clough to Thomas Burbridge, 11 November 1844. See Lowry, op. cit., p. 29.

29 MA to Uncle Trevenen, 8 April 1845. See Lang, op. cit., Vol. 1, pp. 66–8.

30 Ibid.

31 A.G. Butler, *The Three Friends: A Story of Rugby in the Forties*, London, 1900, p. 102.

32 Ibid.

33 Ibid.

34 Ibid.

35 MA to Arthur Hugh Clough, 28 March 1845. See Lowry, op. cit., p. 56; Lang, op. cit., Vol. 1, pp. 64–5 (dated ?5 March 1845).

36 See Tinker and Lowry, op. cit., pp. 25–6.

6 'Days of *Lélia* and *Valentine*'

1 Bishop Edward Coplestone to Edward Hawkins, 1843. See Geoffrey Faber, *Oxford Apostles: A Character Study of the Oxford Movement*, Faber, 1974, p. 62.

2 Stanley, op. cit., p. 21.

3 McCrum, op. cit., p. 4.

4 Honan, op. cit., p. 84.

5 MA to Arthur Hugh Clough, December 1844. See Lowry, op. cit., p. 57; Lang, op. cit., Vol. 1, pp. 62–3.

6 Stanley, op. cit., Vol. 1, p. 160.

7 Patricia Thomson, *George Sand and the Victorians*, Macmillan, 1977, pp. 11–27.

8 Ibid., pp. 21–2.

9 W.E. Houghton, *The Victorian Frame of Mind*, New Haven, 1959, p. 564.

10 MA, 'George Sand', *Mixed Essays*, London, 1880, pp. 315–47.

11 MA to Arthur Hugh Clough, 1845. See Lowry, op. cit., pp. 58–9; Lang, op. cit., Vol. 1, pp. 62–3.

12 MA, 'George Sand', op. cit.

13 MA to Frances Arnold (sister), June 1876. See George W.E. Russell, *Letters of Matthew Arnold, 1848–1888*, Macmillan, 1895, Vol. 2, p. 131.

14 MA, 'George Sand', op. cit.

15 MA to Arthur Hugh Clough, 24 May 1848. See Lowry, op. cit., p. 81; Lang, op. cit., Vol. 1, pp. 108–9.

16 Charlotte Brontë to Ellen Nussey, 24 June 1852; Rebecca Fraser, *Charlotte Brontë*, Methuen, 1988, p. 405.

Notes

17 Iris Esther Sells, *Matthew Arnold and France: The Poet*, Cambridge University Press, 1935, p. 9.

18 Charlotte Brontë, *Villette*, Pan, 1973, p. 250.

19 Charlotte Brontë to Ellen Nussey, 24 June 1852. Quoted in Fraser, op. cit., p. 405.

20 'Rachel', I, II, III. See Allott, op. cit., pp. 521–4.

21 See Harris, op. cit., pp. 498–509.

22 Arthur Hugh Clough to Anne Clough. See Mulhauser, op. cit., Vol. 1, p. 181.

23 Thomas Arnold the Younger to his mother, 16 March 1848. See James Bertram (ed.), *New Zealand Letters of Thomas Arnold the Younger*, University of Auckland and Oxford University Press, 1964, p. 30.

24 Ibid., p. 218.

25 Ibid., pp. 215–16.

26 Ibid., p. 218.

27 Ibid., pp. 218–19.

28 William T. Arnold, 'Thomas Arnold the Younger', *Century Magazine*, LXVI, May 1903, pp. 118–28.

29 Mrs T. Arnold (mother) to William Delafield Arnold, 18 May 1847. See Woodward, op. cit., p. 185.

30 Jane Arnold (K) to Thomas Arnold the Younger, 27 June 1848. See Bertram, op. cit., p. xxx.

31 'Resignation'. See Allott, op. cit., p. 88.

32 Étienne de Senancour, *Obermann*, translated and edited by A.E. Waite, London, 1903.

7 Lansdowne, Clough and Marguerite

1 MA to Thomas Arnold, 28 February 1848. See Lang, op. cit., Vol. 1, pp. 83–5.

2 MA to Arthur Hugh Clough, 1 March 1848. See Lowry, op. cit., p. 69; Lang, op. cit., Vol. 1, pp. 86–7.

3 MA to Arthur Hugh Clough, 24 February 1848. See Lowry, op. cit., p. 66; Lang, op. cit., Vol. 1, p. 82.

4 Harriet Martineau, *Biographical Sketches*, London, 1869. Quoted in Nicholas Murray, *A Life of Matthew Arnold*, Hodder, 1996, p. 66.

5 Charles Lacaita (ed.), *An Italian Englishman: Sir James Lacaita, KCMG, 1813–1895*, London, 1933, p. 93.

6 See Mulhauser, op. cit., Vol. 1, p. 306.

7 MA to his mother, 7 March 1848. See Lang, op. cit., Vol. 1, p. 91.

8 MA to Jane Arnold (K), 10 March 1848. Ibid., pp. 94–5.

Notes

9 J.A. Froude to Arthur Hugh Clough, 6 March 1849. See Mulhauser, op. cit., Vol. 1, pp. 250–1.

10 MA to Arthur Hugh Clough, 24 February 1848. See Lowry, op. cit., p. 66; Lang, op. cit., Vol. 1, p. 82.

11 MA to Arthur Hugh Clough, December 1847. See Lowry, op. cit., p. 64; Lang, op. cit., Vol. 1, p. 76.

12 MA to Arthur Hugh Clough, 6 December 1847. See Lowry, op. cit., p. 63; Lang, op. cit., Vol. 1, p. 77.

13 MA to Arthur Hugh Clough, 12 February 1853. See Lowry, op. cit., p. 130; Lang, op. cit., Vol. 1, pp. 252–4.

14 MA to Arthur Hugh Clough, 29 November 1848. See Lowry, op. cit., p. 95; Lang, op. cit., Vol. 1, pp. 126–7.

15 MA to Arthur Hugh Clough, February 1849. See Lowry, op. cit., p. 98; Lang, op. cit., Vol. 1, pp. 130–1.

16 MA to Jane Arnold Forster (K), 31 October 1853. See Lang, op. cit., Vol. 1, p. 277.

17 Matthew Arnold, 'Maurice de Guérin', *Essays in Criticism*, 1st Series, edited by Sister Thomas Marion Hoctor, University of Chicago Press, 1964, p. 68.

18 'The Strayed Reveller'. See Allott, op. cit., p. 67.

19 MA to Jane Arnold Forster (K), May 1849. See Lang, op. cit., Vol. 1, p. 150.

20 MA to Arthur Hugh Clough, 29 September 1848. See Lowry, op. cit., pp. 91–3; Lang, op. cit., Vol. 1, pp. 119–21.

21 Ibid. See also Allott, op. cit., p. 639.

22 'A Horatian Echo'. See Allott, op. cit., p. 58.

23 MA to Arthur Hugh Clough, 29 September 1848. See Lang, op. cit., Vol. 1, p. 119.

24 'To My Friends, who ridiculed a tender Leave-taking'. See Allott, op. cit., pp. 113–15, titled 'A Memory-Picture'.

25 'A Modern Sappho'. See Allott, op. cit., pp. 216–17.

26 Ward, op. cit., p. 59.

27 MA to Jane Arnold Forster (K), 17 March 1849. See Lang, op. cit., Vol. 1, p. 143.

28 MA to Jane Arnold Forster (K), 7 March 1849. See Lang, op. cit., Vol. 1, p. 141.

8 *The Strayed Reveller, Obermann* and Marguerite, Once More

1 Jane Arnold Forster (K) to Thomas Arnold, 26 October 1848. See Lang, op. cit., Vol. 1, p. 123.

2 Ibid.

3 Ibid.

Notes

4 Charles Kingsley, in Carl Dawson (ed.), *Matthew Arnold: The Poetry*, in the Critical Heritage series, Routledge and Kegan Paul, 1973, p. 41.

5 W.E. Aytoun, *Blackwood's Magazine*, September 1849, LXVI, pp. 340–6. Quoted in Dawson, op. cit., p. 50.

6 MA to his mother, quoted by Mary Penrose Arnold to Thomas Arnold, 14 March 1849. See Lang, op. cit., Vol. 1, p. 143.

7 See Tinker and Lowry, op. cit., p. 287.

8 MA to Arthur Hugh Clough, March 1849. See Lowry, op. cit., p. 104; Lang, op. cit., Vol. 1, p. 134.

9 MA to Jane Arnold Forster (K), 7 March 1849. See Lang, op. cit., Vol. 1, p. 141.

10 Note on 'Empedocles': Yale MS.

11 MA to Arthur Hugh Clough, 23 September 1849. See Lowry, op. cit., p. 109; Lang, op. cit., Vol. 1, p. 155.

12 'Parting'. See Allott, op. cit., p. 121.

13 'A Farewell'. Ibid., p. 131.

14 'Isolation: To Marguerite'. Ibid., p. 127.

15 'To Marguerite – Continued'. Ibid., p. 129.

16 'Human Life'; 'Courage'; 'Destiny'; 'Self-Dependence'. Ibid., pp. 145–51.

17 William Delafield Arnold (brother) to Walter Arnold (brother). Quoted in Kenneth Allott's Introduction to William Delafield Arnold's *Oakfield*, Leicester University Press, 1973, p. 11.

18 MA to Arthur Hugh Clough, 15 December 1849. See Lowry, op. cit., p. 113; Lang, op. cit., Vol. 1, p. 167.

19 Jane Arnold Forster to Thomas Arnold, spring 1849 [?], quoted in David Hopkinson, *Edward Penrose Arnold: A Victorian Family Portrait*, Alison Hodge, 1981, p. 33.

20 Jane Arnold Forster to Thomas Arnold, 23 and 30 November 1849. See Lang, op. cit., Vol. 1, p. 159.

9 Marriage to Miss Wightman

1 MA to Herbert Hill, 5 November 1852. See Lang, op. cit., Vol. 1, p. 247.

2 MA to Wyndham Slade, late spring or summer 1850. See Lang, op. cit., Vol. 1, p. 175.

3 Ibid.

4 Patrick J. McCarthy, 'Mrs Matthew Arnold: Some Considerations and some Letters', *Texas Studies in Literature and Language*, 12, 1971, pp. 647–62.

5 MA to Jane Arnold (K), May 1850. See Lang, op. cit., Vol. 1, p. 171.

Notes

6 Thomas Arnold the Younger, *Manchester Guardian* obituary, 18 May 1888.

7 'A Summer Night'. See Allott, op. cit., p. 282.

8 'The Buried Life'. Ibid., p. 286.

9 'The River'. Ibid., p. 243.

10 'Calais Sands'. Ibid., p. 247.

11 Mary Arnold to Thomas Arnold, 15 April 1851, Balliol College MS. Extract quoted in Lang, op. cit., Vol. 1, p. 203.

12 Ibid.

13 Frances Arnold to Thomas Arnold, 28 April 1851, Balliol College MS. Ibid.

14 Jane Arnold Forster (K) to Thomas Arnold, 30 December 1850. See Lang, op. cit., Vol. 1, pp. 180–1.

15 MA to Jane Arnold Forster (K), 25 January 1851. Ibid., p. 188.

16 MA's 1851 diary quoted in Lang, op. cit., Vol. 1, pp. 190–201.

17 Arthur Hugh Clough to Thomas Arnold, 16 May 1851. See Bertram, op. cit., pp. 202.

18 MA to Jane Arnold Forster (K), 10 May 1851. See Lang, op. cit., Vol. 1, pp. 206–7.

19 Ibid.

20 T. Wemyss Reid, *Life of W.E. Forster*, London, 1888, Vol. 1, pp. 283–4.

21 Thomas Arnold to Arthur Hugh Clough, 14 September 1851. See Bertram, op. cit., p. 205.

22 MA to Thomas Arnold, 2 July 1851. See Lang, op. cit., Vol. 1, p. 211.

23 MA to F.T. Palgrave, 9 June 1851. Ibid., p. 210.

24 Arthur Hugh Clough to Thomas Arnold, 14 June 1851. See Bertram, op. cit., p. 203.

25 MA's 1851 diary, quoted in Lang, op. cit., Vol. 1, p. 210.

26 Frances Lucy Wightman to Charlotte Mary Baird Wightman (her mother), 2 September 1851. See Lang, op. cit., Vol. 1, pp. 214–15.

27 Frances Lucy Wightman to her mother, 14 September 1851. See Lang, op. cit., Vol. 1, p. 216.

28 'Stanzas from the Grande Chartreuse'. See Allott, op. cit., p. 301.

29 'Dover Beach'. Ibid., p. 253.

30 MA to Arthur Hugh Clough, 7 January 1852. See Lowry, op. cit., p. 122; Lang, op. cit., Vol. 1, p. 232.

10 *Empedocles* Renounced

1 Epictetus, *Enchiridion*, viii, translated by G. Long, 1877, p. 382. See Allott, op. cit., p. 171.

2 'Empedocles on Etna'. See Allott, op. cit., pp. 154–206.

Notes

3 MA to Frances Lucy Arnold (wife), 15 October 1851. See Lang, op. cit., Vol. 1, p. 227.

4 MA to Arthur Hugh Clough, 8 April 1852. Ibid., pp. 236.

5 MA to Arthur Hugh Clough, 28 October 1852. Ibid., p. 246.

6 MA to Arthur Hugh Clough, 10 January 1852. Ibid., p. 233.

7 MA to his mother, 19 August 1852. Ibid., p. 240.

8 MA to Herbert Hill, 5 November 1852. Ibid., p. 247.

9 MA to Arthur Hugh Clough, 28 October 1852. Ibid., p. 245.

10 MA to Arthur Hugh Clough, 14 December 1852. Ibid., p. 266.

11 MA to Thomas Longman, 27 August 1852. Ibid., p. 272.

12 MA to his mother, 9 May 1853. Ibid., p. 266.

13 Preface to the first edition of *Poems* (1853). See Allott, op. cit., Appendix A, pp. 654–71.

14 Ibid.

15 'Sohrab and Rustum'. Ibid., pp. 319–55.

16 'The Scholar-Gipsy'. Ibid., pp. 355–69.

17 Dwight Culler, *Imaginative Reason: The Poetry of Matthew Arnold*, Yale University Press, 1966, p. 193.

11 'This for our wisest!'

1 MA to John Duke Coleridge, 22 November 1853. See Lang, op. cit., Vol. 1, p. 179.

2 MA, 'A Guide to English Literature', *Mixed Essays*, op. cit., p. 199.

3 Preface to the second edition of *Poems* (1853), published in 1854. See Allott, op. cit., Appendix A, p. 673.

4 G.H. Lewes, 'Schools of Poetry, Arnold's Poems'. Quoted in Dawson, op. cit., pp. 77–84.

5 Preface to *Poems* (1854).

6 Arthur Hugh Clough, 'Recent English Poetry', *North American Review*, July 1853, LXXVII, pp. 12–24. Quoted in Dawson, op. cit., pp. 77–84.

7 See Dawson, op. cit., pp. 96–113.

8 MA to Wyndham Slade, 3 August 1854. See Lang, op. cit., Vol. 1, p. 289.

9 MA, Note on 'Sohrab and Rustum' in *Poems* (1854). See Allott, op. cit., Appendix C, p. 679.

10 MA to Arthur Hugh Clough, 25 November 1853. See Lang, op. cit., Vol. 1, p. 280.

11 MA to Arthur Hugh Clough, 12 February 1853. Ibid., p. 252.

12 MA to Arthur Hugh Clough, 1 and 3 May 1853. Ibid., p. 263.

13 MA to his mother, 9 November 1853. Ibid., pp. 277–8.

Notes

14 MA to his mother, 22 October 1854. Ibid., p. 296.

15 MA to his mother, 27 February 1855. Ibid., p. 304.

16 MA to William Arnold (brother), 31 March 1856. Ibid., p. 332.

17 Ibid.

18 MA, address to Westminster teachers on occasion of his retirement. See Fraser Neiman (ed.), *Essays, Letters and Reviews by Matthew Arnold*, Harvard, 1960, pp. 306–11.

19 MA to his mother, 27 February 1855. See Lang, op. cit., Vol. 1, p. 304.

20 MA to Arthur Hugh Clough, 12 February 1853. Ibid., p. 252.

21 MA to Arthur Hugh Clough, 1 and 3 May 1853. Ibid., p. 263.

22 MA to William Arnold (brother), 31 March 1856. Ibid., p. 332.

23 MA to Jane Arnold Forster (K), 10 October 1854. Ibid., p. 294.

24 Jane Arnold Forster (K) to Thomas Arnold, 30 May 1855. Ibid., p. 316.

25 MA to Jane Arnold Forster (K), 17 February 1856. Ibid., p. 330.

26 MA to William Arnold, 31 March 1856. Ibid., pp. 331–3.

27 Harriet Martineau to 'Mr Chapman', 11 February 1854. See Honan, op. cit., p. 285.

28 Harriet Martineau, *Daily News*, 26 December 1853. Quoted in Dawson, op. cit., pp. 134–7.

12 A Professor of Poetry

1 MA to his mother, 22 March 1849. See Lang, op. cit., Vol. 1, p. 145.

2 J.A. Froude, unsigned review in *Westminster Review*, LXI, 1 January 1854, pp. 146–59. See Dawson, op. cit., pp. 85–95.

3 'Balder Dead'. See Allott, op. cit., p. 376.

4 MA to Jane Arnold Forster (K), 12 December 1854. See Lang, op. cit., Vol. 1, pp. 301–2.

5 MA to Wyndham Slade, 29 December 1855. Ibid., p. 327.

6 MA to his mother, August 1856. Ibid., p. 339.

7 MA to Jane Arnold Forster (K), 6 December 1856 (from 101 Mount Street). Ibid., pp. 348–9.

8 MA to Jane Arnold Forster (K), 29 April and 6 May 1856. Ibid., pp. 337–8.

9 MA to his mother, August 1856. Ibid., p. 339.

10 See Honan, op. cit., p. 295.

11 MA to Jane Arnold Forster (K), 10 August 1856. See Lang, op. cit., Vol. 1, pp. 340–1.

12 MA to Jane Arnold Forster (K), 2 May 1857. Ibid., pp. 355–6.

13 MA to his mother, 10 May 1857. Ibid., pp. 357–8.

14 MA to Thomas Arnold, 15 May 1857. Ibid., p. 359.

Notes

15 MA to his mother, 10 May 1857. Ibid., pp. 357–8.

16 MA to Richard Lynch Cotton, 22 May 1857. Ibid., pp. 361–2.

17 Fragments from 'Lucretius'. See Allott, op. cit., p. 649.

18 Ibid.

19 MA, 'On the Modern Element in Literature'. See Super, op. cit., Vol. 1, p. 23.

20 Ibid., p. 28.

21 Ibid., p. 20.

22 MA, 'Preface to *Merope*'. See Super, op. cit., Vol. 1, p. 39.

23 Super, op. cit., Vol. 1, p. 225.

24 MA to Jane Arnold Forster (K), 28 January 1858. See Lang, op. cit., Vol. 1, p. 324.

25 MA to Jane Arnold Forster (K), 8 January 1858. Ibid., p. 386.

26 MA to Helena Faucit, 6 March 1858. Ibid., p. 386.

27 Ibid., p. 387.

28 J.A. Froude to MA, 10 January 1858. Ibid., pp. 375–6.

29 Max Müller to MA, 8 January 1858. Ibid., pp. 372–3.

30 MA to his mother, 2 April 1858. Ibid., pp. 387–8.

31 W.R. Roscoe, *National Review*, April 1858, pp. 259–79. See Dawson, op. cit., pp. 154–5; Lang, op. cit., Vol. 1, p. 388, footnote.

32 MA to Jane Arnold Forster (K), 6 September 1858. See Lang, op. cit., Vol. 1, pp. 401–2.

33 Ibid.

34 Ibid.

35 Ibid.

13 Last Poems

1 MA to his mother, 18 January 1858. See Lang, op. cit, Vol. 1, p. 379.

2 MA to Thomas Arnold, 11 February 1858. Ibid., p. 385.

3 Ibid.

4 'Rugby Chapel'. See Allott, op. cit., p. 481.

5 MA to his mother, 16 February 1859. See Lang, op. cit., Vol. 1, p. 414.

6 MA to his mother, 21 November 1859. Ibid., p. 507.

7 MA to Jane Arnold Forster (K), 31 July 1861. See Lang, op. cit., Vol. 2, p. 87.

8 MA to his mother, 14 April 1859. See Lang, op. cit., Vol. 1, p. 435.

9 Woodward, op. cit., p. 195.

10 Ibid., p. 204.

11 'A Southern Night'. See Allott, op. cit., p. 495.

12 'Heine's Grave'. Ibid., p. 507.

13 MA to his mother, 29 October 1863. See Lang, op. cit., Vol. 2, p. 238.

Notes

14 MA to Henry Dunn, 12 November 1867. See Tinker and Lowry, op. cit., p. 272.

15 'Obermann Once More'. See Allott, op. cit., p. 559.

16 'The Terrace at Berne'. Ibid., p. 518.

17 MA to Arthur Hugh Clough, December 1857. See Lowry, op. cit., p. 148.

18 MA to his mother, 20 November 1861. See Lang, op. cit., Vol. 2, p. 101.

19 MA to Blanche Smith Clough, 2 December 1861. Ibid., p. 105.

20 MA to Blanche Smith Clough, 2 January 1862. Ibid., p. 121.

21 'Thyrsis'. See Allott, op. cit., p. 537.

22 MA to his mother, 15 August 1861. See Lang, op. cit., Vol. 2, p. 89.

23 MA to his mother, 4 February 1863. Ibid., p. 187.

24 MA to Frances Arnold (sister), 20 March 1886. See Russell, op. cit., Vol. 2, p. 325.

25 'Growing Old'. See Allott, op. cit., p. 582.

26 MA to his mother, 4 February 1863. See Lang, op. cit., Vol. 2, p. 187.

27 Thomas Burnett Smart (compiler and editor), *The Bibliography of Matthew Arnold*, London, 1892, p. 7.

28 MA to his mother, 24 December 1868. See Russell, op. cit., Vol. 1, p. 401.

Index

'Alaric at Rome' 40–1, 61

Allott, Kenneth 39, 200

Ambervalia (Clough & Burbridge) 97

Arnold, Edward 31, 86, 87, 142, 169

Arnold, Frances 38, 87, 138

Arnold (née Wightman), Frances Lucy ('Flu'): courtship 129–31, 133, 136, 140; engagement 138; K on 174; marriage 142–4; motherhood 150, 153, 175

Arnold, Jane, *see* Forster, J.

Arnold, Lucy 185

Arnold (née Penrose), Mary 18, 138: and Clough 34; health 15; marriage 13; MA and 16, 19, 26–9, 37, 40, 67, 83, 176; and Stanley's *Life* 63

Arnold, Mary ('Bacco') 38, 84, 87, 107, 138, 142

Arnold, Matthew: at Balliol 43, 45–52, 66–7, 73; birth 15; career 67–9, 83, 92–6, 126, 133, 137, 150–3, 169–71, 173, 200–1, 214; childhood 16–18, 22, 26–9; and critics 198; death 217; diary 150; as dramatist 191–2, 197–8; early poems 28, 37–41, 58–62, 87–90; as father 154, 171; finances 133, 151, 186, 214; friends 49–51, 75, 151, 209–10; health 16, 60, 103, 215; home-life 175, 185, 200–1, 214–15; marriage 129–31, 133, 137–8, 140–4; Oriel fellowship 66, 70, 73–4, 103, 133; pastimes 215; personality 26, 29, 30, 34, 37, 42, 47–8, 65, 69–70, 74, 96, 124, 172, 186; as poet 61, 71–2, 93, 99, 100–2, 151–2, 154–5, 157–8, 196, 212; politics 95–6; Professorship 187–8, 191–2, 197, 205, 214; as prose-writer 214, 217; reading 56, 76–80, 90, 97, 140, 180, 189; relations with father 17, 19–20, 22, 30, 35,

Index

37, 54, 57, 59; and religion 113; schooldays 18–20, 27–8, 31, 33–7, 60; sexuality 75–6, 103; social concerns 146–7; travel journal 31–3; and women 103–5

Arnold, Susannah 38, 87

Arnold, Dr Thomas (MA's father): biography of 62–3, 74; and Carlyle 55–6; and Church reform 9, 10–12, 73; and Clough 33–5; death 53–4, 57, 59–60; as father 15–20, 22, 27, 52–3, 171–2; MA on 169, 199–200; marriage 13; Oriel fellowship 9, 73–4; Oxford professorship 47, 51–2; as poet 23–5; pre-Rugby days 9, 13–14; publications 10, 40; at Rugby 1–10, 75, 144–5, 198–9; as scholar 4, 10; sermons 6–8, 10, 44, 46; social concerns 55, 71

Arnold, Thomas (MA's brother) 53; birth 15; career 83–4, 169; childhood 15, 16, 18, 20, 22, 42; on Clough 36, 50; emigration 85, 126; on MA 17, 46, 48, 52, 60, 133, 142; marriage 137; personality 83–5; relations with MA 84, 86; and religion 15, 74, 86; schooldays 27, 31; social concerns 146

Arnold, Thomas (MA's son) 153–4, 201, 215

Arnold, Walter 38, 87

Arnold, William 38, 87, 126, 137, 142, 170, 202–4

Athenaeum 175–6, 185

Athenaeum 193, 216

Aytoun, William 99

Bailey, Philip James 98

'Balder Dead' 180–4, 185, 191

Bhagavadgita 97

'The Birthday' 38–40

Blackett, John 142, 186

Bode, John Ernest 187

The Bothie of Toper-na-fuosich (Clough) 99

Bowood House 83

Bright, Richard 139

Brontë, Charlotte 81–2

Browning, Robert 216

Buckland, Martha 28

Buckland, Mrs 14, 28

Buckland, John 13–14, 18, 20

Burbridge, Thomas 97–8

'The Buried Life' 134–6, 154, 157, 184

Butler, A.G. 69

Byron, Lord 37, 40, 196

Calais 137

'Calais Sands' 137, 154

Carlyle, Thomas 55–9, 62, 70, 71, 126, 180, 181

'Chartism' (Carlyle) 55

Chartists 95

The Christian Duty ...(T. Arnold) 10

The City of the Sultan (Pardoe) 37

Clough, Arthur Hugh 75; career 97; as critic 168; correspondence with MA 117–18, 169, 173; death 209–10; emigration 151, 209; on MA 82, 83, 142, 201; at Oxford 44–5, 49–50, 66, 74, 83, 97; personality 172; as poet 58, 97–100; politics 96, 97; relations with MA 50–1, 66–7, 69–70, 75, 98–100, 140–1, 209–10; religion 97; at Rugby 33–6; in 'Thyrsis' 210–11

Coleridge, Hartley 37

Coleridge, John Duke 49–50, 64–5, 110, 140, 168

Coleridge, Sir John Taylor 129

'Constantinople' 38

Cotton, George 52–3, 88

'Courage' 125

Crabb Robinson, Henry 37, 192

Croker, John W. 76, 142

'Cromwell' 58–9, 60–1, 107

Index

Cromwell (Carlyle) 56
Culler, Dwight 163
Culture and Anarchy 215, 217
'Culture and its Enemies' 215

Daily News 177
The Decade 49–50
Description of the Lake Country (Wordsworth) 21
'Destiny' 125
Discourses in America 217
'Dover Beach' 143, 144–6, 154, 155, 215
Dublin University Review 193

Edinburgh Review 199
Electra (Sophocles) 194
Eliot, T.S. 181
Emerson, Ralph Waldo 61–2, 70–1
'Empedocles' 115–16, 148–50, 154, 157, 184–5, 189, 215–16
Empedocles on Etna 154–6, 166
England and the Italian Question 201
Essays in Criticism 217

'Faded Leaves' 136, 154, 184
'A Farewell' 121–3
Faucit, Helena 192
'Forsaken Merman' 157
Forster (née Arnold), Jane (K) 202; betrothals 52–3, 88, 131–2; childhood 15–16, 18; correspondence 126–7, 173–4; health 139, 141; on MA 47; on MA's poetry 100, 107–8, 110–11, 174; marriage 132, 137; relations with Flu 174; relations with MA 87, 108, 111, 127, 131–3, 138–41, 174, 209; and 'Resignation' 87–9, 132; and Wordsworths 47, 110
Forster, William Edward 131, 141–2, 174, 176, 202
Fox How 20–3, 34, 36–7, 126, 132, 137, 169

Fox How Magazine 22, 27, 38–9, 47, 51
France 31–2, 78–82, 95–6, 143
Fraser's Magazine 111, 132
French Revolution (Carlyle) 71
Froude, James A. 96–7, 100, 179–80, 193, 195

Goethe, J.W. von 71, 72, 165, 168, 196, 209
Gray, Thomas 180
'Growing Old' 212–13
Guérin, Maurice de 79, 100

'The Harp Player on Etna' 184
Hawker, Manley 65
'Haworth Churchyard' 177
'Heine's Grave' 204–5
Heroes and Hero-Worship (Carlyle) 56–7, 180
Hill, Herbert 20, 28
History of Rome (T. Arnold) 40, 163
Honan, Park 28, 192
'A Horatian Echo' 104
Hughes, Thomas 2, 198
'Human Life' 125
Hutchinson, Sara 21

In Memoriam (Tennyson) 165–6
'In Utrumque Paratus' 114
'The Incursion' 51–2
Indiana (Sand) 77–8
Ireland 94
'Isolation: To Marguerite' 123
Italy 97

Jenkyns, Richard 49
Johnson, Samuel 182
Jowett, Benjamin 49

Keble, John 11, 15, 36
Kingsley, Charles 84, 111–12

Lake, William 41–2, 49, 54

Index

Lake District 14, 21–3, 36–7, 88
Laleham 9–10, 13–14, 17, 18, 28
Lang, C.Y. 75
Lansdowne, Lord 83, 92–5, 133, 138
'Leaving' 184
Lélia (Sand) 76, 77, 90
Letters (ed. Lang) 75–6
Letters of Ortis (Foscolo) 105
Lewes, G.H. 76–7, 167
'*A Life-Drama*' (Smith) 167
Life of Thomas Arnold (Stanley) 62–3
'Lines written on first leaving home...' 30
'Lines Written on the Seashore...' 29
Lingen, Ralph 138
Longman, Thomas 156
Lucan, Lord 13
'Lucretius' 116, 185, 189

Mallet, P.H. 180
Marguerite 105–6, 116, 117, 119–23, 133, 207–8
Martineau, Harriet 94, 176–8
Masson, David 167
Maurice, F.D. 84
'Memorial Verses' 132
Merope 191, 192–5, 197–8, 209
Milton, John 182
Moberly, George 27, 31
'The Modern Element in Literature' 192
'A Modern Sappho' 106
Moorman, Mary 21
Müller, Max 60, 193
'Mycerinus' 59–61

National Review 193
The Nemesis of Faith (Froude) 96, 179
New Poems 215–16
'The New Sirens' 100, 114
New Zealand 85
Newcastle Commission on Elementary Education 200

Newman, John Henry 11–12, 15, 43–4, 46, 57, 58, 67, 73, 74
Norse Edda 180
Northern Antiquities (Mallet) 180

Oakfield (W. Arnold) 170, 203
Obermann (Senancour) 79–80, 90–1, 116–17, 206
'Obermann Once More' 206–7
'On the Rhine' 136, 154, 184
'On Translating Homer' 192
Oxford 43–52, 58, 60, 74, 76, 77; Balliol 40, 42, 43–6, 48–9; History Professorship 47, 55–6; Newdigate Prize 58, 60; Oriel 9, 11, 66, 70, 73–4, 133; Poetry Professorship 187–8, 191–2, 197, 205, 214
'Oxford Malignants' (T. Arnold) 11–12, 36, 43
Oxford Movement 11, 43, 57, 74

Palgrave, Francis 142
Pardoe, Julia 37
Paris 80–2
'Parting' 119–20
Pilgrim's Progress 17
Penrose, Mary, *see* Arnold, M.
'The Philosopher and the Stars' 184
Poems (1853) 156–60, 167–8, 177, 179; *Preface* 157–9, 163, 167–8, 174, 176, 178, 179, 185, 191, 216
Poems: First Series 184
Poems: Second Series 184

Queen's Volunteers 201

Rachel 80–2
'Resignation' 87–9, 132, 184
'The River' 136, 154, 184
Roscoe, W.R. 193
'Rugby Chapel' 172, 199–200
Rugby Magazine 35
Rugby School 1–9, 10, 31, 33–5, 52, 56, 67–8, 75, 126, 144
Russell, Lord John 83

Index

Sainte-Beuve, C.-A. 79, 168
Saintsbury, George 162
Sand, George 76–80, 83, 90
'Say this of Her...' 104, 105
'The Scholar-Gipsy' 160–5
'Self Dependence' 125–6, 149
Senancour, Etienne de 79, 90, 116, 206
'Separation' 136, 184
Shairp, J. Campbell 48, 49, 100, 112–13, 115, 168
Slade, Wyndham 129–30, 142, 186, 191
Smith, Alexander 98, 166–7, 168
Smith, Blanche 209, 210
'Sohrab and Rustum' 156, 159, 165, 168, 174, 185, 191
Sophocles 189–91, 193
'A Southern Night' 203–5
Southey, Robert 37
Spasmodics 98–9
Stanley, Arthur 44, 45, 49, 52, 54, 168; biography of Dr Arnold 2, 6, 11, 51, 62–3, 74, 75
'Stanzas from the Grande Chartreuse' 143–4
'Stanzas in Memory of the Author of Obermann' 116–17, 119, 157
Stephen, Fitzjames 199, 200
Strachey, Lytton 2, 5
'The Strayed Reveller' 100–2
The Strayed Reveller 106–14, 127
'A Summer Night' 133–4, 154, 157
Swinburne, Algernon Charles 215
Switzerland 105, 116, 133, 196, 207
'Switzerland' poems 119, 136

Tait, Archibald 49, 67
Temple, Frederick 49, 63

Tennyson, Lord Alfred 58, 99, 165–6, 168, 196
'The Terrace at Berne' 207–8
Thirty-Nine Articles 9, 73–4, 97
The Three Friends (Butler) 69
Thun 105, 116, 128–9
'Thyrsis' 210–11, 215
The Times 60–1
'To a Gipsy Child by the Seashore' 90
'To Marguerite - Continued' 123
'To My Friends...' 106
'To Shakespeare' 62
Tom Brown's Schooldays (Hughes) 2, 4, 6–7, 17, 52, 56, 198–9
'Too Late' 184
Tract 90 (Newman) 43
Tractarians, see Oxford Movement
'Tristram and Iseult' 128–9, 154
Twining, William 87

Villemarqué, Theodore de la 128
Villette (Brontë) 81
'The Voice' 46

Walrond, Theodore 50, 142, 196
Ward, W.G. 44–5, 74
Whately, Henrietta 83, 87
Wightman, Frances, see Arnold, F.L.
Wightman, Sir William 129, 133, 136, 138, 150, 174–5
Wilhelm Meister (Goethe) 72
Winchester School 20, 27–8, 31, 34, 36
Woodward, Frances 203
Wordsworth, Dorothy 21, 36
Wordsworth, William 14, 21, 23, 36, 40, 53, 67, 72, 110, 114, 132–3, 196
'Written in Emerson's Essays' 61–2

ABOUT THE AUTHOR

Ian Hamilton has published two collections of poetry and his other books include *Robert Lowell: A Biography*, *In Search of J. D. Salinger*, *Writers in Hollywood*, *Keepers of the Flame*, and *Walking Possession*, a collection of essays published by Bloomsbury in 1994.